Faith
and
Fertility

of related interest

Third-Party Assisted Conception Across Cultures
Social, Legal and Ethical Perspectives
Edited by Eric Blyth and Ruth Landau
ISBN 978 1 84310 084 3

Experiences of Donor Conception
Parents, Offspring and Donors through the Years
Caroline Lorbach
Foreword by Eric Blyth
ISBN 978 1 84310 122 2

Making Babies the Hard Way
Living with Infertility and Treatment
Caroline Gallup
ISBN 978 1 84310 463 6

Sexuality and Fertility Issues in Ill Health and Disability
From Early Adolescence to Adulthood
Edited by Rachel Balen and Marilyn Crawshaw
ISBN 978 1 84310 339 4

The Adoption Experience
Families Who Give Children a Second Chance
Ann Morris
ISBN 978 1 85302 783 3

Faith
and
Fertility

Attitudes Towards Reproductive Practices in

Different Religions from Ancient to Modern Times

Edited by Eric Blyth
and Ruth Landau

Foreword by Richard Harries

Jessica Kingsley Publishers
London and Philadelphia

First published in 2009
by Jessica Kingsley Publishers
116 Pentonville Road
London N1 9JB, UK
and
400 Market Street, Suite 400
Philadelphia, PA 19106, USA

www.jkp.com

Copyright © Eric Blyth and Ruth Landau 2009
Foreword copyright © Richard Harries 2009

Library of Congress Cataloging in Publication Data
A CIP catalog record for this book is available from the Library of Congress

British Library Cataloguing in Publication Data
A CIP catalogue record for this book is available from the British Library

ISBN 978 1 84310 535 0

Printed and bound in Great Britain by
Athenaeum Press, Gateshead, Tyne and Wear

Eric Blyth wishes to dedicate this book to his parents Bernard and Joan and to his sons Ian and Stuart.

Ruth Landau wishes to dedicate the book to her husband Yoram, her daughter Orna, her son Ori, and their children.

Acknowledgements

We wish to thank everyone who willingly contributed to this book, and staff at Jessica Kingsley Publishers for their support and encouragement. We wish to give special thanks to Sue Hanson at the Centre for Applied Childhood Studies at the University of Huddersfield, who provided admirable administrative support to finalise the manuscript.

Eric Blyth and Ruth Landau

Contents

Foreword

In the same way it was once said that love and marriage go together like a horse and carriage, it used to be the case that there was a continuum from the time when that love was expressed in sexual intercourse, through fertilisation and implantation in the mother's womb, to that same mother eventually giving birth to her baby. Now that continuum can be broken at almost every point. There can be sexual intercourse without fertilisation and fertilisation without intercourse; motherhood without pregnancy and pregnancy without having one's own child. Fertility and how we bring about the future of the human race is more and more in our hands, not simply left to the vagaries of chance and nature.

This new power in human hands has raised and continues to raise some fundamental ethical questions. Furthermore, in almost every culture in the world the ethical norms that seek to guide the answers owe a great deal to the dominant religion of the culture in which the questions are being asked. Moreover religion, far from dying out, as theorists of secularisation suggested 40 years ago, is an increasingly important player on the world stage. So what religion has to say about fertility and the new scientific advances in relation to it is of great importance, not just for clinicians and counsellors at the front line of treatment but for those responsible for social policy.

At the moment there is a high level of vagueness about what a particular religion does or does not teach in this area. So it is very good to have this timely, authoritative and helpful book. Drawing on the latest research about how religions are in fact impinging on fertility issues, it also sets out clearly, in separate chapters, the basic structure and beliefs of each of the major world religions and how this ought to guide the views of its adherents on assisted reproduction. It is comprehensive in its scope, not just confining itself to what are usually called the world religions and some of the different approaches within them, for example between the Roman Catholic and Anglican churches. It also includes the impact of traditional Chinese practices and traditional African religion on issues of fertility and its modern associated techniques.

We now live in a world in which different cultures and religions impinge and impact on one another as never before. This book will be invaluable for anyone who is wanting to look at these issues from a rounded perspective and who wishes to reflect critically not only from within but also from outside the ethical framework provided by their own culture.

Richard Harries,
Professor Lord Harries of Pentregarth,
Gresham Professor of Divinity and Honorary Professor of Theology,
King's College, London.

Introduction

Ruth Landau and Eric Blyth

Advances in human reproductive technology

The invention of the contraceptive pill in 1960 and the *in vitro* fertilisation (IVF) procedure in 1978 are among the most important technological advances of the second half of the twentieth century. The Pill dramatically changed the fate of women, who, until its invention, were exposed to unplanned and often unwanted pregnancies due to lack of autonomous control over their fertility. The Pill for the first time enabled women themselves – without the need for co-operation of their partner – to determine whether they conceived children at all, the timing of their first birth and the spacing of their consequent births. The easy and convenient use of oral contraception brought women a long sought-after freedom from their dependence on men.

A further significance of this invention was that it allowed a total separation between the realisation of human sexual drives and human reproduction. In other words, the Pill offered women sexual liberty without the penalty of an unwanted pregnancy or the need for an abortion. This convenient and independent ability to control and limit their fertility has had a major effect on, at least, Western women's lives, including their relationships with men. The Pill allowed women, at least theoretically, to enter the labour market and compete with men, without being threatened by the possibility of an unplanned pregnancy. The consequent changes in gender roles have had an impact not only on the institution of marriage but also on fertility patterns around the world.

The major reason for developing the Pill was to allow 'family planning', primarily birth timing and spacing, and thus to limit the number of children a woman bore.

In contrast, IVF initially aimed to help couples suffering from infertility problems who could not fulfil their wish for a child. IVF enables a woman to become pregnant and give birth to a child without sexual intercourse, but the procedure still requires male sperm, a female egg and a woman in whose uterus the embryo must be implanted to develop. Medically assisted conceptions now include gamete intra-fallopian transfer (GIFT), zygote intra-fallopian transfer (ZIFT), intra-cytoplasmic sperm injection (ICSI), 'genetic' and 'gestational' surrogacy, prenatal genetic diagnosis, and post-menopausal and posthumous human reproduction. These modern 'high-tech' methods of assisting conception not only eliminate any need for sexual intercourse but − by the use of gamete donations − also provide the possibility of breaking the genetic connection between the children and the woman who bears them. Moreover, now that sperm, eggs and embryos can be frozen and thawed for subsequent use, the time-span between conception and birth can extend to years and has become dependent on social, rather than purely biological, variables.

These new technologies and forms of medical assistance thus have the potential to change human reproduction dramatically. They offer humankind unprecedented possibilities and seemingly unlimited control over women's fertility. Yet, at the same time they pose endless moral, ethical, social and legal questions regarding the legitimacy of their use. Ogburn (1964) observed that 'material technology' (inventions and advances) develops much earlier than 'spiritual technology' (norms, ideologies and laws) and that it may take 'spiritual technology' many years to react to a new technology, sometimes even decades. This observation seems particularly pertinent to the new human reproduction technologies.

Faith and human reproduction

Spirituality, formalised as religion, is an intrinsic part of all human cultures, feeding into a culture's norms, laws and ideologies. Religion also influences civil authority in many fields, especially those concerned with the prevention or promotion of procreation, such as abortion and infertility treatments (Schenker 2000). The impact of religion in directing societal responses to the new human reproductive technologies in various countries around the world was brought home to the editors of this volume by the thirteen chapters of *Third-Party Assisted Conception Across Cultures: Social, Legal and Ethical Perspectives* (Blyth and Landau 2004). Neither 'faith' nor 'religion' were explicitly thematised. Yet the impact of dominant belief systems, regardless of whether based on organised religion or folk beliefs, was highlighted by several contributors as providing the context in which third-party assisted conception was legitimate (or not) in their country. Even different streams within one religious community may develop quite different interpretations of their authoritative official teachings, greatly affecting their attitude to third-party assisted conception.

These various chapters, together with other sources (reviewed in the following pages), indicate that different faith communities have different theories about what constitutes the authoritative official teaching of their community at a given time in history.

The recent developments in the science and technology of human reproduction create new challenges for the various religions, particularly for their spiritual and theological leaderships. Religious leaderships cannot ignore these challenges; to serve their communities they need to develop theological approaches to clarify accepted attitudes toward the new developments. Thus, one question about the relation between faith and fertility is: how indeed do the religions and their formal leadership respond to and cope with these challenges?

An even more pressing question concerns the place of faith and religion in the lives of women and men at the beginning of the twenty-first century. Do they really have an impact on the way family unions are formed? Are they still important in affecting the fertility patterns of individuals around the world? Does religion affect the number of children a couple desires? Does religion really influence the use or lack of use of contraception, the acceptability of abortion or the willingness to make use of the various new forms of assisted conception?

Extending these questions leads us to a comparison between the various religions and faiths. What do we actually know about the attitudes toward reproductive practices in the different faiths and belief systems and their norms? Are there indeed major differences among various faith or religious communities in beliefs and practices related to the issues of fertility, infertility and assisted conception? And if there are, what are these differences and how do they influence everyday practice in the context of reproduction?

Strangely, there is a great paucity of academic literature on the association between religion and fertility, infertility and assisted conception. Woas (2007) claims that religion has survived a period of comparative neglect in the social sciences at the time when it can affect, among others, various aspects of family formation and patterns of fertility. The literature mainly focuses on the association between faith and fertility patterns from the economic and population perspective. For example, religious affiliation as a determinant of demographic behaviour, particularly among Roman Catholic communities, was at the forefront of demographic research in the 1960s (McQuillan 2004), after which demographers' interest in religion decreased. The contrast between the current decline of fertility in all industrialised countries and in many developing countries, and the various fertility patterns in the Muslim world, have renewed interest in the old question of the influence of religion on fertility patterns (Adsera 2006; Derosas and van Poppel 2006; United Nations 2003). Even so, hardly any attention has been paid to the relationship between religion and assisted conception.

Faith, religion and fertility

Regardless of their religion, people's religiosity may affect their fertility patterns. Religiosity may be expressed in various forms and levels of religious participation, such as attendance at religious services within a congregation, family observance, individual devotion, as well as by the salience of religion for life decisions (Waite and Lehrer 2003). Religiosity generally has far-reaching positive effects. For example, Waite and Lehrer cite reports into cancer risk that show a difference of more than seven years at age 20 in life expectancy between those who attend religious services more than once a week and those who never attend. They cite studies suggesting an association between religious involvement and better mental health outcomes, educational attainment and subsequent economic well-being. Furthermore, studies of young people growing up in developed countries with some religious involvement show a lower probability of substance misuse and juvenile delinquency, delayed sexual debut and more positive attitudes toward marriage and having children (Bearman and Bruckner 2001; Donahue and Benson 1995; Marchena and Waite 2001).

McQuillan (2004) argues that the ideological influence of a religion goes beyond its specific rules; it includes values touching on gender, sexuality and family life as issues of religious identity and the role of religious institutions in different societies. This has been shown in depth by Evelyn H. Lehrer, a Chicago University professor of economics. Based on US data, she suggests that religions differ in their fertility norms, leading to differences in the perception of the desired number of children and of the expectations from children (Lehrer 1996a).

Comparisons between Roman Catholic, Protestant and interfaith couples suggest that fertility was significantly influenced by the religious affiliation of both wife and husband, as well as by the degree of the intra-family division of labour and specialisation (Lehrer 1996b). In a more recent study, Lehrer (2004a) found that religious affiliation continues clearly to affect entry into marriage and cohabitation by the post-baby-boom cohort in America, with significant differences among mainline Protestants, conservative Protestants, Roman Catholics, Mormons, Jews,[1] and the unaffiliated.

Her findings confirm that the faith in which a woman is brought up has important effects on the decisions she makes over her life, including schooling, employment and fertility. For example, Mormons show high fertility rates. Roman Catholicism also exemplifies strong pronatalist ideologies. In contrast, Jews in the US show unusually low fertility.

Lehrer (2004b) interprets the high fertility rates of Mormons as a rational response to the psychological and social rewards granted by this religion to couples with many children. In contrast, she notes that since the Jewish religion *per se* does not encourage small families, explanations for the low Jewish fertility rates must be sought in other aspects of Judaism, the Jewish community and its interactions with the broader community. Lehrer suggests that women raised as conservative Protestants or Mormons have incentives to marry earlier because their faith encourages home-based activities and higher fertility. These faiths make a sharp distinction between male and female social and economic roles, encouraging the traditional division of labour within a household with young children. Consequently, there is a lower level of female employment among members of these faiths. Furthermore, women in conservative Protestant households spend about 4.5 hours per week more than men performing tasks classified as typically female, while the overall hours of household work are nearly identical to those of families of other religions (Ellison and Bartkowski 2002, cited by Lehrer). At the other end of the spectrum, Jewish mothers are more active in the labour market. Religion also influences the education and upbringing of children, allocation of time and money, the cultivation of social relationships and often even place of residence.

All of these, in turn, affect fertility patterns (Waite and Lehrer 2003). For example, parents who attach importance to religion and its teachings are more likely to send their children to schools and/ or after-school activities emphasising the values cherished by their own religion. As noted above, religious exposure in childhood influences later fertility patterns.

In the US, the mean years of schooling are highest for Jews, lowest for conservative Protestants, with Roman Catholics and mainline Protestants at the centre of the distribution. Lehrer explains this difference by suggesting that Jews place a high priority on investing in the human capital of their children and, considering the small size of the family, invest more resources, especially maternal time, in each child during its formative years. The lower level of schooling of conservative Protestants may result from Protestants preferring to comply with authority (parents and teachers), with a concomitant rejection of novel ideas. Thus, conservative Protestants prefer their children's education to resemble their own, and particularly discourage them from attending 'liberal' schools that encourage critical thinking, thus making their children more likely to accept the teachings of their leaders regarding use of modern contraceptives or of abortion. This rejection of critical inquiry and the greater asymmetry in household labour exert a particular effect on women in this community that provides them with less choice. They receive less encouragement to continue their education; this reduces their opportunities in the labour market and encourages them to marry and have more children instead. As a consequence of their lower level of schooling and higher fertility, they have less capacity to attend to their children's needs.

Although Lehrer's surveys show that religious affiliation clearly correlates with fertility, religious values are likely to play a critical role in affecting fertility patterns only 'when three conditions are satisfied: first, the religion articulates behavioural norms with a bearing on fertility behaviour; second, the religion holds the means to communicate these values and promote compliance; and, third, religion forms a central component of the social identity of its followers' (McQuillan 2004, p.25). For example, in 22 low fertility industrialised countries (where the mean fertility rate results in families of one or two children) Rindfuss, Benjamin Guzzo and Morgan (2003) documented a dramatic drop in fertility levels as women's participation in the labour force increased. The lowest national total fertility rates in the countries studied are in Italy (1.19) and Spain (1.16), perhaps because of their strong religious and family institutions. The increase in women's education and employment in Italy and Spain in the past two decades was met with resistance by society as a whole, but especially by men, who preferred that women continue to fulfil their traditional role of mothers and homemakers. However, societal responses are important if women are to fill motherhood and work roles simultaneously. Rindfuss et al. (2003) argue that lack of appropriate responses led women in Italy and Spain to refrain from marrying and having children. Considering that women still desire to have children, what changed is the preference for a traditional marriage. In other words, women may want to have a child or two, but not necessarily within a formal marriage. Whether a woman will end up having children within a formal union with the father or not may be dependent on her religious upbringing.

The significant effects of religion on fertility are not confined to the Judeo-Christian traditions. A comparative study of Muslim and non-Muslim wives in India, Malaysia, Thailand and the Philippines showed that Muslim wives usually have more children, are more likely to desire additional children and are less likely than non-Muslim wives to use contraception when they want no more children (Morgan *et al.* 2002).

Comparing differences in fertility between Muslims and Hindus in India, Dharmalingam and Morgan (2004) found that Muslims are more likely than Hindus to intend to have another child. Specifically, Muslims with two or more living children are twice as likely as Hindus to intend to have another child. If they intend to have no more children, Muslim women are half as likely as Hindu women to use contraceptives and thus are at a higher risk of having an unwanted child. The pronatalist attitudes of Muslims cannot be explained by female autonomy, women's education or measures of household consumption. Instead, the differences may be explained by group identity and political disadvantage (Morgan *et al.* 2002); the pervasive Muslim–Hindu fertility differences in India may be a consequence of the fact that Muslims are a minority group (Dharmalingam and Morgan 2004).

In the Central Asian part of the former Soviet Union, including Uzbekistan and Kazakhstan, the Muslim majority has always married at an earlier age and showed higher fertility than Russians and other peoples of European origin and Judeo-Christian cultural roots (Agadjanian 1999; Agadjanian and Makarova 2003). However, this observed fertility gap between Muslims and Hindus/ Christians may relate more to gender roles and education than to a particular faith (Hussain 2001; Alagarajan 2003) – or possibly there are differences among the faiths: the results of a study on Roman Catholics in the US indicate that the effects of exposure to religion at a young age outweigh the effects of socio-economic factors, pointing to religion as an important factor in the formation of child-bearing preferences (Pearce 2002).

The importance of religion in the context of assisted conception is also evident in the Arabic-speaking world, where the regulations relating to assisted reproduction are derived mainly from the Islamic religious regulations (Aboulghar, Serour and Mansour 2007). However, Tober, Taghdisi and Jalali (2006), using the example of the successful family planning programme of the Islamic Republic of Iran, point out that different interpretations of a religion may or may not influence reproductive health-related behaviours.

In Israel, the Jewish population has maintained a more or less constant total fertility rate over the last 30 years (2.8 children per woman). The total fertility rate of Arab Muslim women in Israel is much higher, currently 4.6 births per woman, although it has decreased dramatically (Landau 2003). The relatively high Jewish fertility rate principally reflects the very high fertility rate amongst the ultra-Orthodox Jews (7–7.5 births per woman) and the high fertility rate of the national-religious Jewish population (4.5 births per woman), as against the low, European level of fertility among the secular Jews in the country. These significant differences in fertility patterns within one religious group point to the importance of level of religiosity, as expressed by active religious participation in the community (Landau 2003).

Mozambique, with a *per capita* gross national product for 1999 estimated at US $210 and total fertility rate of almost six children per woman, exemplifies the impact of traditional belief systems on fertility. As elsewhere in sub-Saharan Africa, fertility remains a fundamental social value in Mozambique for both women and men. In the rural-origin Bantu traditions of the country, a woman's status is largely determined by her marital fertility and even when marriage ties weaken, a woman's fertility remains, at least subjectively, her major asset for a future relationship (Agadjanian 2001). The impact of religion on attitudes to fertility and infertility is similarly significant in South Africa. Within African culture, premarital sexual relations are acceptable; pregnancy is seen as a proof of fertility and children as a sign of wealth. Infertility is perceived as punishment for wrongdoing (Carbonatto 2004; Sewpaul 1999).

Considering the importance attached to the value of fertility in all societies, and relevant to the introduction of the new reproduction technologies, the question that arises is: what are the effects of these pronatalist views on infertile women? In an illuminating book on infertility and patriarchy in Egypt, Inhorn (1996) writes, 'the contemporary interpretations of Islamic doctrine threaten to increase the stigmatisation of women who are unable to comply with the "multiplication of offspring" tenets prescribed by Islamist groups in contemporary Egyptian society' (p.259). It is plausible to assume that similar attitudes also prevail in other faiths, devaluing infertile women, with all the social and psychological consequences.

At first sight, religious stigmatisation of infertility could appear to encourage the acceptance and use of modern assisted conception technology. Yet religious and cultural factors may still oppose the use of these technologies. For example, the Confucian heritage in Japan regards marriage as the means for continuing the paternal line, requiring a husband to be the genetic father of his wife's children. Similarly in Hong Kong, the strong belief in intergenerational family and blood ties rooted in traditional Chinese culture results in very low acceptance of any form of third-party assisted conception (Ng *et al.* 2004).

The Roman Catholic Church, while strongly pronatalist, has consistently opposed third-party assisted conception on theological grounds. Countries like Argentina and Poland, where the Church has a strong impact, thus show a relatively low incidence of third-party assisted conception (Baron 2004; Bielawska-Batorowitz 2004). European countries where the various Christian religions have a weaker impact, such as the Nordic countries, show relatively high rates of cohabitation and non-marital fertility. Women here clearly show an increased reluctance to marry and to stay married and are prepared to bear children either with a cohabiting partner or alone. Their fertility rates, however, remain rather low, but this may be due to differences in levels of gender equality in various social institutions (Morgan and Berkowitz King 2001; Rindfuss *et al.* 2003). Denmark, Finland and Sweden lead not only in non-marital fertility but also in acceptance of assisted conception. These countries show the highest rate of IVF cycle treatments per million inhabitants in Europe (Landau 2005) and the highest proportion of IVF births in relation to total births globally; while IVF births represent about one per cent of total births in most industrialised countries, they represent 2.7 per cent of all births in Finland, 2.8 per cent of all births in Norway, 2.9 per cent of all births in Sweden, 3.3 per cent of all births in Iceland and 3.5 per cent of all births in Denmark (Andersen *et al.* 2009).

It seems that a woman's decisions on how many children to bear depend on the normative and religious structure of her country. If the normative and practical environments permit it, then a woman who wants a child but not a husband (or who has difficulties in finding a suitable partner) may have a birth outside of a marital re-lationship and may use assisted conception technologies (Rindfuss *et al.* 2003). For example, in Israel the culturally pronatalist attitude is that children have a social value; apart from other benefits, they create social capital by establishing new relations among members of the family and the community (Morgan and Berkowitz King 2001). This pronatalist norm, as well as the encouraging stance of some religious leaders, enable even Orthodox Jewish single women to bear a child through medically assisted conception (Rotem 2004).

Western women now have greater flexibility in how they struc-ture their lives, but they have difficulty finding standards against which to judge their own progress or success. In such a situation, raising a child can bring a predictability to daily life that promotes well-being and provides some continuity to a woman's 'narrative'. Unlike other relationships, the mother–child bond is still strongly enforced by societal norms and perceived to have an enduring character (Morgan and Berkowitz King 2001). For some women, having children has assumed a quasi-religious function of provid-ing solutions to the meaning of life and the question of how to live as an adult. Children can fulfil such a quasi-religious function of making sense of a woman's life partly because of the capacity biological relationships have for symbolising social relationships

(Morgan and Berkowitz King 2001). It is still not clear, however, how a child can fulfil such a function in cases of third-party assisted conception where the child has no genetic or biological relationship to the mother.

Immerman and Mackey (2003) argue that religions in the twenty-first and twenty-second centuries will have one of three main trajectories: (1) they can encourage gender egalitarianism and occupational mobility for women; (2) they can be indifferent to gender roles, or (3) they can encourage gender complementarity, confining women primarily to the role of motherhood with minimal opportunities outside that role. Immerman and Mackey assume that the different courses taken by various religions will differentially influence the fertility level of the relevant communities.

Faiths and religions

Since the 1800s, Western scholars of comparative religion increasingly regard Buddhism, Christianity, Hinduism, Islam and Judaism as the most significant 'world religions'. Even today, these are considered the 'Big Five' and are the religions most likely to be covered in world religion books (Adherents.com 2008). According to the main database at Adherents.com (October 2008), Christianity is the largest religious group in the world (2.1 billion adherents), followed by Islam (1.5 billion), Hinduism (900 million), Chinese traditional religion (394 million), Buddhism (376 million), primal-indigenous (300 million), African traditional and Diasporic (100 million), Sikhism (23 million), Juche (19 million) and Judaism (14 million).

Since most religions undergo countless redefinitions, each of these 'world religions' is actually a collection of distinct movements, sects, divisions, denominations, and so on. Yet all adherents of the same religion share at least some commonalities, such as a common historical heritage and some shared doctrines, practices or texts. Emile Durkheim classically defined religion as 'a unified system of beliefs and practices relative to sacred things, that is to say, things set apart and forbidden – beliefs and practices which unite into one single moral community' (Adherents.com 2008). The major divisions within Christianity are the Roman Catholic Church, various Orthodox Churches and a number of Protestant denominations. These may differ widely in their views on marriage and procreation; for example, Sutton (1996) has explored the differences in this context between the Roman Catholic Church, the Church of England and the Presbyterian Church of Scotland. Islam also comprises numerous branches, the largest and best known being Sunni and Shi'ite.

Adherents.com (2008) regards Chinese traditional religion as the common religion of the majority Chinese culture. It consists of a combination of Confucianism, Buddhism and Taoism, as well as the traditional non-scriptural, local practices and beliefs. For most religious Chinese, these different ancient Chinese philosophies and traditions form a single, seamless, composite religious culture and worldview. Similarly, Japanese Shinto is one of the 'classic' 11 or 12 'major world religions'. But adherent counts for this religion are problematic and often misunderstood. Shinto is the indigenous ethnic practice of Japan and its importance is almost entirely historical and cultural (Adherents.com 2008). African traditional religions have spread considerably beyond their region of origin and they remain influential, identifiable religions. Of these, probably the largest African traditional religious/tribal complex is Yoruba. This was the religion of the vast Yoruba nation states in West Africa which existed before European colonialism. Today, adherents of African Diasporic religions typically have no real tribal affiliation; they may be converts to African-based religion and are not necessarily either African or black.

Finally, the number of secular or non-religious people is given by Adherents.com as around 1.1 billion. This number may be arguable. While China probably does have the largest number of actual atheists of any country in the world and many Russians clearly remain atheists, Adherents.com notes that it is difficult to determine accurately how many of those classified as atheists or non-religious in the Communist-era USSR and by the current Chinese government are actually atheists according to their personal beliefs.

In this book we trace the development of the challenges that new technologies in the area of fertility currently present to the prevalent faith systems of the world. The chapters in the book are listed in order of the magnitude of the faith systems in terms of the number of their adherents.

Christianity has the largest number of adherents in the world. In Chapters 1 and 2 we present the views of the Roman Catholic Church and the Anglican Church.

In Chapter 1, Jim Richards introduces the basic values and morals of the Roman Catholic Church, also referred to as the 'Latin' Church and sometimes abbreviated simply as the 'Catholic' Church. The Roman Catholic Church, tracing its founding to the coming of Jesus Christ over two thousand years ago, has a hierarchical structure, based at the bottom on parishes led by a priest under the jurisdiction of a bishop. The highest authority of the Church is the Pope, the Bishop of Rome, with his seat in the Vatican. The Vatican Council, consisting of bishops, formulates the Church's doctrines, which are assembled in what is referred to as the Catechism. The Catechism is periodically revised, updated and approved by the Pope. According to the Catechism, every human being has the right to life from conception, the family is the original cell of social life, and marriage is an unbreakable union. Based on these core values, Richards discusses the Roman Catholic Church's categorical views of abortion, the use of contraception, third-party assisted conception, sex selection and the use of other fertility-related technologies. On a continuum of restrictive–permissive approach to issues in the area of fertility, the Roman Catholic Church in its doctrines and teaching is on the restrictive side.

The Anglican faith has been known as such since 1534 when Henry VIII, King of England, split from the Papacy. In contrast to adherents of the Roman Catholic Church, Anglicans do not refer to one central authority to make decisions regarding morals in an ever-changing world. The Church of England, the Anglican Church of Canada, the Episcopal Church of the United States of America and the Anglican Church of Australia, based on independently carried out studies on their views of fertility issues, advise their respective governments. The titular head of the Anglican communion is the Archbishop of Canterbury and its leadership comprises bishops who, since 1868, meet once a decade within the framework of the Lambeth Conference. A scrutiny of the Lambeth Conferences over time reveals that the Anglican approach to fertility issues tends to be pragmatic. The Anglican view of the use of contraception, which underwent a process from rejection to approval, exemplifies this best. The volume of studies published by the Anglican Churches in order to adjust the core Anglican values on centrality of marriage, the child's well-being and the individual's responsibility towards society in fertility issues is not only impressive but has also exerted an important impact on the laws in different countries. Phyllis Creighton describes in Chapter 2 the approaches of the Anglican Churches to issues such as abortion, surrogacy and sex selection.

Like Christianity, Islam is a monotheistic religion originating with the teachings of the Prophet Muhammad, an Arab leader from the seventh century. In Islam there are two principal denominations, the Sunni and the Shia'a, although there is no central authority to decide on fertility issues. The first and principal source to guide Muslims on these issues is the holy Qur'an. While the Qur'an does not provide explicit answers to problems of family formation, it is expected that each generation exercises judgment to find solutions to the problems that arise. However, according to the Qur'an, a free individual is someone who belongs to two entities, to the larger community of Islam and to the family. Being part of a family and having responsibilities, duties and obligations towards the family are central values in Islam. Procreation in Islam is a sign of God's will and a large family is perceived to be a blessing. In Chapter 3 Mohammad Iqbal and Ray Noble identify additional sources that guide Islamic thinking and actions: Sunnah, the Prophet's actions, Hadith, the Prophet's sayings and Shariah, the jurists' decisions. Based on core Islamic values and these sources, they then specify Islamic views of birth control and family planning, abortion and artificial reproductive technologies, pre-implantation genetic diagnosis and selection of embryos, surrogacy and human cloning.

Hinduism is unique among the religions in that it has no known founder or exact date of origin; its roots dating back four thousand years and the authors of its sacred texts unknown, Hinduism is a principal religion of the people of India. Hinduism's approach to family and fertility issues is greatly affected by the Hindu belief in rebirth, viewing life from a perspective that encompasses not just this life but many other lives that preceded it, as well as lives that will succeed it. Based on ancient Sanskrit epics of India and other sacred scripts and ancient tales, in Chapter 4 Gautam N. Allahbadia, Swati G. Allahbadia and Sulbha Arora familiarise the reader with the basic Hindu concepts of *dharma* and *karma*, with the deities Brahma, Vishnu and Shiva, and a variety of rituals customary in Hindu families. Although, unlike other faith systems, Hinduism is very tolerant of abortion and the use of reproductive technologies, the ancient preference for male children still significantly affects the structure of Hindu society. Female children may still be subjected to gender bias. Female infanticide and killing of infants born with physical impairments soon after birth have been frequent practices in India owing to lack of law enforcement, and are now augmented by sex selection procedures that are used to forestall the births of female infants.

Geok Ling Lee, Celia Hoi Yan Chan, Elizabeth Wai-Hing Choi Hui and Cecilia Lai Wan Chan, in Chapter 5 on Chinese traditional religious beliefs, portray the importance of these beliefs on the behaviours of Chinese people. Although the beliefs have ancient roots, the rationale for them has been forgotten or lost over time.

Chinese traditional beliefs can be divided into institutionalised beliefs (religion) and non-religious beliefs (folk belief systems and cultural practices). Confucianism, Daoism and Buddhism are the institutionalised traditional Chinese beliefs that form the basis of daily living for Chinese people. Although Buddhism, which underwent a transformation when entering China, appealed more to women because of its creed of universal compassion, in both Confucianism and Daoism the emphasis is on men. In the Chinese folk beliefs, likewise, the male is predominant. In a patrilineal and patriarchical Chinese society, only giving birth to a son endows a woman with status in her extended family. The strong cultural preference for sons, coupled with the state's 'one child policy', has resulted in an unprecedented imbalanced gender ratio in China. In the past this took an enormous toll in terms of female babies being aborted, abandoned or killed. It is unclear whether the current shortage of females will improve their lives or perpetuate existing discrimination, such as exposure to the risk of kidnapping or being sold into marriage, neither of which practices has been unusual in the past.

Buddhism is another ancient belief system originating in India. 'Buddha' means 'enlightened one' in the ancient Indian languages. The earliest source of Buddhist literature is the Indian Pali Canon, a Sanskrit text. In Chapter 6, drawing on Sigala Discourse (a dialogue between Buddha and the layman Sigala on the question of proper conduct in family relationships), Michael G. Barnhart discusses Buddhism's views of family and fertility. The main emphasis in Buddhism, in Barnhart's view, is on the overall manner in which one should conduct oneself in living and the degree of compassionately motivated reciprocity that can lead to freedom from suffering. As Barnhart introduces the basic values and concepts of Buddhism, the reader gradually learns that Buddhism is not a dogmatic belief system; Buddhists are relatively free to determine what sorts of rites and socially sanctioned relationships with others support the idea of living in a way that promotes peace and freedom from fear through compassionate reciprocity. Considering that Buddhism is very adaptive, and that historical precedent is of limited value in determining what Buddhist ethics demand, an apparently more 'liberal' approach to fertility control, diverse family structures (including 'alternative' families) and assisted reproduction are also possible from a Buddhist perspective.

The contribution of Titilayo O. Aderibigbe on African traditional religion (Chapter 7) focuses predominantly on the Yoruba traditional religion in Nigeria. According to Aderibigbe, for Africans their belief encompasses the very essence of their whole being and neither 'imported' Christianity nor Islam has succeeded in eroding their worldview. What is common to all African traditional religions is belief in a supreme, omnipotent and omniscient creator, and the fact that almost all adherents worship the supreme deity through lesser gods, who they believe intercede between humans and the supreme God. Traditional religions all share a common belief in spirits, divinities and ancestors who form a link between the present and the past. One of the basic tenets of the Yoruba traditional religion, that women and children belong to men, has often been interpreted to mean that men can also control their reproduction. Since children are regarded as the blessing of the gods and a source of a man's wealth, the Yoruba traditional religion rejects the ideas of contraception and abortion. Aderibigbe describes in detail the Yoruba traditional religion's views on involuntary childlessness, protection of the unborn, the status of women in a patriarchical society that allows polygamy and assisted conception.

Judaism, the first monotheistic religion, dates back over five thousand years. Judaism believes in a single, omnipotent God who created the universe and governs it. In this collection the views of Orthodox and Reform Judaism on family and fertility issues are presented.

Rabbi Gideon Weitzman, in Chapter 8, indicates that while there are different groups in Orthodox Judaism, all of them are committed to following and acting upon the Halachah, the Jewish legal system that guides the actions of an Orthodox Jew. The Halachah comprises the Five Books of Moses and the Oral Law that is the interpretation of the law. In Orthodox Judaism, the normative religious behaviour is based on an ongoing explanation of the Halachah. There is no one central authority that determines the daily behaviour of Orthodox Jews, which is rather guided by the rich halachic literature that includes previous decisions and their interpretations pertaining to issues in everyday life, and the examination of new situations in view of those precedents. While each rabbi may participate in the halachic debate, there are some rabbis whose opinions carry greater weight and cannot be ignored. The first commandment of the Torah – 'be fruitful and multiply' – reflects the great importance of having and raising children in the Jewish tradition. Based on various halachic sources, Rabbi Weitzman examines the halachic views, as perceived by Orthodox Judaism, on fertility testing, modern fertility treatments, third-party assisted conception, the status of the embryo and related issues.

Reform Judaism reflects modern Jewish thought. Its beginning is traced to the late eighteenth century in central Europe and nowadays it flourishes particularly in North America. While the traditional Jewish Halachah does retain a significant influence upon Reform religious practices, Reform Judaism is also committed to 'informed choice' and the religious autonomy of the individual. The teaching and practices of Reform Judaism are basically guided by the growing body of Reform responsa, essentially finding new and more permissive interpretations of the traditional Halachah. In Chapter 9 Mark Washofsky illustrates this interaction between the Orthodox traditional and Reform Jewish values in relation to the first commandment concerning procreation. In contrast to the Orthodox view, Reform Jewish thought does not hold that procreation is a duty more incumbent upon males than upon females. The egalitarian approach towards women in Reform Judaism significantly distinguishes it from Orthodox Judaism, and has an impact on its views on abortion, the status of the embryo, assisted conception, surrogacy and sex selection. Washofsky concludes that the tension between Orthodox Jewish thought and the need to reconcile it with the challenges of social changes and technological innovations results in a plural conception of moral truth in Reform Judaism.

This overview has clearly shown the significance of religion for family formation and fertility patterns, and for gender roles in the family and in society. However, there has not, hitherto, been a single text systematically presenting current interpretations of the teachings of the world's main religions on these issues. This volume aims to fill that gap and provide the reader with reliable information on the perceptions of various faiths regarding the issues of gender equity, marriage, use of modern means of contraception and assisted conception technologies. The contributors to this volume, regarded as authorities in their religion or belief system, were requested to provide a new overview of these issues and of the related debates within their respective faiths.

We believe that exposure to the current teachings on these important issues in the world's major religions and belief systems can significantly improve the intercultural understanding of values influencing fertility-related practices. Furthermore, the global level of migration in recent decades has given many societies a multi-cultural make-up. The present volume will provide professionals in these societies with essential cultural background information for intervening in issues pertaining to family life.

Note

1   In common with other American researchers, Lehrer does not distinguish between Orthodox, Conservative and Reform Judaism, treating it as a single community, although the Reform community is the largest Jewish community in the USA.

References

Aboulghar, M., Serour, G.I. and Mansour, R.T. (2007) 'Ethical aspects and regulation of assisted reproduction in the Arabic-speaking world.' *Reproductive Biomedicine Online 14*, 143–146.

Adherents.com (2008) www.adherents.com/

Adsera, A. (2006) 'Religion and changes in family-size norms in developed countries.' *Review of Religious Research 47*, 3, 271–286.

Agadjanian, V. (1999) 'Post-Soviet demographic paradoxes: ethnic differences in marriage and fertility in Kazakhstan.' *Sociological Forum 14*, 3, 425–446.

Agadjanian, V. (2001) 'Negotiating through reproductive change: gendered social interaction and fertility regulation in Mozambique.' *Journal of Southern African Studies 27*, 2, 291–309.

Agadjanian, V. and Makarova, E. (2003) 'From Soviet modernization to post-Soviet transformation: understanding marriage and fertility dynamics in Uzbekistan.' *Development and Change 34*, 4, 447–473.

Alagarajan, M. (2003) 'An analysis of fertility differentials by religion in Kerala state: a test of the interaction hypothesis.' *Population Research and Policy Review 22*, 5–6, 557–574.

Andersen, A.N., Goossens, V., Bhattacharya, S., Fervaretti, A.P., Kupka, M.S., de Mouzon, J. and Nygren, K.G. (2009) 'Assisted reproductive technology and interuterine inseminations in Europe, 2005. Results generated from European registers by ESHRE.' *Human Reproduction 24*, 6, 1267–1287.

Baron, L. (2004) 'Argentina: hopes, results and barriers.' In: E. Blyth and R. Landau (eds) *Third Party Assisted Conception across Cultures: Social, Legal and Ethical Perspectives*. London: Jessica Kingsley Publishers.

Bearman, P.S. and Bruckner, H. (2001) 'Promising the future: virginity pledges and first intercourse.' *American Journal of Sociology 106*, 4, 859–912.

Bielawska-Batorowitz, E. (2004) 'Poland: provision and guidelines for third-party assisted conception.' In: E. Blyth and R. Landau (eds) *Third Party Assisted Conception across Cultures: Social, Legal and Ethical Perspectives*. London: Jessica Kingsley Publishers.

Blyth, E. and Landau, R. (eds) (2004) *Third Party Assisted Conception across Cultures: Social, Legal and Ethical Perspectives*. London: Jessica Kingsley Publishers.

Carbonatto, C.L. (2004) 'South Africa: cultural diversity.' In: E. Blyth and R. Landau (eds) *Third Party Assisted Conception across Cultures: Social, Legal and Ethical Perspectives*. London: Jessica Kingsley Publishers.

Derosas, R. and van Poppel, F. (eds) (2006) *Religion and the Decline of Fertility in the Western World*. Dordrecht: Springer.

Dharmalingam, A. and Morgan, S.P. (2004) 'Pervasive Muslim–Hindu fertility differences in India.' *Demography 41*, 3, 529–545.

Donahue, M.J. and Benson, P.L. (1995) 'Religion and the well-being of adolescents.' *Journal of Social Issues 51*, 2, 145–160.

Ellison C.G. and Bartkowski, J.P. (2002) 'Conservative Protestantism and the division of household labour among married couples.' *Journal of Family Issues 23*, 8, 950–985.

Hussain, S. (2001) 'Do women really have a choice? Reproductive behavior and practices of two religious communities.' *Asian Journal of Women's Studies 7*, 4, 29–69.

Immerman, R.S. and Mackey, W.C. (2003) 'Religion and fertility.' *Mankind Quarterly 43*, 4, 377–408.

Inhorn, M.C. (1996) *Infertility and Patriarchy: The Cultural Politics of Gender and Family Life in Egypt*. Philadelphia, PA: University of Pennsylvania Press.

Landau, R. (2003) 'Religiosity, nationalism and human reproduction: the case of Israel.' *International Journal of Sociology and Social Policy 23*, 12, 64–77.

Landau, R. (2005) *The Policy of Assisted Conception Treatments in Israel.* Jerusalem: Hebrew University of Jerusalem, Paul Baerwald School of Social Work, The Social Policy Research Group.

Lehrer, E.L. (1996a) 'Religion as a determinant of marital fertility.' *Journal of Population Economics 9*, 2, 173–196.

Lehrer, E.L. (1996b) 'The role of husband's religious affiliation in the economic and demographic behaviour of families.' *Journal for the Scientific Study of Religion 35*, 2, 145–155.

Lehrer, E.L. (2004a) 'The role of religion in union formation: an economic perspective.' *Population Research and Policy Review 23*, 2, 161–185.

Lehrer, E.L. (2004b) 'Religion as a determinant of economic and demographic behavior in the United States.' *Population and Development Review 30*, 4, 707–726.

McQuillan, K. (2004) 'When does religion influence fertility?' *Population and Development Review 30*, 1, 25–33.

Marchena, E. and Waite, L.J. (2001) *Marriage and Childbearing Attitudes in Late Adolescence: Gender, Race and Ethnic Differences.* Revised version of paper presented at the meeting of the Population Association of America, March 2000, Los Angeles, CA, USA.

Morgan, S.P. and Berkowitz King, R. (2001) 'Why have children in the 21st century? Biological predisposition, social coercion, rational choice.' *European Journal of Population 17*, 1, 3–20.

Morgan, S.P., Stash, S., Smith, H.L. and Oppenheim Mason, K. (2002) 'Muslim and non-Muslim differences in female autonomy and fertility: evidence from four Asian countries.' *Population and Development Review 28*, 3, 515–537.

Ng, E., Liu, A., Chan, C. and Chan, C. (2004) 'Hong Kong: a social, legal and clinical overview.' In: E. Blyth and R. Landau (eds) *Third Party Assisted Conception across Cultures: Social, Legal and Ethical Perspectives.* London: Jessica Kingsley Publishers.

Ogburn, W.F. (1964) *On Culture and Social Change.* Chicago, IL: University of Chicago Press.

Pearce, L.D. (2002) 'The influence of early life course religious exposure on young adults' dispositions toward childbearing.' *Journal for the Scientific Study of Religion 41*, 2, 325–340.

Rindfuss, R.R., Benjamin Guzzo, K. and Morgan, S.P. (2003) 'The changing institutional context of low fertility.' *Population Research and Policy Review 22*, 5–6, 411–438.

Rotem, T. (2004) 'That's the way we want it.' *Haaretz Weekend Supplement*, 11 June, 42–46.

Schenker, J.K. (2000) 'Women's reproductive health: monotheistic religious perspectives.' *International Journal of Gynecology and Obstetrics 70*, 1, 77–86.

Sewpaul, V. (1999) 'Culture, religion and infertility: a South African perspective.' *British Journal of Social Work 29*, 5, 741–754.

Sutton, A. (1996) 'Three Christian views on assisted conception and marriage – the Roman Catholic Church, Church of England and Presbyterian Church of Scotland.' *Eubios Journal of Asian and International Bioethics 6*, 105–107.

Tober, D.M., Taghdisi, M.H. and Jalali, M. (2006) '"Fewer children, better life" or "As many as god wants?" Family planning among low-income Iranian and Afghan refugee families in Ishfahan, Iran.' *Medical Anthropology Quarterly 20*, 1, 50–71.

United Nations (2003) *World Fertility Report 2003.* Geneva: Department of Economic and Social Affairs: United Nations.

Waite, L.J. and Lehrer, E.L. (2003) 'The benefits from marriage and religion in the United States: a comparative analysis.' *Population and Development Review 29*, 2, 255–275.

Woas, D. (2007) 'Does religion belong in population studies?' *Environment and Planning A 39*, 5, 1166–1180.

1

A Roman Catholic Perspective on Fertility Issues

Objective Truths, Moral Absolutes and the Natural Law

Jim Richards

The Catholic Church – adherents, organisation and doctrine

The Roman Catholic Church traces its founding to the coming of Jesus Christ and his conferring on the 12 apostles the mission to take his teaching to the whole world. The tradition is that the Church was founded 50 days after his crucifixion, death and resurrection, at Pentecost. The present Church consists of what we know as the Roman Catholic Church, together with 22 'particular churches'. These include the church in the West, sometimes known as the Latin Church, and churches in the East, such as the Maronites, who originated and are still numerous in Lebanon, and the Syro-Malabar Church, which springs from Kerala, in India. All of these are in full communion with one another and accept the Pope and his authority as Bishop of Rome.

Numerically it is estimated that there are 1,114,966,000 Catholics (Central Statistics Office 2007), comprising one sixth of the world's population, and so making it the largest religious organisation in the world, as well as the largest Christian church. The organisational structure is based on parishes, which are normally led by a priest under the jurisdiction of a bishop, who will have in his charge a group of parishes, called a diocese. Worldwide there are 2,782 such episcopal areas, also known as 'sees'. The bishops are able to trace their origins, and thus their authority, back to the 12 apostles chosen by Jesus. This historical continuity is known as the Apostolic Succession. The bishops, convened by the Pope in an Ecumenical Council, are thus able to make infallible statements and, when they are so convened, share in the Magisterium, the infallible teaching office of the Church.

Membership of the Church is via baptism, followed by confirmation and the Eucharist. The beliefs and doctrines of the Church come from the Bible, especially the four Gospels, which recount Jesus' life and teachings. These have been developed through the Magisterium.

The early Church was notable for its diversity. Many languages were used, reflecting the range of peoples joining the Church, and a variety of rites were employed. Rome, as the place of martyrdom of both Peter and Paul, was always regarded as a special place, but it did not in those early days possess the jurisdictional authority it was later to acquire and which it still holds. This growth in the influence of Rome was particularly noticeable from the eleventh and twelfth centuries. This could be evidenced by Latin becoming the universal language of the Church and the growing complexity of laws governing all aspects of Church life, known as Canon Law. This period also saw the greater separation of clerics from laity. These elements remained, and to some extent deepened, following the Counter-Reformation in the sixteenth century, which developed in reaction to the establishment of the Protestant Churches, following Martin Luther's break with Rome.

Aspects of the above changed rapidly after the Second Vatican Council (1962–1966), not least in the use of the vernacular in worship, the ordination of married men as deacons, and the opportunities, not yet fully realised, for women to play a greater part in the running of the Church. The Council also brought about a greater sense of the collegiate nature of the episcopacy, as may be seen in the decisions made at the Council and the subsequent establishment of national Conferences of Bishops (Hastings 2000).

Despite the vast size of the Church and its spread across the world, the way it is organised and how it formulates and makes known its doctrines means that one is able to understand clearly the voice of the Church on all major matters and, in particular, with regard to the topics covered below. An accessible vehicle for this is the Catechism of the Catholic Church, which provides a comprehensive collection of Catholic 'doctrine regarding both faith and morals' (Catechism 2002, p.5). It was revised, updated and approved by the late Pope John Paul II, who in doing so incorporated in it the works of the Second Vatican Council. In giving his approval to the text Pope John Paul II described its doctrinal value in the following terms: 'I declare it to be a sure norm for teaching the faith and thus a valid and legitimate instrument for ecclesial communion' (Catechism 2002, p.5). He went on to assert that it is 'a sure and authentic reference for teaching Catholic doctrine'.

The family and its wider role

Given that the Church has stated that 'The family founded on marriage is truly the sanctuary of life' (Pontifical Council for Justice and Peace 2004, p.136) and that marriage is based on men and women giving a lifelong commitment to each together, it can readily be seen that this unit is the basis of family formation. The family should be seen as a 'domestic church' (Catechism 2002). Consequently it is from within the family that familial gender relationships are formed and links across generations established. Thus most of the important relationships in life spring from the family, and it is from this family experience that we reach out to the wider community to forge other relationships. This makes the family the 'original cell of social life' (Catechism 2002, p.476). The Church sees the family as the unit which should do its very best to care for the old, the young, the sick and those with disabilities within it, while recognising that this is not always possible.

More specifically with regards to relationships within the immediate and wider family, children are expected to 'honour' their mothers and fathers (*New Jerusalem Bible* 1990, p.70, p.817, Ecclesiasticus 7:27), an obligation springing from the love they should have for each other, and from the fact it is parents who give to children the gift of life. As roles reverse and parents age and become infirm, their now adult offspring are able to repay the gift of life, affection, care and support they received, by helping and caring for their parents. The Church also stresses the importance of the relationships forged between brothers and sisters. Grandparents have a special place in family life as well: 'The crown of the aged is their children's children' (*New Jerusalem Bible* 1990, p.744).

The role of parents extends beyond the physical and emotional care of their children. Children are seen as the 'supreme gift of marriage' (Catechism 2002, p.509) and the norm of marriage is to expect and hope for children. With specific regard to the number of children a husband and wife have, this is a decision for them alone. This position is based on the principle of subsidiarity, that is that decisions within the wider community and within families should be made at the lowest level possible. Therefore any form of state interference in the number of children parents have is an attack on a fundamental right and it is to be resisted. Consequently it is the duty of the state to ensure that families have this freedom (Catechism 2002). With regard to limitation of the number of children that are conceived, the Church recognises that spouses may wish 'to space the birth of their children' (Catechism 2002).

More widely, with regard to population growth, the Church condemns any programme which has as its purpose a campaign to deliver contraception or sterilisation as constituting 'an affront to the dignity of the person and family' (Pontifical Council for Justice and Peace 2004, p.138). Population growth is instead to be tackled by 'promoting greater justice and authentic solidarity' (Pontifical Council for Justice and Peace 2004, p.138). The link between population growth and poverty is to be seen in the context of the growing inequalities between rich and poor countries and between the rich and poor within countries.

There is recognition that in parts of the world, particularly Europe, there is a falling birth rate, whereas in other parts of the world there are sharp increases. The Church sees the use of contraception, sterilisation and abortion as a cause of the former. The decline in birth rates in these countries will only cease when these practices cease. The Church does not see the use of these three practices as the solution to the 'demographic explosion' in other countries.

The Church's teaching on marriage

To understand fully the position the Catholic Church holds in relation to contraception it will be helpful to explore first the Church's beliefs regarding marriage: 'God himself is the author of marriage' (Second Vatican Council 1998a, p.590). The Church recognises how marriage between men and women as a social institution has been affected by social and other changes, but in essence it demonstrates that the condition of marriage is firmly lodged within human nature and that it 'comes from the hand of creator' (Catechism

2002). The Church also believes that man and woman are created one for the other, and that each one of us is also created in the image of God. Moreover, God is love, and the love a married couple have for each other is a mirror of God's love for us. Marriage itself creates an unbreakable union: 'So they are no longer two therefore, but one flesh' (Matthew 19:6). Furthermore, there is within each of us a unity of body and soul. The consummation through and in the bodies of husband and wife itself becomes a holy act, with any children created being a result of the full expression of their married love (Richards 2003). It is in this context that the Church is able to describe parents as 'ministers of life' (Pontifical Council for Justice and Peace 2004, p.140).

Thus the married couple 'become two people inextricably linked in an understanding from God' (John Paul II 2005). It is a covenant relationship, one based on a promise of lifelong love and fidelity to each other, and the grace that was bestowed on the couple on the day of marriage is to be drawn on throughout that marriage. Their mutual love deepens, as does their love for God and for any children born to them (Richards 2003). The family created within marriage is 'the primary vital cell of society' (Second Vatican Council 1998b, p.779).

Children are seen as 'The supreme gift of marriage' (Catechism 2002, p.370), not as a right, or as something 'owned' (Catechism 2002, p.509). They come from the mutual giving of the couple. Indeed, in the words of Pope Paul VI's still controversial Encyclical, *Humanae Vitae*, 'it is necessary that each and every marriage act remain ordered *per se* in the procreation of human life' (Catechism 2002, p.507). The basis of this teaching springs from the call of conjugal love, which means that each should give to the other totally. In other words, there are to be no artificial barriers used during sexual intercourse. It has to be recognised that the available evidence suggests this is a doctrine honoured more in the breach than in the observance, with countries regarded as Catholic, such as Italy, Spain and France, having fertility rates of 1.33, 1.32 and

1.9 respectively. In contrast, the UK rate is 1.87. All these rates are below that needed for population replacement (Curtin and Branigan 2007).

Further evidence of the opposition of some Catholics to the Church's teaching on abortion, contraception and the creation of life by artificial means can be seen in the controversy over the London Catholic Hospital of St John and St Elizabeth. The move in 2007 to install on the site an NHS GP practice where the above three treatments would need to be offered or advised (since state money supports the practice) has led to the resignation of some Board members despite the fact that they wanted the practice installed, because this would be an infringement of the Catholic Hospital's code of ethics. In similar vein, a former advisor to Cardinal Cormac Murphy-O'Connor, the Archbishop of Westminster, has openly criticised the Church's stance on IVF as being an instance of 'disregarding its duty of love' (Wall 2007).

There is recognition that involuntary childlessness is a cause of great suffering, and research into reducing sterility is encouraged. However, and this will be considered more fully below, this should not be done in such a way as to entail 'the dissociation of husband and wife' (Catechism 2002, p.509). The sexual act is not to be separated from the procreative act. If all means have been employed to conceive that are within the Church's teaching, then one possible alternative is seen as adoption (Catechism 2002). It is, though, recognised that 'marriage was not instituted for the sole reason of procreation' (Pontifical Council for Justice and Peace 2004, p.128). There is, in other words, great value in the mutual love of husband and wife and their love for others, even when children are not born to them (Pontifical Council for Justice and Peace 2004).

The Church's teaching regarding the creation of life by artificial means has not changed over the years in response to technological developments. This does not mean that the Church does not encourage scientific research into the causes and treatments of infertility. Indeed, it is strongly supportive of what is referred to as the Billings Method, pioneered by Professors John and Evelyn Billings. This method allows women to have knowledge of and control over their menstrual cycle by learning how to sense the changes in the amount and texture of cervical mucus, and thus assists in determining both the optimum timing for conception, and conversely a woman's infertile periods. So much admired was this work that the late Professor John Billings received a Papal Knighthood for his achievements, most notably in the organisation he and his wife set up, WOOMB (World Organisation Ovulation Method Billings).

Despite the Church's clear teaching on such procedures as IVF, even when the gametes are from the husband and wife, there are, and no doubt will continue to be, parents who take this route. It is therefore legitimate to enquire as to the reception given, both to the children so conceived and to their parents, by the Church.

The children are regarded in exactly the same way as a child born by natural means, and they are equally welcomed within the Church. The position with regards to the parents in daily parish practice is no different than with any other group of parents. As with the latter, should they feel they have done wrong in this regard, or on any other matter, then they have available to them the Sacrament of Reconciliation, more commonly known as Confession.

A different view is more likely to be taken if someone makes public their views of, for instance, IVF. If their stated pronouncements contradict the Church's teaching, it is possible for that person to be denied communion.

Family forms other than marriage

The above has clear implications as to how the Church regards family diversity. The key point here is that it is only within marriage, between a man and a woman, that the full expression of physical love should take place, and so the Church opposes any sort of same sex partnership, whether or not sanctioned by law, just as it also opposes cohabitation by heterosexual couples. It perhaps goes without saying that it is opposed to such practices as polygamy because of its views regarding the exclusivity of marriage.

Its doctrines concerning same sex cohabitation and sexual acts within such unions are clear: 'They are contrary to the natural law...under no circumstances can they be approved' (Catechism 2002, p.505). However, alongside this is the recognition that all of us are made in the image of Christ, and therefore 'Every sign of unjust discrimination in their regard should be avoided' (Catechism 2002, p.505).

The Church is similarly opposed to single women who deliberately seek to conceive a child with no intention of living with the father. The single-parent family thus formed is also a misnomer, for all children have two parents. The Church recognises that there is family breakdown but it does not believe it is helpful to describe the families that are often formed following breakdown as 'recomposed' or 'reconstituted'. The reality is that there is a 'broken' family that remains, which may still be of importance to the child of the family, who may suffer as a result of that breakdown. These family types are essentially adult creations, primarily aimed at meeting adults' needs. Ultimately they are not child centred (Trujillo 2003).

The human embryo and storage of embryos

With regard to embryos, the Church teaches that life must be protected and recognised as if it was a human person, and it is able to cite biblical authority for this position. This fundamental right to protection is not dependent on the views of the parents, society or the state. They are inalienable and cannot be taken away: 'they belong to human nature and are inherent in the person by virtue of the creative act from which the person took his origin' (Catechism 2002, p.490). One such fundamental right is 'every human being's right to life and physical integrity from the moment of conception until death' (Catechism 2002, p.490).

Flowing from this is the clear implication that the human embryo, as a person, must be cared for, as far as it is possible, just like any other human being (Catechism 2002). Therefore prenatal diagnosis, so long as it is part of a process that leads to healing and the hoped-for eventual life outside the womb, is morally acceptable. It is not acceptable, though, if it is used as a reason to seek an abortion – if, for instance, it is thought that the unborn child may have disabilities: 'children have the right to their parents' unconditional acceptance at every stage of life' (Catholic Bishops 2005).

The Church does not approve of the storage of embryos. Embryo cryopreservation, apart from the objections that the conjugal act within marriage is the only way to produce children, can have other negative consequences. Stored embryos can sometimes be discarded by parents, who may fail to respond to requests from clinics as to their wishes with regards to them. There can also be cases involving courts as to who 'owns' the embryo and who may determine how it is to be disposed of, following the separation of a man and a woman, after the embryos have been produced, as occurred in the dispute between a British couple, Natalie Evans and her former fiancé, Howard Johnson. Ms Evans had six eggs fertilised by Mr Johnson and then stored, as she was about to undergo medical treatment for ovarian cancer, which would leave her infertile. Subsequently Ms Evans and Mr Johnson separated and Mr Johnson withdrew his consent to Ms Evans' use of the embryos. Ms Evans took her case to the European Court of Human Rights which ruled against her, and consequently the embryos were destroyed (European Court of Human Rights 2006).

Abortion and contraception

The Church's teaching on abortion is clear and the Catechism states in unflinching language that 'abortion willed whether as an end or a means, is gravely contrary to the moral law' (Catechism 2002, p.489). Moreover 'formal co-operation' is a 'grave offence' (Catechism 2002, p.489) and those who procure an abortion do by that very act excommunicate themselves.

This stance is taken given the belief and the Church's doctrine that there must be absolute protection for all human life from the 'point of conception' (Catechism 2002, p.489). The Church also charges society as a whole in its various structures, and especially elected politicians, to have regard to what the Catechism describes as every human being's right to life (Catechism 2002), which is innate in a person's origins, being created in the image of Christ. Flowing from this is the injunction that from conception the unborn child is to be treated as human. Such a child is by definition highly vulnerable and the state has a special responsibility to care (Catechism 2002).

The above teaching is also especially addressed to those who hold elected office. The role of an elected person and adherence to Church doctrine is a controversial area, summed up in the question as to whether that person is a representative of the electorate or of his or her church. The response might be that as long as the electorate knew of the candidate's position on relevant matters, in this case abortion, then they should have known, in effect, what they were voting for. In any case, the Church has stated that, 'there should be no support given to legislation in respect of unjust laws or laws that are contrary to the moral order' (Cat. 1903). This would include abortion.

However, in certain circumstances it would be permissible, for example, to vote for a measure involving abortion if the law was being changed so that some of its negative consequences, as perceived by the Church, were being mitigated. This might involve a reduction in the number of weeks beyond which an abortion could not take place (John Paul II 2005). Within the UK this position has been voiced by Church leaders. Cardinal Keith O'Brien, Archbishop of Edinburgh, has spoken of the need for those who support abortion to examine their consciences, stating that if they continue in their position they should exclude themselves from receiving communion (Farmer 2007). He stated this in the context of Scotland's 2006 abortion figures being at an all-time high of 13,081, despite the fact that when the Abortion Act was passed in 1967, supporters of the legislation had stated that its use would be rare. England and Wales also experienced the highest ever number of abortions at 193,700 in 2006, whereas it was 186,400 in 2005, and 148,000 in 1986 (Ward 2007). Cardinal O'Brien's position is also supported by Cardinal Cormac Murphy-O'Connor, Archbishop of Westminster (Murphy-O'Connor 2007).

The Church is criticised for not tolerating abortion and contraception. Opponents argue that allowing the latter would reduce the need to have recourse to the former. The counter-argument to this is what has been described as the negative impact of the 'contraceptive mentality' (Joh Paul II 2005). By this it is meant that using artificial contraceptive methods implies a pre-existing disposition not to have a child. If nevertheless a child is conceived, that would tend to strengthen a subsequent wish to seek an abortion. It is also argued that the 'contraceptive mentality' has an essence of self-centredness based on an essentially selfish notion of freedom, where a child would be seen as a curtailment of that freedom.

It is also to be noted in this context in relation to destroying the embryo, that the embryo also has a soul, which the Church teaches is not produced by parents but is created immediately by God (Catechism 2002). The body and soul of a person do not have a separate existence. They are seen as a unity, although the soul is seen as being of greater value to a person.

Third-party assisted conception

There is a range of procedures available to assist couples in conceiving a child. The Church permits only those procedures which facilitate conception via natural means. This means that third-party assisted conception is not approved. Indeed, it is described as 'gravely immoral' to employ techniques that in effect separate husband and wife from each other in procreation by the intrusion of a third party. This would embrace surrogacy and techniques which involve the donation of either sperm, eggs or embryos. Surrogacy would include instances even where the embryo implanted was created using the sperm and egg of the husband and wife. These 'third party' procedures 'infringe the child's right to be born of a father and mother known to him and bound to each other by marriage' and deny the right of the couple only to become parents through each other (Catechism 2002, p.509).

Techniques which involve the married couple only are, unlike the above, deemed to be 'less reprehensible' but are still 'morally unacceptable' (Catechism 2002, p.509). Again there is a dissociation between the married couple. The life created is produced by medical practitioners and 'establishes the domination of technology over the origin and destiny of the human person' (Catechism 2002, p.509). The child is not created by an act of love between two people but is produced by others.

Apart from these objections the Church is also concerned that many of these techniques have a high failure rate, both with regards to the initial fertilisation and then subsequently with the development of the embryo. Because of these factors there is an over-production of embryos, leading to the problem of 'spare embryos'. Consequently, stored and unused, there is then a call for them to be used for research purposes (John Paul 2005).

Surrogacy, whether the surrogate selected is within the family, for example a sister, or chosen as a result of a financial transaction, is considered to be 'gravely immoral' because it means that the spouses' right to become parents only through each other is negated. Moreover, the child also has rights and these too are negated in that the child has not been born of parents 'bound to each other by marriage' (Catechism 2002, p.509). This teaching applies, whatever might be the genetic constitution of the child born as a result of surrogacy, and it should be recognised that this procedure can complicate parenthood, with up to five adults involved, depending on circumstances: there may be the two commissioning parents, the man who donated sperm, or the women who donated eggs, and the surrogate. Nor should the womb be seen as a neutral space. It is now much better known that in the in-utero environment, what the mother eats and drinks, her emotional disposition, all have the potential for a positive or negative impact on the child.

Surrogacy also inverts our conception of motherhood because the 'good' surrogate relinquishes the child, whilst the 'bad' surrogate keeps the child. Thought has also to be given to any existing children of the surrogate and the possible impact on them, particularly if they are of tender years, of seeing their mother pregnant, give birth and then have that baby given away. Her older children might also receive a distorted concept of parenthood as a commercial transaction. Intra-family surrogacy, whilst not necessarily involving a commercial element, has its own distortions, whereby the surrogate, if a sister to one of the commissioning parents, becomes the 'aunt' of that baby (Richards 2003).

The Church has made clear its opposition (Pontifical Academy for Life 2004) to egg donation because, amongst other things, it offends the conjugal unity of the couple by the introduction of a third party and negates the right of a child to be born to parents who share his or her biological structure. Egg donation has within it, at first glance, a commendable altruistic aspect, particularly as a woman has more eggs than she will ever need. Closer examination reveals serious problems. Eggs may be donated for two reasons. One is for the creation of embryos for therapeutic cloning. The other is so that a woman who is unable to produce eggs may have one donated, then fertilised by her husband or partner and subsequently implanted in her womb. There are, though, dangers to the woman who donates because the hormone treatment needed to produce a large number of eggs in one cycle has the potential to make a woman sterile, or possibly lead to her death (Sutton 2007), and the long-term effects of these stimulative drugs are unknown. There is the additional possibility that this type of stimulation may lead to abnormalities in children born to the women who have undergone this treatment (Steigenga, Helmerhorst and Koning 2006). There are also commercial aspects to this where women undergoing fertility treatment may be offered 'free' IVF treatments in exchange for eggs. If it is straight payment then this might encourage young women in difficult financial circumstances to donate. It could be argued that reduced fees for infertility treatment could be construed as tantamount to the sale of body parts. This would appear to be outlawed by the Council of Europe Convention on Human Rights and Biomedicine, where Article 21 states that: 'The human body and its parts shall not, as such, give rise to financial gain' (Council of Europe 1997).

The Church's view is that IVF as a process is wrong because by its very nature it leads to the destruction of embryos. But in addition there is also a clear element of selfishness in embarking upon artificial methods of reproduction in old age.

Prenatal tests, selection and saviour siblings

The Church has no objections to prenatal diagnosis so long as this is for the purpose of safe-guarding the health of the child in-utero (John Paul II 2005). It is, though, concerned with the growth of practices involving an eugenic mindset. This may manifest itself in two ways. One is where the child is in the womb and a test is carried out for certain conditions. Such a test 'all too often becomes an opportunity for proposing and procuring an abortion' (John Paul II 2005, p.9). Tests may also be carried out on embryos created outside the womb with those that do not pass these tests being destroyed. Again the Church sees this as the unwarranted death of an unborn child. Particularly within the European context, the Church has expressed fears that these practices have very close echoes with Europe's Nazi past (Trujillo 2003).

Closely linked to this practice is prenatal selection, which has been used to create so-called 'designer babies', where would-be parents have an embryo implanted in the mother which has the particular characteristics they seek, such as race, personality and intelligence. There are also procedures to test for the gender of a future child. One such test kit is called 'Pink or Blue'. The kit can be ordered on the internet and it has been criticised both for the commercialisation that it encourages in childbirth and the fact that a child of the undesired gender may be aborted. The 'wrong sex' aspect, it is reported, is often to the detriment of females, given the desire of some groups to have boys rather than girls (Prynn 2007).

Another reason for pre-selection is so that 'saviour siblings' may be created. One example of this was in respect of a six-year-old boy suffering from beta thalassaemia, which necessitated having a blood transfusion about once a month and being on a drip five days out of seven for twelve hours each time. A child was conceived with matching characteristics to the existing one so that this subsequent child's umbilical cord blood might be used to cure the older child (Sutton 2005).

The Church is clear that all the above are morally wrong. Pre-selection of embryos inevitably leads to the destruction of some embryos, either prior to implantation or, post implantation, as a result of abortion. Furthermore, the child who eventually is born has not been created for his or her own intrinsic value but to meet other needs, either the social ones of the parents, or, as in the case of 'saviour siblings', to meet the needs of another child. With this last category one also has to ask what might happen if the cure hoped for by giving birth to the 'saviour' did not work. There are also the feelings of that child, in knowing that he or she was born not for himself or herself but to assist a sibling. Pressure might also be put on the 'aide' child in later years but before reaching the age of majority, to donate, for example, bone marrow, given the perfect match. Again, if this procedure does not work, one has to reflect on possible adverse family dynamics, with the 'saviour' perhaps being made to feel a failure, resentment from the sibling to be saved, and the parents having a different regard for their two children, one to be saved, the other to be used.

It has been argued that there is a stronger moral argument against 'saviour' babies as opposed to 'designer' babies. The former are conceived because of what they offer to another child, whereas at least the latter are conceived because the attributes selected are thought to be intrinsically advantageous to the child (Sutton 2005).

Posthumous conception

Posthumous conception, where a child is conceived following the death of one spouse, is opposed by the Church because the child will not be born into a family comprising husband and wife and because there is, by definition, a total absence of any loving sexual relationship between husband and wife at the time of fertilisation. Posthumous conception also deprives the child of a parent and distorts the natural order, a distortion only made possible by technological discoveries. In addition the deceased parent is objectified, because all that is needed of him or her is the relevant gamete, not the love and care of the parent. There is, of course, huge sympathy for the predicament and anguish of the surviving partner, but the ultimate good of society and the welfare of the child may not necessarily be best served by allowing the moral pace to be set by technicians and interested parties.

Secrecy and donor-assisted conception

Donor-assisted conception, of whatever type, inevitably gives rise to questions as to how the legal parents explain to the child his or her own origins. All children at some time are likely to ask of their parents 'Where do I come from?' The response, where a child is conceived and born naturally, will inevitably vary, based on the age and understanding of the child and the attitudes of the parents. The response, though, will fall within a broadly acceptable framework whose history is as long as parenthood itself. However, where the biological and social parents are not the same, there is but a relatively short period of experience on which we may call. What studies have revealed, though, is a common theme of secrecy (McWhinnie 2003). The research suggests that although pre-birth there will have been discussions between the parents, this often ceases post-birth and the impression is given of a child conceived naturally, often both to the wider family and to friends. Once set on this path it becomes almost impossible to reveal the truth to the child. The problems this may cause can be immense, such as when a child has a medical condition and a doctor asks whether there is a history of this in the family. Socially, complications arise when questions are asked about eye or hair colour. Even more devastating can be the discovery of one's true parentage as an adult and the consequent realisation that, although one's legal parents gave one love, they also brought one up within a lie.

Although parents might be put in this position by what they see as the severe social stigma attached to infertility, family life based on the flawed foundations of falsehood is inherently insecure. This situation is enabled to endure because the technology, which the Church identifies as immoral, exists. The Catholic Bishops of the British Isles have stated that donor-conceived children should, as a right, be provided with information about their genetic background at the age of 16 (Catholic Bishops 2005).

Cloning

Human cloning is here defined as a procedure whereby an embryo is produced with near identical genetic make-up to the organism used to make the clone. Resulting from this might be the birth of a person (although there is no evidence that, so far, this has ever happened), or the embryo might be used for research purposes, or for therapeutic reasons for the production of stem cells. With regard to these last two, the procedures involved take what is required from the embryo and result in its destruction. Hence, it has been pointed out, it is hardly therapeutic for the clone (Murphy-O'Connor 2001). In making a human clone to help cure someone else there is the deliberate intention of destroying life and treating that life as a product (Catholic Bishops 2005). It needs also to be realised that using cloned tissues or organs for transplantation in order to reduce the risk of rejection can, nevertheless, still carry the risk of rejection, particularly as the cloned embryo's make-up may not be an exact copy of the recipient's. The Church's objections to this process, beyond those already examined, include the fact that cloning takes place outside of marriage and in the absence of any act of love between two people. It is also something which essentially involves domination and control by the person carrying out the cloning over the person cloned (Pontifical Academy for Life 1997).

Conclusion

In the positions that the Church has taken on matters discussed in this chapter, it can be seen that there are three 'golden' threads running through its teachings. The first is that all human life is created in the image of God. The second is that all human life is precious from the moment of conception and that the child, at whatever stage of his or her existence, has an absolute right to protection. The third is the teaching on marriage, where within a particular marriage nothing should be done which comes between the couple giving to each other totally and exclusively. From this it is clear that on these issues of faith and fertility the Church starts from the belief that there are objective truths, moral absolutes and a natural, or external, law – the last meaning that there is a universal, divinely given wisdom with which, guided by reason, we may discern good from evil. By application of the natural law, we can judge the laws passed by governments. There is, in other words, 'an objective moral code implanted in human nature' (Murphy-O'Connor 2002). This overall stance is in direct conflict with a code based on moral relativism, whereby morality is something that is subjective, changeable and individualised, this last based on an individual's views in his or her own situation. Relativism places a high value on personal freedom and choice. Exercising what is described as a person's right to choose − as in abortion, or in becoming a parent even if in the process embryos (or in other words, other potential children) are destroyed − enables the strong to overcome the most vulnerable.

Relativists also argue that these positions often represent the will of the majority and that they offer the greatest benefit for the greatest number. This Benthamite approach, however, also produces the intolerance, or dictatorship, of the majority (Richards 2003). In the case of unborn persons, it affords them little or no protection. The most vulnerable in society are thus given less protection than the strong. In allowing the strong to overcome the weak, democracy becomes the tool of the powerful. It negates what the Church sees as the principal duty of a democracy, which is to safeguard the rights of each person, including those yet unborn.

Within the UK, the Catholic Church has expressed concern at the narrow remit of the Human Fertilisation and Embryology Authority (HFEA), which exercises only regulatory and inspectoral powers within the framework of the existing legislation, and whose ethics committee, consisting of only five members, advises only the HFEA itself. Recognising the weakness of this type of arrangement, many European countries now have independent standing bio-ethics committees of between 15 and 35 members, with some of the committees having the duty, not only to advise governments, but actively to engage the public in their deliberations. These committees are given the remit to seek views from a wide range of organisations, including religious ones. If we had a similar body in the UK it would go some way to broadening and deepening the process by which the country as a whole, and the government in particular, come to conclusions on these issues.

Finally, in all that has been outlined in the above, relating to the Church's clear teaching on matters of faith and fertility, this does not mean that the Church is unsympathetic to those unable to have children by natural means. The local minister is likely to be all too painfully aware of a couple's anguish over unfulfilled parenthood. Also there is clear evidence to show that there are many services run under the auspices of the Church to help with post-abortion counselling and assistance (Caldwell 2007). Moreover, any children born by artificial means are as welcome in the Church as those born by natural methods.

The pastoral care and understanding for the individual does not mean though that we should simply 'acquiesce in the current "post-modern" assumption that all truths are relative and all moral precepts provisional' (Murphy-O'Connor 2002). The divine norms are seen to be timeless. Nor are they arbitrary. Instead, they are best seen as providing a foundation on which to inform our consciences, a map and compass to lead us through life's journey.

References

Caldwell, S. (2007) 'Boom in numbers of working women seeking abortion trauma counselling.' *Catholic Herald* 22/06/07, 2.

Catechism of the Catholic Church (2002) London: Burns Oates.

Central Statistics Office (2007) *Statistical Yearbook of the Church 2005*. Vatican City: Libreria Editrice Vaticana.

Catholic Bishops' Joint Bioethics Committee (2005) *Submission to Department of Health Review of the HFEA*. London. Accessed 02/07/07 at www.linacre.org/HFEA%20Review%202005.html

Council of Europe (1997) 'Oviedo – Convention for the protection of human rights and dignity of the human being with regard to the application of biology and medicine: Convention on Human Rights and Biomedicine.' Accessed 15/05/08 at cc.msnscache.com/cache.aspx?q=73356206229821&mkt=en-GB&lang=en-GB&w=d7932b27,3b07a6a1&FORM=CVRE

Curtin, P. and Branigan, T. (2007) 'Hints of a baby boom as fertility rate hits highest level for 26 years.' *Guardian* 08/06/07, 11.

European Court of Human Rights (2006) *Case of Evans v. The United Kingdom (Application no. 6339/05).* Accessed 07/03/07 at http://cmiskp.echr.coe.int/tkp197/view.asp?item=1&portal=hbkm&action=html&highlight=United%20%7C%20Kingdom&sessionid=7677594&skin=hudoc-en

Farmer, H. (2007) 'Cardinal warns pro-choice churchgoers of the "barrier to receiving Holy Communion".' *Tablet* 02/06/07, 35.

Hastings, A. (2000) 'Catholicity.' In A. Mason, A. Hastings and H. Pyper (eds) *The Oxford Companion to Christian Thought.* Oxford: OUP.

John Paul II (2005) *Evangelium Vitae. Encyclical Letter.* London: Catholic Truth Society.

McWhinnie, A.M. (2003) 'Disclosure and development: "taking the baby home was just the beginning".' In D. Singer and M. Hunter (eds) *Assisted Human Reproduction.* London: Whurr.

Murphy-O'Connor, C. (2001) *Briefing,* 12/12/01, p.22, 23.

Murphy-O'Connor, C. (2002) *Briefing,* 16/01/02, p.11.

Murphy-O'Connor, C. (2007) *Cardinal Reflects on Annual Day for Life.* Roman Catholic Diocese of Westminster. Accessed 28/06/07 at http://www.rcdow.org.uk/cardinal/default.asp?content_ref=1342

New Jerusalem Bible. Reader's Edition (1990) London: Darton, Longman and Todd.

Pontifical Academy for Life (1997) *Reflections on Cloning.* Vatican City: Libreria Editrice Vaticana.

Pontifical Academy for Life (2004) Tenth General Assembly (Feb 2004). Accessed 19/09/2007 at www.vatican.va/roman_curia/pontifical_academies/acdlife/documents/rc_pont_acd_life_doc_20040316_x-gen-assembly-final_en.html

Pontifical Council for Justice and Peace (2004) *Compendium of the Social Doctrine of the Church.* Vatican City: Libreria Editrice Vaticana.

Prynn, J. (2007) 'Sex test kit will lead to parents playing God.' *Evening Standard* 04/05/07, 8.

Richards, J. (2003) 'Ethical issues – the major faiths: a personal view.' In D. Singer and M. Hunter (eds) *Assisted Human Reproduction.* London: Whurr.

Second Vatican Council, *Apostolicam Actuositatem* (1998a) *The Conciliar and Post-conciliar Documents Vol. I.* Dublin: Dominican Publications.

Second Vatican Council, *Guadiam et Spes* (1998b) *The Conciliar and Post-conciliar Documents Vol. I.* Dublin: Dominican Publications.

Steigenga, M.J., Helmerhorst, F.M. and Koning, J. (2006) 'Evolutionary conserved structures as indicators of medical risk: increased evidence of cervical ribs after ovarian hyperstimulation in mice.' *Animal Biology 56,* 63–68.

Sutton, A. (2005) 'Moral dilemma of the saviour siblings.' *The Catholic Times* 08/05/05, 11.

Sutton, A. (2007) 'No miracle from embryonic stem cells.' *The Catholic Times* 14/01/07, 11.

Trujillo, A.L. (2003) *The Family and Life in Europe.* Vatican City: Pontifical Council for the Family. Accessed 06/03/07 at www.vatican.va/roman_curia/pontifical_councils/family/documents/rc_pc_family_doc_20030614_family-europe-trujillo_en.html

Wall, S. (2007) 'Rendering unto Caesar.' *Tablet* 01/12/07, 12.

Ward. L. (2007) 'Abortion increase by four percent in one year.' *Guardian* 20/06/07, 12.

Watt, H. (1997) *The Diane Blood Case.* Accessed 03/07/07 at www.linacre.org/Diane%20Blood.pdf.

2

Anglican Faith and Reasoning
Wrestling with Fertility Issues

Phyllis Creighton

The Anglican polity and ethos

Anglicanism, made possible as we know it by King Henry VIII's split from the Papacy in 1534, traces back to early missionaries to the British Isles, a Celtic church whose bishops attended the Council of Arles in 314, and the mission of St Augustine from Rome or Gaul in 596–597. The most widespread Christian denomination after the Roman Catholic, the Anglican Communion has some 80 million members in 164 countries; the Church of England (CofE) is the largest (26 million), but the fastest growing part is in the global south, with a majority of Anglicans in Africa (Anglican Communion Office 2008; Church of England Year Book

2007). The Communion's symbolic head is the Archbishop of Canterbury.

Spiritual leadership and legislative authority are exercised by both clergy and laity in various ways, including participation in diocesan, provincial, and national synods. Unity, interdependence, and communication have been fostered since 1868 by the Lambeth Conference (LC), a meeting of bishops held every ten years at the call of the Archbishop of Canterbury; since 1971 by the Anglican Consultative Council, which convenes bishops, priests, and laity of provinces every two or three years; and since 1979 by meetings of the Primates, who head the 34 self-governing provinces.

Influenced by the sixteenth-century theologian Richard Hooker and his approach to meaningful appropriation of faith in changing historical circumstances, the Anglican Communion sees itself as bound by the three-fold cord of scripture, reason, and tradition, Anglicans in a continuing process of reasoning have interpreted the Bible afresh in light of sacred and secular knowledge to shape faith, conscience, and action in changing contexts. Broad and multicultural, with believers of evangelical, catholic, liberal, and charismatic bent, the Communion has been tolerant of diversity and ambiguity and has had presence and engagement in the world.

Issues related to human reproduction have been studied in the CofE, the Anglican Church of Canada (ACC), the Episcopal Church of the United States of America (TEC), and the Anglican Church of Australia (ACA), together embracing some 33 million Anglicans. They have published studies and advised governments. Indeed, the CofE, as the 'Established Church' in the land, participates in lawmaking, since its senior bishops hold seats in the British House of Lords. This chapter will sketch this work, with the ACC as primary lens, to reveal characteristic Anglican insights.

Understandings drawing on the Bible shape Anglican perspectives: belief in the worth of human life as created in God's image, the need to heal, the importance of marriage as a lifelong, loving partnership of man and woman, and of the family as the place where the child belongs. Heterosexuality, chastity, and marital faithfulness have been norms of the Communion (Lambeth Conference Resolutions Archive, LC 1978, Resolution 10; LC 1998, Res.1.10).

Contraception: from rejection to approval

Procreation of children was traditionally seen as the purpose of marriage and contraception was denounced by the LC in 1908 (Res.41) and 1920 (Res.68). Growing understanding of sexual love as strengthening marital love, and of family limitation as benefiting children, brought a dramatic shift. The 1930 LC named the functions of sex God-given, the duty of parenthood the glory of married life, and the family a vital contribution to the nation's welfare (LC 1930, Res.9, 14). But it declared that, given 'clearly felt moral obligation to limit or avoid parenthood' and 'a morally sound reason for avoiding complete abstinence,' other methods might be used (LC 1930, Res.15). Anxious about the spread of birth control among the unmarried, it also urged prohibition of unrestricted advertising or purchase of contraceptives (LC 1930, Res.18). By 1958, when population growth, linked to falling death-rates, was of concern, the LC held that parents had the God-given moral responsibility for deciding upon the number and frequency of children (as well as the choice of birth control method), a responsibility requiring 'wise stewardship' of the family's resources but also 'thoughtful consideration of the varying population needs and problems of society and the claims of future generations' (LC 1958, Res.115).

Sterilisation to prevent conception had been judged by a CofE expert group in 1951 to be a grave decision, but it rejected compulsory sterilisation (then legal in parts of the US and Canada), holding the power of generation a human right (CofE Moral Welfare Council 1951). By 1962 another committee suggested that, in light of Christian missionary doctors' responsibility in burgeoning regions such as India and of the social dimension of morality, voluntary sterilisation might legitimately be carried out in some circumstances (Church Assembly Board for Social Responsibility c1962).

In Canada, the 1967 ACC General Synod (GS) urged parliament to legalise dispensing of contraception under medical or professional guidance and to support population control and family planning programmes in countries seeking assistance (ACC GSJ 1967, p.72). The 1994 TEC General Convention (GC) (Res. D009) took action with the UN Cairo Conference on Population and Development. Reaffirming the 1930 LC resolution, it commended to its dioceses and agencies provision of relevant information and services, and encouraged governments to seek remedies to reverse rapid population growth adversely affecting women's lives, prospects for peace, and environmental resource depletion, its resolution to be forwarded to the US government, UN Secretary-General, and Cairo conference chair (TEC GCJ 1995, pp.281–282).

Pregnancy termination: compassion and responsibility

Pregnancy termination, abhorred by the 1908 LC (Res.42) and 1930 LC (Res.16) as repugnant to Christian morality, was countenanced by 1965, when a CofE group published *Abortion, an Ethical Discussion*. This study accepted termination of a pregnancy threatening a woman's health or well-being as morally licit, but rejected rape or risk of foetal deformity as grounds. The CofE played a part in securing British legislation permitting abortion, but since the 1967 statute admitted rape, foetal deformity, and social indications as grounds, the outcome was regarded in the CofE as a defeat (Dunstan 1974, p.37).

An ACC brief to parliament in 1967 drew on *Abortion, an Issue for Conscience* (Creighton 1974). The book noted problems caused by population growth, increased historical knowledge and new insights into Christian tradition, and Western culture's recognition of the place of women as factors prompting reassessment of Christian opposition to abortion. Regarding absolute prohibition of abortion and abortion on demand as indefensible positions, it urged termination be legally permissible on grounds of serious threat to the pregnant woman's life or health in its broadest sense. It cautioned that abortion should not be used to solve problems requiring socio-economic measures. With rape, incest, or substantial risk of foetal abnormality, it was prevention of breakdown of a woman's health that might be a valid ground for abortion. In 1969 serious threat to the pregnant woman's life or health became the legal grounds for abortion in Canada.

The 1973 GS (Act 18) adopted the stand of the brief, urging its dissemination and rigid enforcement of the law to prevent abortion on demand (ACC GSJ 1973, p.M-12). Then in 1974 the GS-appointed interdisciplinary Task Force on Human Life (TFHL) produced *Abortion, an Issue for Conscience*, which set out socio-economic circumstances, changing attitudes, abortion concerns (reported growing numbers, loose interpretation of the law, need for more facilities for, and promotion and use of, contraception), as well as scientific and theological understandings of unborn human life. Abortion was accepted as sometimes justifiable and necessary, but fraught with moral ambiguity, and to be considered only if the mother's well-being, seen in the full circumstances of her life, could be secured in no other way. Asserting a woman's need for skilful comprehensive counselling, it urged Christians to be a caring community. The TFHL saw the Church's role as shaping conscience, providing family life and sex education, supporting those caught in the problem, and pressing government for broad socio-economic action.

Its claim that 'to resort to abortion lightly or casually is to degrade our humanity, to deny the responsibility and responsiveness of human nature' (Creighton 1974, p.33) was echoed by a 1976 Anglican Consultative Council declaration that 'irresponsibility in the creation or termination of life is incompatible with a true understanding of human nature' (Parke-Taylor 1983, p.13). In the ACC, and the Anglican Communion, a right-to-life minority accepts abortion as moral only where the mother would otherwise die. After the 1980 ACC GS (Act 42) rejected the principle of abortion on demand or for reasons of convenience or economic or social hardship (ACC GSJ 1980, pp.29–30), the ACC published another group study in 1982. Noting resort to abortion by many on socio-economic grounds and loose interpretation of the law, it sought a more careful interpretation of health, suggesting the medical profession develop guidelines (Alton 1983). When the Supreme Court in 1988 struck down the abortion provisions as unconstitutional, another commissioned study, *Abortion in a New Perspective*, was sent to every Member of Parliament. The ACC, it noted, 'accepted abortion with great moral caution, while hoping to render it unnecessary through making the community more welcoming' (ACC Task Force on Abortion 1989, pp.7–8). It called, in vain, for new legislation to make abortion legal for women whose pregnancies endanger their life or physical or mental health, and to establish a supportive process involving professional counselling and two physicians. Urging an upper time limit for termination prior to reasonable prospect of foetal viability, it rejected abortion for genetic defect, rape, or incest. It again urged (as had the previous study) more church-based family life education, more socio-economic justice measures for women and families, more birth control services and research. As for Canada's solution – no law on abortion, the study observed that it 'isolates the burden as the woman's choice; it does not engage the community in its responsibilities for the new generation or provide support to women in difficulties' (*ibid.* p.25).

Abortion, a continuing issue of conscience

The CofE has continued to back safe legal termination, accepting it as a legitimate moral choice in limited circumstances. General Synod (GS) resolutions (CofE GSR 1966, 1974, 1975, 1979, 1983, 1993, 2002) based on expert group reports also called for social support for pregnant women in difficulty, and sought to narrow the grounds for abortion and reduce its incidence by stricter application of the law (CofE Mission and Public Affairs Division 2005). In 1990 all 11 Anglican bishops in the House of Lords unsuccessfully opposed a Commons measure to allow late abortions beyond the then 24-week limit (Church Times 1990). GS in 1993 urged that post-24-weeks termination for serious foetal handicap be interpreted as applying to conditions where the foetus would survive only briefly. Gravely concerned about the numbers of abortions, in 2002 it urged legislation to restrict abuses (CofE Mission and Public Affairs Division 2005). In 2007 Archbishop of Canterbury Rowan Williams expressed uneasiness at the increasing normalisation of abortion as a private decision (Williams 2007).

The ACA GS in 1989 (Res.72) also expressed concern about growing acceptance of abortion on demand, calling on Australian legislatures to uphold the unborn child's rights, and provide human relations education, pregnancy support, and care of single-parent families (ACA 'Social issues: Reproduction – IVF and Abortion' 2008). TEC's 1967 GC had urged law reform in the US to permit pregnancy termination on broad grounds – serious threat to the woman's physical or mental health, rape, forcible incest, or substantial reason to believe the child would be born seriously deformed in mind or body (TEC GCJ 1968, pp.308–309). GC reaffirmed a similar stance in 1976 (Res.D095), excluding abortion for convenience (TEC GCJ 1977, p.C-3), and again in 1979 and 1982 (Res. B009. TEC GCJ 1983, p.C-156). Emphasising the duty to practise responsible birth control, a further 1982 resolution (Res.A065) condemned abortion for sex selection (*ibid,* p.C-157). By 1988 GC (Res.C047) was urging that abortion be used only in extreme situations, Episcopalians help women explore alternatives, and the Church form members' conscience about God-given procreative powers, affirming responsible family planning (TEC GCJ 1989, p.683). But the 1994 GC (Res.A054s) continued unequivocally to oppose legislative, executive, or judicial abridgement of a woman's right to decide about pregnancy termination or limitation of her access to safe means (TEC GCJ 1995, pp.323–325).

Reproductive technologies: donor insemination rejected

Anglicans have long questioned new reproductive technologies. In 1948 a CofE commission, in *Artificial Human Insemination*, held a woman's insemination with her husband's semen to be moral, but considered use of donor semen wrong in principle and contrary to Christian standards (Church of England 1948). Urging that donor insemination (DI) be criminalised, they deemed it wrongful indulgence of a woman's parental desires, depersonalisation of sex extracting procreation from relationship, and adultery for both woman and semen donor, while secrecy, fraud in birth registration and deception about kinship, risks with disclosure, and donor's motives and intentions raised further concerns (Creighton 1977, pp.7–9). A decade later, Archbishop of Canterbury Geoffrey Fisher asserted that this report, though not officially adopted, commanded the church's general approval. He saw DI as an offence making the child the lifelong victim of deception and leaving the family in a relationship of secret make-believe (Fisher 1958, pp.154–157).

Wrestling with DI issues in Canada

The ACC Task Force on Human Life (TFHL) approached new reproductive technologies cautiously. Probing whether DI might morally be used within a marriage, its 15 members agreed DI should not be deemed adultery and should have legislative protection, while donor-conceived offspring should be considered children of their mother's husband and given full legal standing as lawful children of their family. The majority thought DI a humane, moral response of marital love faithful to God's will, the desire and need legitimate, children a blessing for the couple and society, and, where responsibly undertaken by the pair, the donation of sperm humane and responsible.

But a strong minority held that marriage, as a one-flesh unity, means a commitment to a mutual life with no guarantee of children, and believed a childless couple could find fulfilment through self-giving love within the human family. Regarding as an important value a man's acceptance of full responsibility for the life his sperm creates, they doubted semen donation was moral. They found the view of DI as merely the technical introduction of a fertilising agent difficult to reconcile with Christian understanding of the person as a body self (a psychosomatic unity), and questioned whether this technical view takes into full account the human dimensions – the anonymous biological father and the partial genetic otherness of the child. They concluded that life should be created by a husband and wife through sexual union.

Some TFHL members suggested that neither church nor society should stress that woman's fulfilment lies chiefly in maternity, and that the church might have a responsibility, given overpopulation, to refrain from building social pressures on couples to have children. All agreed DI should not be given to single women, considering it unwise and unjust deliberately to create a child who can have no expectation of having a father. They expressed uneasiness about donor motivation and donor payment. To prevent unregulated commercial enterprise, they urged government regulation of the frozen semen banks likely to be established.

Donor anonymity and the resulting practice of secrecy were questioned as either possible, right, or necessary, given the known risks of damaging discovery by the child in marital or family quarrels, adoption experts' concern about the serious problems from secrecy, and abandonment of it in adoption practice, with adopted people's right to information about biological parentage established in Britain. Some members suggested honesty and openness would help DI families. The 1977 GS (Act 56) commended to church and community the book incorporating the TFHL findings, written by one of its members, Phyllis Creighton, *Artificial Insemination by Donor: A Study of Ethics, Medicine, and Law in our Technological Society* (ACC GSJ1977, p.43).

The Church of England's focus on the child

By 1987 the CofE, in a health department consultation, had advised adapting the adoption pattern to DI: full genetic and identity records should be kept, and the child on maturity, with counselling, should have access to this information, 'with the *possible* exception of the name of the donor' (Church of England Board for Social Responsibility 2002, p.3). Its November 1997 GS declared that children are not commodities to be bought or sold, that the welfare of the child created by third-party gametes is of overriding importance (including the child's need for a father), and that marriage is the ideal context for procreation and rearing of children. GS welcomed the Human Fertilisation and Embryology Authority (HFEA) decision to phase out donor payments, and asserted that fertility treatment should be limited to pre-menopausal years (*ibid*, p.1). By 2002, observing that openness is essential to the child's sense of being wanted in the family, the CofE advised that future offspring should be able to obtain identifying information about their donor, and that only donors agreeing to disclosure of their identity to any offspring should be recruited. Believing that 'sperm and eggs are not commodities to be bought or sold but are God-given means of making possible the gift of new life' *(ibid, p.2)*, the CofE, the submission noted, had repeatedly urged abolition of payment for donation, including remuneration of expenses. In 2004 the CofE advised a parliamentary committee that need for a father should be retained in the legislation and not be dropped without serious debate weighing the long-term social consequences (Church of England and Community Public Affairs Unit 2004). Its 2005 response in a consultation on the Human Fertilisation and Embryology Act proposed: the child's need for a father and a mother should replace this clause and a full parliamentary debate be required before allowing use of artificial gametes, the creation of a child with only one genetic parent being a significant ethical concern; payment for gametes (except for expenses or inconvenience) should be prohibited in all circumstances, including research; operation of internet gamete procurement services should be regulated to prevent commercial practices; and information, including identifying, should be provided to donor-conceived people at 16 and also entered in the birth register, as a means of ensuring that parents tell children they are donor-conceived (Butler 2005).

The Episcopal Church and reproductive technologies

The Episcopal Church (TEC) has not undertaken in-depth study of reproductive technologies, but various commissions on human affairs and health put forward views. Supporting husband insemination by 1970, a 1973 report questioned the propriety of DI (Smith and Granbois 1992, pp.41–42). A 1982 report, however, affirmed use of anonymous male donors. Just as Anglicans held artificial human insemination (AIH) to be moral, it saw IVF for a married couple using their gametes as in principle acceptable, and the 1982 GC (Res.A067) approved that usage (TEC GCR, A-101a). The commission condemned use of DI or IVF to provide a child for a single person as American narcissism and self-indulgence, and (it added in 1988) as deliberately causing the child the deprivation and risks of having only one known biological parent (Smith and Granbois 1992, p.45). It urged the 1982 GC to strongly condemn surrogacy as exploitative of the natural mother, since child-bearing forges strong ties between the mother and the newborn (Episcopal Church GC 1982, p.133), and to take the stand that 'human semen should not be bought and sold for reproductive use' (*ibid*, p.141). Its 1985 report also rejected the purchase of embryos for IVF implantation (Smith and Granbois 1992, p.43). With payment of surrogates routine in the US, it expressed concern about the surrogate's ties to her newborn, about the recipient parents' attitude, and about the surrogate's other children's possible anxiety that they might also be given away, and in light of the Church's long-standing opposition to the selling of sexual services, it opposed surrogate parenting for hire. The 1985 GC received this report, but, in the end, did not endorse the stance (Episcopal Church GC 1985, pp.141–142). In 1988 the commission affirmed that surrogate motherhood is not a moral option for Episcopalians, but the 1991 report neither endorsed nor condemned surrogacy or use of donated sperm, ova, or embryos; it urged Episcopalians considering these options to become informed about the ethical issues involved and seek priestly counsel, a stand GC adopted (Res.A-101a) (Smith and Granbois 1992, pp.45–46).

Surrogacy examined

Commercial promotion of surrogacy had led the executive of the ACC General Synod to call for a study. Its task force (TF) 1990 report *Whose Child Is This? Ethical, Legal, Social, and Theological Dangers of 'Surrogate Motherhood'* (Baycroft 1990) took note of TEC's views and of a 1985 CofE study, *Personal Origins* (Church of England Board for Social Responsibility 1985). The CofE group saw gestational surrogacy, especially where remunerated, as 'undermining the dignity of women in the bearing of children they have no intention of mothering'. Acknowledging 'strong bonding' to the foetus during pregnancy might make the surrogate unwilling to relinquish her child, they held that 'in surrogate motherhood the Christian institution of the family is endangered and thus it cannot be morally acceptable as a practice for Christians' (Church of England Board for Social Responsibility 1985, p.41). The February 1988 CofE GS had supported the British Government decision to leave surrogacy arrangements outside the law (Church of England Mission and Public Affairs Council (2003), pp.12–13).

The ACC TF pointed out the reported long-range goal of surrogacy agencies to cut costs by IVF and embryo transfer to women in poverty-stricken parts of the US and Third World countries. Citing research on bonding in pregnancy, it questioned 'enabling women to conceive children as a money-making venture and bargain away the commitment to their care that has a visceral basis in bonding'. By applying biblical values of love and justice, and theological insights, it asserted, 'we should identify surrogate motherhood as corrosive of our very humanness' (Creighton 1990, pp.30, 32).

The TF also raised troubling questions about intergenerational family creation by surrogacy. If the self-identity of people, as social beings, is embedded in relations with others, the study observed, profound re-arrangement of the 'nexus of relationships' through intergenerational family surrogacy may result in 'overwhelming irresoluble confusion concerning their very self-understanding' (Hewitt 1990, p.40).

Principles and values relevant to surrogacy

The TF advised: 'Human beings must be treated as ends, not means. The humanity of women must not be subordinated to their reproductive capacities. Nor may children be deliberately created for sale…The buying and selling of human beings, for whatever purpose, incorporates the evil present in slavery and is just as offensive.' Church and society must re-evaluate the general attitude toward childlessness as failure that underpins such market exploitation. The inadequacy many women feel in not being able to bear children stems in part from society and the Church identifying motherhood as the essence of femininity. 'Christians must rethink their images of women and their attitudes toward them in order to affirm their full humanity as not contingent upon maternity' (Baycroft 1990, pp.93–94).

Agreeing to publish and commend the report (Act 70), the 1989 ACC GS affirmed marriage as a lifelong exclusive union of two persons, held its integrity and value not compromised by the absence of children, and found both remunerated and altruistic surrogacy a dehumanising and unacceptable means of acquiring children (Act 71) (ACC GSJ 989, pp.58–60). Thus 'as a matter of public policy surrogate parenting should be discouraged...surrogacy contracts should be unenforceable in Canada', and initiating, arranging, or agreeing to a surrogacy arrangement for payment should be banned (Act 112) (*ibid.* pp.86–87). With GS authorisation, these principles and recommendations shaped ACC advice to the government. The book was the ACC submission to the Royal Commission on New Reproductive Technologies (RCNRT) in 1990. A TF member served on the subsequent Health Canada Advisory Committee on Reproductive and Genetic Technologies that influenced the 2004 Assisted Human Reproduction Act, which essentially banned commercial surrogacy.

Questioning *in vitro* fertilisation

On IVF, the 1994 ACC report *Suspended in Time: the Frozen Human Embryo* (Creighton 1994) noted claims of low success rate and of questionable use for unexplained infertility; risks of ovarian hyper-stimulation, and unknown long-term consequences of hormonal cocktails; high risks facing IVF children (more multiple and premature births, neonatal and perinatal deaths, other health problems); high costs of IVF drugs and pharmaceutical companies' promotion of IVF (by clinic sponsorship, professional conferences, and so on). 'As a humanitarian response IVF is deceptive', it judged (Creighton 1994, p.28). The needs of far more women would be met by measures to prevent infertility – reproductive health care services including contraceptive programmes, especially for teenagers, early diagnosis and treatment of pelvic inflammatory disease and sexually transmitted diseases, good sex education, and research for better contraceptives.

The human embryo and moral limits

Initiated by the 1989 GS, this report set out the two Anglican views of the embryo – that it is either, in all important respects, a human being entitled to full protection from the time of conception, or a potential person entitled to deep respect. Anglican recognition of unborn human life as having high though not absolute value, and of the need for beneficence might, it argued, morally ground use of 'spare' IVF embryos for important research on fertilisation mechanisms and embryonic development or transfer. But to create an embryo for research is to deny it the intrinsic value due a human life and accord it merely instrumental value – a morally repugnant approach. The report reiterated a 1983 CofE call for protection of the embryo from use for toxicological or pharmacological research, but suggested that concern for health and well-being in an over-populated world provided moral grounds for using it in research into a contraceptive vaccine.

Pre-implantation genetic diagnosis and genetic manipulation

The same report saw moral issues in pre-implantation genetic diagnosis (PGD) of embryos and resulting genetic-based selection, and expressed concern about the slippery slope of the developing genetics, genetic enhancement and germ-line alteration (which it considered speculative, rife with complexities) and positive eugenics, which historically led to abuses of power. The search for genes deemed superior gives the manipulators 'emerging power of unknown dimensions over the very stuff of life' (Creighton 1994, p.31). Urging that our benchmark be enhancing the wholeness and dignity of human beings, it held that 'assuming ultimate power to reshape the roots of our being is arrogance, not wisdom, for humankind' and we must continue to raise moral issues, focusing on fundamental human values (*ibid.* p.32). The study recommended the Church pay close attention to the pending RCNRT report, and looked to it recommending bars to creation of identical human beings by cloning, and of chimeras, ectogenesis, parthenogenesis, embryo fusion, and eugenics through germ-line alteration, as well as creating an IVF register and a regulatory agency with a lay and professional board to monitor reprogenetic developments. 'The churches have a strong interest, as the claimed voice of the defenceless – and of prophecy – to monitor this vital field… We need to remember that new occasions teach new duties and it is up to us to shape their pattern' (*ibid.* p.33).

Human cloning

In 1997, the ACC ethicist, the Reverend Canon Eric Beresford, proposed a moratorium on human cloning to enable analysis and debate, but thought outright rejection premature. He noted the potential for enormous profit and abuse and the need to weigh who stands to gain or lose, and he flagged implications for the parent–child relationship and the child's psychosocial development. He questioned the cloning of a sibling for matched bone marrow or organ donation to a sick child, as producing one child for the sake of another (Beresford 1997). Around the same time Sir John Polkinghorne, a physicist and CofE priest engaged in its genetics and ethics study, found suggested uses of cloning to restore a deceased relative, or create a close genetic match for someone needing a 'spare part', morally repulsive instrumental proposals. He rejected cloning of human beings, noting it would require 'radical human manipulation' and the 'production of experimental human beings', and asserted that a legal ban should be considered (Polkinghorne 1997, pp.38, 41). The 1998 ACC GS (Act 50) decided to urge the Canadian government to prohibit the cloning of human beings and ask the bishops to raise the issue at the imminent LC (ACC GSJ 1998, pp.72–73). In TEC, Cynthia Cohen, chair of a diocesan interdisciplinary group, urged that creating children by cloning would 'destroy the very meaning of human procreation as a biological and relational partnership between two people in a committed union. It would fail to honor human parameters and God's purposes' (Cohen 1997, p.24). But the chair of TEC's science, technology and faith committee, the Reverend Jake Keggi, thought cloning merely another aspect of human reproduction, humans being co-creators with God in an evolving universe (Ashworth 1998). A 2007 CofE memorandum to a parliamentary joint committee endorsed the legal prohibition of implanting cloned embryos (Church of England Mission and Public Affairs Council 2007).

Sex selection and the saviour sibling

A 2003 CofE submission to the Human Fertilisation and Embryology Authority (HFEA) advised sex selection through sperm sorting and PGD should be permitted only in the case of significant risk of serious sex-linked genetic diagnosis. It rejected sperm sorting for non-medical reasons, citing, among social harms, a gradual shift in people's perception of what children are. With a religious tradition regarding children as gifts from God, the proper role of parents is as nurturers open to the unexpected, not controllers (Church of England Mission and Public Affairs Council 2003). A 2004 CoE response to a genetics consultation expressed concern about use of

PGD for trivial conditions and non-therapeutic genetic enhancement as 'increased commodification' of babies. The Anglicans remained 'concerned that the acceptability of "saviour siblings" tips us on to a slippery slope, where individuals are increasingly seen only as a means to an end' (Church of England Mission and Public Affairs Council 2004). In a 2005 consultation on the HFE Act, the CofE advised that PGD to identify a saviour sibling be explicitly named a last resort procedure and restricted to serious and life-threatening conditions, and that a protocol for limiting future demands on this sibling should be explored (Butler 2005, para.35). A 2007 submission reiterated the restrictions and approved a proposed legal ban on 'social' sex selection (Church of England Mission and Public Affairs Council 2007, para.10).

The Church of England: embryo research and cloning

An official 2001 CofE submission on embryo stem cell research urged that wanton creation of specially cloned human embryos not be permitted in the event that cell transplants from them should prove to be a viable treatment method, and considered an international ban on reproductive cloning desirable (Church of Englnd Board for Social Responsibility 2001). A 2003 Mission and Public Affairs Council report for GS declared that the embryo is not separable from the web of human relations and that the principle of the sanctity of human life embraces the mutuality of all human life. The report asserted the principle that ends do not justify means, as well as a developmental view of the embryo (day 14 and the primitive streak being seen as the beginning of an individual) – both of which are present in Christian thinking and tradition – underlay the permission provided by the 1990 HFE Act for limited embryo research (Church of England Mission and Public Affairs Council 2003, p.9). But a 2005 memorandum, commenting on the desirability of allowing embryos to be created for treatment of serious diseases, declared that producing and destroying a tissue-matched embryo 'would be entirely unacceptable instrumentality' (Butler 2005, para.65).

The Episcopal Church: genetic diagnosis and engineering

Long interested in genetics, the 1985 TEC GC (Act A090) encouraged genetic engineering research, establishment of an expert theological genetics education group, and seminary provision of basic training in genetics and ethics (TEC GCJ 1986, p.179). A 1998 book by the Diocese of Washington Committee on Medical Ethics dealing with genetic prenatal and pre-implantation diagnosis saw genetic testing as part of our role as co-creators with God and healers with scientific knowledge (Episcopal Church 1998). Given GC's stance that human life should be initiated only advisedly, couples have a responsibility, they suggested, not to bear children who would face a life of serious incurable illness. But they also worried about dangers inherent in the emphasis on babies without disability: developing a quality-control mentality, social pressures, government coercion, and production of designer children, with a revival of eugenics overshadowing growing capacities to discover and manipulate human genes. Christians, they asserted, embrace diversity, hold all human beings of equal significance, and should work to eliminate discrimination and stereotyping.

TEC's presiding bishop's bioethics consultation in 1998 raised further concerns and proposed a regular genetics forum. These Episcopalians questioned privileging genetic technologies with investment of resources while public health care and distribution of basic medical care went unaddressed; they saw at issue the nature of Christian responsibility to the neighbour and who the neighbour was (Wood, Mathewes, and Griffiss 1999).

Australian Anglicans: embryo research and cloning

In 1985, the ACA GS (Act 72), noting issues raised by its Social Responsibilities Commission's book, *Making Babies: The Test Tube and Christian Ethics* (Nichols and Hogan 1984), had opposed live human embryo research, and so advised government authorities (ACA 'Social Issues: Reproduction – IVF and Abortion'). Noting that the Anglican Communion had made no definitive statement on cloning, a 1999 GS submission to a parliamentary committee sought a five-year moratorium on cloning human body parts and tissues and use of human embryonic stem cells, plus extensive public discussion before its review (Anglican Church of Australia 1999, *Submission*). A 2000 Diocese of Melbourne submission declared that cloning to alleviate suffering would violate the Christian principle that human beings may never be treated merely as a means to an end; 'it would be morally demeaning and psychologically damaging for someone to learn that the primary reason for their existence lay not in their own value, but in their utility for another purpose' (Melbourne Anglican 2000).

Much of the best stem cell research in the world was being done in Australia. Bishop George Browning of the Diocese of Canberra and Goulburn, whose synod had urged the Commonwealth government in 2001 to ban research into cloning of human persons, in a 2005 submission told a parliamentary legislative review committee that it still supported that ban, but that, given the hopes of many suffering people, research using embryonic stem cells for cloning human tissue should be allowed, utilising 'spare' IVF embryos, with regulation and registration. Non-implanted human embryos, before the primitive streak develops, should be considered ethically the same as other live human tissue (Anglican Church of Australia 2005, Browning). The submission relied on a 2002 report to the diocesan Synod by its appointed expert committee, which had rejected cloning of human beings as unsafe and disrespectful of human dignity, treating embryos as means not ends, and opening up the risk of eugenic manipulation. That report asserted that the 'era of biotechnology holds promise of being one of the greatest of all co-creative adventures of the human spirit', but, given the ambivalence of all use of human creativity, and the potential for unethical pursuit and application of science, the Church needs to exercise vigilance (Anglican Church of Canada 2002).

But a 2005 Diocese of Sydney submission to an official review disagreed that the genetic parents could donate their leftover embryos, the embryo not being their property to destroy, but a gift to be nurtured, and it opposed all destructive embryo research. Asserting alternative stem cell therapies to be the more feasible option, it claimed that once therapeutic cloning techniques are developed, 'it will not be possible to 'police' their use against reproductive cloning' (Anglican Church of Australia. Diocese of Sydney. Social Issues Executive 2005). When the Commonwealth Parliament passed legislation in December 2006 banning reproductive cloning but providing for creation, use, and destruction of human embryos for research, an impassioned protest was written for the Diocese of Melbourne's Social Responsibilities Commission, lamenting that the law 'allows us to treat life as a commodity to be created and destroyed and used at our convenience and desire', empowering medical researchers and scientists by a precedent with the potential for extension in unpredictable directions (Pullin 2006).

Anglicanism: adaptation and questioning

Within the Anglican Communion, on the fertility issues, save contraception, modernists and traditionalists differ. Adaptation to the culture shows in English bishops' acceptance of post-menopausal older women's use of IVF with donor eggs (Fay 1994; Henderson, Rumbelow and Miles 2006). Cultural unease shows in repeated efforts to limit abortion, to reform DI practice, and to oppose commercial surrogacy. Anglicans take seriously the task of shaping law in this field, and sometimes they influence it, open to science and accepting of technological advances, but not uncritically. An attitude that 'we have to keep steady nerves and plot our way rationally through it', as Richard Holloway, then Bishop of Edinburgh, said in relation to genetic developments (Ashworth 2000), and the view that regulating their use is more feasible than banning it, are typical Anglican responses. Modernists and traditionalists share uneasiness in confronting the extent and uses of new genetic powers, and concern that with genetic manipulation, 'donor' sperm, eggs, and embryos, and surrogacy, 'babies could become part of our throwaway society, selectable consumer durables', as English bishop Hugh Montefiore put it (1995).

Gender issues and family diversity

On same-gender relationships, the Anglican Communion is in conflict. The ACC, through 30 years of studying homosexuality, has developed understanding and acceptance of gay sexuality. Since 1978, the College of Bishops has insisted that people of homosexual orientation are full, equal members of the Church, but has rejected gay and lesbian sexual practice. Just as the 1978 LC reaffirmed heterosexuality as the scriptural norm, the College since then has upheld sexual abstinence outside the marital union of man and woman, and therefore celibacy for gay and lesbian persons, a stance the 1998 LC also took, 'rejecting homosexual practice as incompatible with Scripture' (LC Res.10, 1978; LC Res.1.10, 1998). But by 1997 some Canadian bishops had recognised that relationships of mutual support, help, and comfort between homosexual persons can be expressions of God's will and purpose (ACC House of Bishops 1997).

The CofE, in the main, holds to the traditional family. Speaking to a parliamentary committee about its 2004 memorandum and the CofE focus on the child, Bishop Michael Nazir-Ali discounted, because of very small samples, research showing no adverse impact on the welfare of children born to loving stable lesbian couples; he cited research of much greater scope on how children fare when they have both a father and a mother (House of Commons Science and Technology Committee 2005). The CofE advised in 2005 that the HFE Act, under review for amendment, stipulate 'the need of a child for a father and a mother' (Butler 2005, para.17). But the CofE in 2007 asserted that removing the requirement to take account of need for a father would send an 'entirely erroneous signal about the significance of fathers'. The welfare and likely best interest of the child to be born, and hence its right not to be deliberately deprived of having a father, must be put first, a step required to 'address the drift towards personal autonomy becoming the only ethical consideration'. The Church argued that, given the paucity and equivocal nature of evidence, the precautionary approach of avoiding the potential harm of identity issues for a child designed to have neither biological nor social father requires retention of the clause (Church of England Mission and Public Affairs Council 2007, Ev 68).

In Canada, in the Diocese of New Westminster, after much study and three synod votes, Bishop Michael Ingham has since May 2003 permitted liturgical blessing of same-sex unions (a small number being performed). The 2004 ACC GS (Act 37) affirmed the sanctity and integrity of same-sex adult committed relationships (ACC GSJ 2004, p.58), but referred to a theological commission the question of whether same-sex blessing is a matter of doctrine (Act 35), and thus under GS jurisdiction (*ibid.* pp.53–54). Same-sex marriage became legal in Canada in July 2005. The ACC House of Bishops agreed, in May 2007, to allow a Eucharist and prayers, without a nuptial blessing, for such couples who seek the Church's reception of their civil marriage, and prayers for committed couples, not including vows or blessing (Anglican Church of Canada 2007a). Then GS held (Act 42), with the commission, that same-sex blessings are not in conflict with core (in the sense of credal) doctrine (ACC GSJ 2007, p.52), but declined to affirm diocesan authority to authorise them (*ibid.* p.55). Ottawa, Montreal,

Niagara, and Huron diocesan synods subsequently voted to allow blessings for civilly married same-sex couples, but their bishops have withheld permission. Some blessings of same-sex unions have taken place in TEC, but these, in fact, have been performed more often in CofE parishes than in North America.

The 2003 election to TEC episcopacy of Gene Robinson, a priest in an openly gay relationship, precipitated a crisis in the Anglican Communion, especially in the global south, where homosexual practice is widely held contrary to the Bible. Under pressure, TEC GC in June 2006 agreed not to authorise public rites for such blessings and pledged restraint by not agreeing to the consecration of bishops 'whose manner of life presents a challenge to the wider church and will lead to further strains on the communion'. This bar includes non-celibate gay or lesbian priests (De Santis 2006). TEC bishops endorsed the stance in September 2007 (De Santis 2007).

Acceptance by the end of 2007 of a draft Covenant developed by a group appointed by the Archbishop of Canterbury, with a drift towards the Primates becoming enforcers in doctrine and practice, had been proposed as the *sine qua non* of Communion membership for provinces (Anglican Communion Office 2007). What impels this shift is a drive for conservative control by the global south (backed by American evangelical money), with same-sex blessings a wedge issue in a broader rejection of historic Anglicanism – openness to change in light of ongoing reasoned biblical interpretation, tolerance of theological diversity, and women's access to priesthood, episcopacy, and primacy. (By 2008, only 13 provinces had ordained women as priests, and three provinces as bishops.)

Following responses, the St Andrew's draft Covenant, wrestling with the tensions between unity and autonomy, was issued in February 2008 (Anglican Communion Office 2008), for consideration by the provinces. Recognising the churches of the Anglican family as autonomous-in-communion, interdependent, and mutually responsible, the Covenant would commit them to 'regard to the Communion's common good'. This would include searching through its councils for a common mind on essential matters; caution in actions deemed threatening to its unity and mission; acceptance of processes for communion-wide evaluation commissioned by any of the Instruments of Unity (Canterbury, LC, Anglican Consultative Council, Primates' meeting); mediation in conflict; and reception of a request from them for a course of action whose rejection they might take as relinquishment of covenant relationship.

But the Communion was dramatically split with the June 2008 Global Anglican Future Conference (GAFCON), which drew 291 bishops (representing millions of Anglicans), and 1148 laity and clergy. The conference issued an arch-conservative Jerusalem Declaration that launched the GAFCON movement as the Fellowship of Confessing Anglicans and encouraged the GAFCON Primates to form a council (GAFCON 2008). Archbishop of Canterbury Rowan Williams insists 'the Anglican Communion will still continue in some form, albeit weakened'; noting that Anglicanism is plural and diffuse, and that diffused authority is part of its model, he said the issue 'is not about establishing a central commissariat, but about establishing mutual covenants of responsible, mutual protocols' (Church Times 2008).

Should present great tensions and conflict shift the Anglican Communion into authoritarian, imposed conservatism, the cautiously liberal response to evolving reprogenetics could become past history for Anglicanism. Would such a Communion nurture the openness to science and technology and the reshaping of ethics in new social contexts that have characterised Anglican perspectives on fertility issues? The 'gospel that welcomes diversity of thought' proclaimed by TEC bishops in March 2007 is the seedbed for such thinking, and this also stands to be rejected (Bates 2007). Will the pattern of wrestling with the reproductive issues posed by science and society, and adapting traditional understandings, fit in tomorrow's Anglican world?

Acknowledgement

The author wishes to acknowledge the invaluable assistance given by Karen Evans, Librarian at National Office of the Anglican Church of Canada, who provided an annotated bibliography of monographs and articles and advice on citation.

References

Alton, B. (ed.) (1983) *The Abortion Question*. Toronto: Anglican Book Centre.

Anglican Church of Australia, 'Social issues: reproduction – IVF and abortion.' Accessed 9/7/08 at www.anglican.org.au/index.cfm?SID=2&SSID==97&PID=242.

Anglican Church of Australia (1999) *Submission to the House of Representatives Standing Committee on Legal and Constitutional Affairs Inquiry into the Scientific, Ethical and Regulatory Aspects of Human Cloning*. Accessed 15/07/08 at www.anglican.org.au/docs/Enquiry-into-Cloning-1999.doc.

Anglican Church of Australia (2005) Browing, J. *A Submission from the Bishop of Canberra and Goulburn...to the Legislation Review Committee* (LRC445). Accessed 15/07/08 at www.anglican.org.au/docs/SICloningBrowning.pdf.

Anglican Church of Australia. Diocese of Sydney. Social Issues Executive (2005) *Submission to the Lockhart Review* (LRC780). Accessed 15/07/08 at www.anglican.org.au/docs/SIcloningSydney.pdf.

Anglican Church of Canada. House of Bishops (1997) Human Sexuality: A Statement by the Anglican Bishops of Canada. Accessed 15/07/08 at www2.anglican.ca/faith/identy/hob-statement.htm.

Anglican Church of Canada (1967) *Journal of Proceedings Twenty-Third Session*, Ottawa, August 22 to August 31.

Anglican Church of Canada (1973) *General Synod Regina Journal of Proceedings 26th Session General Synod/Regina*, May 3 to May 11.

Anglican Church of Canada (1977) *Journal of Proceedings 28th General Synod*, University of Calgary, Alberta, August 11 to August 18.

Anglican Church of Canada (1980) *Journal of Proceedings 29th General Synod*, Trent University, Peterborough, Ontario, June 17 to June 25.

Anglican Church of Canada (1989) *L'Église Anglicane du Canada Journal of the Thirty-Second General Synod*, Memorial University St John's, Newfoundland, June 15 to June 23.

Anglican Church of Canada (1998) *L'Eglise Anglicane du Canada Journal of the Thirty-Fifth General Synod*, McGill University Montreal, Quebec, May 21 to May 29.

Anglican Church of Canada (2002) 'The cloning of human cells: A response to the scientific issues from an ethical and theological perspective.' Accessed 15/07/08 at www.anglican.org.au/docs/SICloningC&G.pdf.

Anglican Church of Canada (2004) *L'Église Anglicane du Canada Journal of the Thirty-Seventh General Synod*, Brock University St Catharines, Ontario, May 28 to June 4.

Anglican Church of Canada (2007) *L'Église Anglicane du Canada. Journal of the Thirty-Eighth General Synod*, The Marlborough Hotel Winnipeg, Manitoba, June 19 to June 25.

Anglican Church of Canada (2007a) 'Bishops' pastoral statement to go to General Synod.' Accessed 12/07/08 at www.anglican.ca/news/news.php?newsItem=2007–05–01_hob.news.

Anglican Church of Canada Task Force on Abortion (1989) *Abortion in a New Perspective: Report of the Task Force on Abortion*. Toronto: Anglican Book Centre.

Anglican Communion Office (2007) 'Preliminary Report – Draft Text.' April. Accessed 11/04/09 at www.anglicancommunion.org/commission/covenant/report/draft_text.cfm.

Anglican Communion Office (2008a) *An Anglican Covenant – St Andrew's Draft Text*. Accessed 07/07/08 at www.aco.org/commission/covenant/st_andrews/draft_text.cfm.

Anglican Communion Office (2008b) 'Welcome.' Accessed 09/07/08 at www.anglicancommunion.org/.

Ashworth, P. (1998) 'Don't play God with clones.' *Church Times* 16 January, 1.

Ashworth, P. (2000) 'First the code, now the moral maze.' *Church Times* 7 July, 1.

Bates, S. (2007) 'US rejects Anglican Ultimatum.' *The Guardian* 22 March, 15.

Baycroft. J. (ed.) (1990) *Whose Child Is This? Ethical, Legal, Social, and Theological Dangers of 'Surrogate Motherhood'*. Toronto: Anglican Book Centre.

Beresford, E. (1997) 'Temporary halt in cloning worth it to allow careful study.' *Anglican Journal* April 1, 18.

Butler, T. (2005) *Review of the Human Fertilisation and Embryology Act: a Public Consultation*. Accessed 30/11/2007 at www.dh.gov.uk/en/Consultations/Responsestoconsultations/DH_4132358.

Church Assembly Board for Social Responsibility (c1962) *Sterilization: an Ethical Enquiry*. London: Church Information Office.

Church of England (1948) *Artificial Human Insemination: the Report of a Commission Appointed by His Grace the Archbishop of Canterbury*. London: SPCK.

Church of England (2007) *Church of England Year Book 2008*. London: Church House Publishing.

Church of England Board for Social Responsibility (1985) *Personal Origins*. London: Board for Social Responsibility.

Church of England Board for Social Responsibility (June 2001) 'Response to the House of Lords Select Committee on stem cell research.'

Church of England Board for Social Responsibility (June 2002) 'Response to the Department of Health donor information consultation: Providing information about gamete or embryo donors.' Accessed 26/06/09 at www.cofe.anglican.org/info/socialpublic/science/hfea/gamete.pdf

Church of England Community and Public Affairs Unit (2004) 'Memorandum from the Church of England Community and Public Affairs Unit to the House of Commons Science and Technology Select Committee: Human reproductive technologies and the law.' In House of Commons Science and Technology Committee (2005) *Human Reproductive Technologies and the Law. Fifth Report of Session 2004–05. Volume II: Oral and written evidence*. Appendix 17, EV 245–246. Accessed 26/06/09 at www.publications.parliament.uk/pa/cm200405/cmselect/cmsctech/7/7ii.pdf

Church of England Mission and Public Affairs Council (2003) *Embryo Research: Some Christian Perspectives*. Accessed 10/07/08 at www.cofe.anglican.org./info/socialpublic/science/hfea/embryoresearch.pdf.

Church of England Mission and Public Affairs Council (2004) 'Choosing the future: the Church of England's response to the Human Genetics Commission's consultation: Choosing the future.' November. Accessed 26/06/09 at www.cofe.anglican.org/info/socialpublic/science/genetics/hgcresponse.pdf

Church of England Mission and Public Affairs Council (2007) 'Memorandum.' In *House of Lords/House of Commons Joint Committee on the Human Tissue and Embryos (Draft) Bill* Vol.II Evidence Ev 68, pp.319–324. Accessed 15/07/08 at www.publications.parliament.uk/pa/jt200607/jtselect/jtembryos/169/169ii.pdf.

Church of England Mission and Public Affairs Division (2005) *Abortion: a Briefing Paper.* Accessed 10/07/08 at www.cofe.anglican.org/info/socialpublic/science/abortion/abortion.pdf.

Church of England Moral Welfare Council (1951) *Human Sterilization: Some Principles of Christian Ethics.* London: Church Information Board.

Church of England Public Affairs Unit (2003) 'Response to the Human Fertilisation and Embryology Authority: Sex selection: Choice and responsibility in human reproduction.' 23 January. Accessed 15/07/08 at www.cofe.anglican.org/info/socialpublic/science/hfea/hfeasexselection.pdf.

Church Times (1990) 'Dr Habgood speaks of "moral dividing line" on embryos.' *Church Times* 26 October, 1.

Church Times (2008) 'Defiant amid the doubters.' *Church Times* 11 July.

Cohen, C.B. (1997) 'Human cloning brings moral hazards.' *Episcopal Life* 24 June, 24.

Creighton, P. (ed.) (1974) *Abortion, an Issue for Conscience.* Toronto: Anglican Book Centre.

Creighton, P. (1977) *Artificial Insemination by Donor: a Study of Ethics, Medicine, and Law in our Technological Society.* Toronto: Anglican Book Centre.

Creighton, P. (1990) 'The world of surrogacy and our humanness.' In J. Baycroft (ed.) (1990).

Creighton, P. (1994) *Suspended in Time: the Frozen Human Embryo.* Toronto: Anglican Book Centre.

De Santis, S. (2006) 'Church makes indirect statement about gay bishops.' *Anglican Journal* 21 June. Accessed 10/07/08 at www.anglicanjournal.com/world/ecusa06/014/article/church-makes-indirect-statement.

De Santis, S. (2007) 'Schism plans develop after U.S. meeting.' *Anglican Journal* 1 November. Accessed 10/07/08 at www.anglicanjournal.com/issues/2007/133/nov/09/article/schism-plans-develop-after-us-meeting/.

Dunstan, G.R. (1974) *The Artifice of Ethics.* London: SCM Press.

Episcopal Church. Diocese of Washington, Committee on Medical Ethics (1998) *Wrestling with the Future: Our Genes and Our Choices.* Harrisburg, PA: Morehouse Publishing.

Episcopal Church (1968) *Journal of the 62nd General Convention of the Episcopal Church, Seattle, Washington, September 17 to September 27, 1967.* New York: General Convention.

Episcopal Church (1977) *Journal of the 65th General Convention of the Episcopal Church, Minneapolis-Saint Paul, Minnesota, September 11 to September 23, 1976.* New York: General Convention.

Episcopal Church (1982) *The Blue Book: Reports of the Committees, Commissions, Boards and Agencies of the Episcopal Church. 67th General Convention, New Orleans, Louisiana, September 5 to September 15.* New York: General Convention.

Episcopal Church (1983) *Journal of the 67th General Convention of the Episcopal Church, New Orleans, Louisiana, 1982, September 5 to September 15, 1982.* New York: General Convention.

Episcopal Church (1985) *The Blue Book: Reports of the Committees, Commissions, Boards and Agencies of the Episcopal Church. 68th General Convention, Anaheim, California, September 7 to September 14.* New York: General Convention.

Episcopal Church (1986) *Journal of the 68th General Convention of the Episcopal Church, Anaheim, California, September 7 to September 14, 1985.* New York: General Convention.

Episcopal Church (1989) *Journal of the 69th General Convention of the Episcopal Church, Detroit, Michigan, July 2 to July 11, 1988.* New York: General Convention.

Episcopal Church (1995) *Journal of the 71st General Convention of the Episcopal Church, Indianapolis, Indiana, August 24 to September 2, 1994.* New York: General Convention.

Fay, P. (1994) 'Fertility body to publish paper.' *Church Times* 7 January, 1.

Fisher, G.F.F. (1958) *The Archbishop Speaks. Addresses and Speeches.* London: Evans Brothers Limited.

GAFCON (2008) 'GAFCON final statement: Statement on the global Anglican future.' Accessed 15/07/08 at www.gafcon.org/index.php?option=com_content&task=view&id+79&Itemid =12.

Henderson, M., Rumbelow, H., and Miles, A. (2006) 'Fertility panel bishop blesses IVF for over-50.' *London Times* 14 October, 1–2.

Hewitt, M. (1990) 'Reflection on the significance and meaning of surrogate motherhood.' In J. Baycroft (ed.) (1990).

House of Commons Science and Technology Committee (2005) *Human Reproductive Technologies and the Law. Fifth Report of Session 2004–5. Vol. II Oral and Written Evidence.* HC 7-II. London: The Stationery Office. Accessed 26/06/09 at www.publications.parliament.uk/pa/cm200405/ cmselect/cmsctech/7/7ii.pdf

Lambeth Conference Resolutions Archive (1878, 1908, 1920, 1930, 1958, 1998). Accessed 10/07/08 at www.lambethconference.org/archives/index.cfm.

Melbourne Anglican (2000) 'Cloning violates Christian principles.' *Melbourne Anglican,* February.

Montefiore, H. (1995) 'Something off-the-peg from Mothercare.' *Church Times 3* March, 10.

Nichols, A. and Hogan, T. (eds) (1984) *Making Babies: the Test Tube and Christian Ethics.* Canberra: Acorn Press.

Parke-Taylor, G.H. (1983) *The Family in Contemporary Society: Theological Considerations and a Canadian Perspective.* Toronto: Anglican Book Centre.

Polkinghorne, J. (1997) 'Cloning and the moral imperative.' In R. Cole-Turner (ed.) *Human Cloning: Religious Response.* Louisville, KY: Westminster John Knox Press.

Pullin, C. 'Embryo experimentation – the future path for our society.' Accessed 11/04/09 at www. melbourne.anglican.com.au/main.php?pg=download&id=19637.

Smith, D.H. and Granbois, J.A. (1992) 'New technologies for assisted reproduction.' In *The Crisis in Moral Teaching in the Episcopal Church.* Harrisburg, PA: Morehouse.

Williams, R. (2007) 'Abortion—fundamental convictions about humanity need to be kept in focus.' Accessed 9/04/09 at www.archbishopofcanterbury.org/1237.

Wood, E., Mathewes, C. and Griffiss, J.E. (1999) 'Report on the bioethics consultation.' *Anglican Theological Review 81* 4, 561–565.

Abbreviations

ACC GSJ – Anglican Church of Canada General Synod Journal

Res. – Resolutions

TEC GCJ – Episcopal Church General Convention Journal

3

Islamic Identity and the Ethics of Assisted Reproduction

Mohammad Iqbal and Ray Noble

Introduction

In this chapter we consider ethical issues arising from the use of fertility treatments in the context of Islamic faith. In so doing we will address first the nature of ethics in Islam, and then the particular problems arising from infertility treatment in relation to core beliefs. The central themes are first, that there is no single authority in Islam giving answers to these ethical issues; fertility has a particular significance in Islamic cultures, and in many communities it is an issue Muslims find difficult to discuss; family structure and lineage have special significance in relation to a sense of belonging and personhood; and finally the inherent role of compassion and mercy in Islamic faith and ethics.

Introduction to Islamic ethics

'Islam' signifies peace and absolute, unconditional submission to God. Nevertheless, Islam is not a monolithic faith with clear prescriptions for all aspects of life. Nor is there a single authority to consider and impose such prescriptions. There is a diversity of views and continued debate, reflecting not only opinion from different sects, cultural backgrounds or schools of jurisprudence but also discourse within these diverse groups. As with other areas of ethics there are differences of view, and not least in relation to problems of fertility and procreation. There are, however, clear threads in the tapestry, strands that link back to core Islamic values and beliefs.

Understanding Islam in a cultural sense requires an appreciation of the way in which behaviour and morality are shaped by the revelations of the Qur'an. This source of knowledge in the Qur'an is given, and not subject to empirical analysis. Muslims believe that the Holy Qur'an is the 'uncreated' or unedited words of God revealed to the Prophet Muhammad (pubh) in 610 AD. It is regarded by Muslims as 'the living miracle' revealed from Allah as guidance to mankind; its validity is a matter of faith, not of rational judgement.

All ethical issues in Islam are considered within the framework and guidance of Qur'anic verses. The Qur'an is not a narrative in the manner of the biblical texts in the Old or New Testaments; each verse can be perceived as a divine command or as a set of obligations on individuals and the ideal conduct required by God (Edge 1996), or, as Reinhart (1983) puts it, 'an unparalleled window into the moral universe'. Nevertheless, as Riffat Hassan states, the Qur'an is not 'an encyclopedia which may be consulted to obtain specific information about how God views each problem, issue or situation' (cited in Maguire 2003).

The types of guidance (*surah*) revealed in the Qur'an are God's injunctions or proscriptions and those Qur'anic verses pertaining to the domain of permissible human actions. God's injunctions are considered absolute, but the human domain is continually changing and developing, not least as a result of human action. Increasing knowledge and human understanding produce changing political, social and moral dilemmas. Humans are considered to be God's vicegerents on earth, gifted with reason and talent which they must apply in the application of faith. An appeal to God does not absolve or abrogate the responsibilities of humans as rational beings.

There are three additional sources that guide Islamic thinking and actions. These are the Prophet's sayings, *Hadith*, the Prophet's actions, *Sunnah*, and the jurists' decisions, *Shariah*. Islam is a progressive faith with a built-in process for responding to change in the human condition. It is a religion with an inherent ethical process, and the study of ethics in Islam is a natural extension of Islamic law (Haleem 1993). Thus, whilst the roots of Islamic law and ethics can be traced to the Qur'an and Sunnah, Islamic scholars also make reference to logic, public interest, and local custom and consensus when addressing unusual or contemporary issues, and before assigning them into the accepted legal spectrum of morals, ethics and law.[1]

Islam has no papal figure or central ruling synod that can impose its views and as such 'Religious truth is a matter of argument and conviction, a cause in which everybody is entitled to contend and everybody is entitled to convince and be convinced' (al-Faruqi 2006). Thus a central feature of Islamic ethics is that it allows the specifics of any current moral problem to be analysed and argued from Qur'anic principles, using analogy and logic to come to the best and most reasonable solution.[2] Islamic Shariah can adapt itself to new issues, provided that these are not contrary to the tenets of Islam. It allows Islamic ethics to respond realistically to new problems where there is no clear answer in the Qur'an and it establishes Islam's respect for the faculty of reason. It becomes mandatory to exercise judgement in finding solutions to problems of our time, and this is not the least so for issues of fertility, infertility, marriage, conception, gender selection, divorce, and women's rights in the light of modern developments in science and medicine. Nonetheless, this process of thought and argument is not a free-for-all where any opinion counts equally, regardless of how it has been reached (Alwani 1993).

Islamic jurisprudence (*fiqh*)[3] comprises the rulings of jurists. These are derived by different methodologies, which can be defined as schools of thought (*madh'hab*). In Sunni Islam,[4] there are four classical schools named historically after the jurists who taught them: Hanafi, Hanbali, Maliki and Shafai. These four schools share most of their rulings, but differ on the particular hadiths they accept as authentic and the weight they give to analogy (*qiyas*) or reason in their methodologies. In Shi'a Islam[5] there is one principal school, that of Jafari, and whilst this branch of Islam has in some cases developed its own interpretations, methodology and authority systems, on the whole its bioethical positions do not differ fundamentally from those of the Sunni (Daar and Khitamy 2001). There is also a school of *Ibadi* Islam, though this is not specifically named. Ibadi Islam, a distinct sect of Islam that is neither Sunni nor Shi'i, exists mainly in Oman, East Africa, the Mzab valley of Algeria, the Nafus mountains of Libya, and the island of Jerba in Tunisia. Whilst these schools interpret the same verses of the Qur'an, they may not necessarily agree. Their interpretations are considered to be either opinions or declarations (*fatwas*),[6] but never as precedents. There is also a consensus of uniform acceptance between the principal Islamic schools, and they may carry equal weight or legitimacy.[7] Thus, in some societies Muslims may draw on or refer to different *madh'hab*, depending on personal views and the specifics of the issues being considered. In this sense, then, these schools contribute to an ongoing ethical discourse.

Islam is culturally pluralistic and the adoption of a Muslim stereotype should be avoided. Whilst there is a strong sense of common identity, Muslims do not form one racial, ethnic or cultural entity; rather there are many cultures influenced by Islam or for which Islam is the core belief. There are in the world today over one billion Muslims living in over 80 countries with over 200 languages or dialects, and in a diverse set of social, political and economic circumstances. Indeed, this pluralism is emphasised in the Qur'an: 'Oh humankind! We created you from a single soul, male and female, and made you into nations and tribes, so that you may come to know one another' (49:13).

Islam instils in its adherent a sense of his or her place and belonging within the family and of a responsibility to that group. Thus, Islamic ethics considers the nature of duty arising from obligations within the family and community. A Muslim woman, for example, regards her responsibilities as necessitating a balance with, or even subordination to, those of the family group. The rampant individualism often experienced in contemporary life, that which treats the goals of the individual in isolation from other factors, or as the supreme goal, runs against a deep Islamic commitment to this social interdependency. This sense of belonging and the central importance of lineage are pivotal to understanding reproductive ethics from an Islamic perspective, particularly in relation to assisted reproductive technologies, as it affects permissibility of adoption, surrogacy and sperm or egg donation. Thus, in Islam, to maintain purity of lineage, not only are adultery and fornication (*zina*) prohibited but also adoption, thus keeping the family line 'unambiguously defined without any foreign element entering into it' (Qaradawi, cited in Irfan 2005). It likewise prohibits artificial insemination of sperm unless it is provided by the recipient's husband.

The Qur'an defines the *free* individual as someone who belongs. This belonging is applied to two communities: 1) the larger community of Islam and 2) the family. This concept of the individual as one who belongs is a key factor in understanding Islamic ethics, and particularly in relation to fertility. Rights, duties and obligations for the individual arise from this identity and sense of belonging. In contrast, Western philosophical concepts of the individual tend to stress rights and obligations in relation to the state or society, setting the individual apart from others rather than establishing an identity with or for others. 'I am because I belong' is strategically dissimilar to the identity of 'I am because I am different'. Thus, Islamic ethics emphasises *community ties* and the obligations and duties arising from them. The family is the foundation of Muslim society. The Islamic family (*rahim*)[8] is extensive and it includes all relatives, whether close or distant, heirs or not, including also for a man those female relatives whom he can marry. The Arabic root from which the word *rahim* is derived indicates mercy, compassion and *justice*, which are core principles of Islamic ethics, and this word encapsulates the interdependence, duties and obligations of the individual.

Autonomy, freedom of will, rational action and the Will of God

Muslims believe in a divine decree or destiny, *qadar*: 'To God belongs the dominion of heavens and earth. He creates what He wills. He bestows females upon whom He wills and bestows the males upon whom He wills. Or He couples them in males and females and He leaves barren whom He wills. For He is All-Knowledgeable All-Powerful' (42:49–50).

But Muslims also believe that Allah gave humans a power and freedom as rational beings.[9] If morality is an expression of duty and obligation, then it follows that the concept of free will is fundamental to morality. No moral judgement could be made where an agent has no freedom to choose, if their actions were directed solely by the 'laws of nature' or by providence. Consequently, each individual is accountable for his or her deeds. The eminent Muslim scholar, Sheikh Muhammad Al-Hanooti (2003), puts it thus: 'There are two circles of *qadr*. One of those circles is called the circle of the lawful will. In that circle, man can decide what to do or what not to do. He has a full free will. There is nothing compulsory for man in that circle. Everything of that circle is his responsibility. He can be praised if he complies with the law. He will be condemned if he violates the law. No one in this circle will justify what he does or what he neglects as a matter of *qadr*.'

Accordingly, in one sense infertility might be seen as God's providence; but God has also charged humans with a responsibility to eradicate disease and human suffering. Attempts to cure infertility are therefore not only permissible, but may also be seen in Islam as a duty to both family and community.

Fertility and birth control in an Islamic perspective

Islam regards procreation as a sign of God's will: 'And we cause who we will to rest in the wombs' (22:5). Interfering with the natural cycle of fertility is forbidden. However, Islamic scholars make a distinction between fertility control (*Tahdid al Nasl*) which is forbidden, and fertility planning or organisation (*Tanzim al Nasl*), which is permissible. Barrier methods such as condoms and diaphragms are encouraged, but there are varied opinions on other methods. Some religious thinkers (for example, Sha'rawi) consider the use of the birth control pill as forbidden because it interferes with the natural cycle of reproduction, whilst other scholars (for example, Al Ghazali) argue that oral contraception can be an encouraged method of fertility organisation as it does not intervene directly with the conception as such. In as much as it may be irreversible, vasectomy for the male or the permanent sterilisation of the woman would be forbidden unless done for medical reasons. This demonstrates an important principle in Islam, that it is the purpose of any given method rather than the type of contraception that determines its acceptability.

The Qur'an describes the process of conception quite clearly as part of procreation, with several passages relating to the conceptus, the developing embryo and the foetus in the womb: 'Man We did create from a quintessence (of clay); then We placed him as (a drop of) sperm in a place of rest, firmly fixed; then We made the sperm into a clot of congealed blood; then of that clot We made a (foetus) lump; then We made out of that lump bones and clothed the bones with flesh; then We developed out of it another creature. So blessed by God the Best to Create!'[10]

In another *Surah* it is revealed that: 'O mankind! If you have a doubt about the Resurrection, [consider] that We have created you of dust; then of sperm; then out of a leech-like clot, then out of a morsel of flesh, partly formed and partly unformed, in order that We may manifest [Our power] to you; and We cause whom We will in the wombs, for an appointed term, then do We bring you out as babes.'[11]

On the same subject, the Prophet Muhammad (pbuh) confirmed that: 'Each of you is constituted in your mother's womb for forty days as a *nutfah*[12] then it becomes *alaqah*[13] for an equal period, then a *mudghah*[14] for another equal period, then the angel is sent and he breathes the soul into it' (Musallam 1983).

We are also told that it is the sperm that determines the sex of the child: 'Allah fashioned both male and female from a drop of sperm, when it was cast forth [ejaculated]' (53:46).

The Qur'an gives no specific guidance on contraception yet it is clear that the preservation of the human species is an objective of marriage. The Prophet Muhammad (pubh) said, 'You merit rewards of charity in your sexual union with your spouses', and he also said, 'Marry and procreate'. Islam encourages having many children, but family planning is allowed (Qaradawi 1994). Having children is recommended (*mandub*) but it is not mandatory. Marriage in Islam is a celebration of sexuality within the bonds of lawful union. It is neither viewed primarily as an outlet for sexual desires and fulfilment; nor is it considered solely for the purpose of procreation. Sexual fulfilment within marriage strengthens the bonds between man and wife in adhering to the divine mandate.

Muslims opposed to birth control cite the Qur'an: 'Kill not your children for fear of want: We shall provide sustenance for them as well as for you. Verily killing them is a great sin' (17:31).

However, supporters of birth control argue that this interpretation is incorrect because this verse clearly refers to infanticide, a practice common in pre-Islamic Arabia (Nicholson 1966), and the Qur'an admonishes Arabs against killing their children for fear of poverty and promises sustenance for them.

During the *Jahilliyya* era (pre-Islamic 'period of ignorance', preceding the revelation of the Qur'an to the Prophet Muhammad) infanticide was frequently committed for a variety of reasons: as a pledge of fulfilment to the idols if their wish came true; due to poverty creating an inability to sustain a newborn child; if the health of the mother was too fragile to carry the pregnancy to term, or if she had a suckling child and the father could not afford a wet nurse.

The Qur'anic revelations guided the Prophet Muhammad (pubh) as follows:

> O Prophet: When believing women come to you to give you their pledge not to associate anything with God in worship, that they shall not steal, that they shall not commit adultery, *that they shall not kill their children*, that they shall not utter slander, intentionally forge falsehood, and that they shall not disobey you in any just cause: then accept this pledge and pray to God for their forgiveness, for God is Oft-forgiving Most Merciful (6:12).

There is a common consensus amongst Muslim jurists that practising birth control for fear of poverty is a manifestation of weakness of faith and trust in Allah, the Provider and Sustainer of all beings. Nonetheless, in practice most Muslim authorities permit contraception to preserve the health of the mother or the well-being of the family. There are a number of hadith which indicate that the Prophet knew of birth control and approved of it in appropriate circumstances. The common method of contraception at the time of the Prophet was *coitus interruptus*, thus preventing the semen from entering the vagina. The Companions of the Prophet engaged in this practice during the period of Qur'anic revelation.

Islam is against family planning if it is carried out for reason of enjoyment and unwillingness to undertake the responsibility of parenthood. However, the right to create a family is equally shared by husband and wife, and neither one of them can resort to contraception unilaterally. It should be done with consensual agreement.

The Islamic approach to contraception is pragmatic. Contraception may be permitted if: 1) both spouses are of young age, or academic students waiting to complete their studies; 2) one or both are suffering from illness which prevents them undertaking parenting responsibility, or it would drain them physically or emotionally; 3) it is done to provide quality and care to existing children; 4) if a pregnancy would be a threat to the life of the woman. Another valid reason which was advocated at the time of the Prophet was that a new pregnancy or a new baby might be harmful for a suckling child.

Personhood, ensoulment and abortion

Most Muslim scholars agree that a foetus in the womb is recognised and protected by Islam as a human life. It is not clear how or whether this extends to embryos produced and maintained *in vitro*, which raises the question of the status of these embryos and any obligations towards them. Whilst there are specific considerations that arise when an embryo or foetus is growing in the womb, and not least a consideration of the life or health of the mother, terminating the life of an embryo *in vitro* is for some Muslim scholars the equivalent to terminating the life of an embryo or foetus growing in the womb.

In Islam, as with most other religions, a central issue is when the developing organism becomes a person, and the nature and existence of a soul. 'Whosoever has spared the life of a soul, it is as though he has spared the life of all people. Whosoever has killed a soul, it is as though he has murdered all of mankind' (5:32).

On this issue there is not a unity of view either historically or currently. Traditionally Islam has regarded personhood as something acquired prior to birth, although scholars have not agreed on when this occurs. Some authorities consider that 'ensoulment' occurs at 120 days of gestation, or about four months into a pregnancy, a time which may relate to when the woman may first 'feel' the movements of the developing foetus.

The 'traditional' Islamic view on abortion held the moment of 'quickening', when the mother first feels the foetus move in the womb, to be significant (Natour, Bakri and Rispler-Chaim 2005). These movements may be detected by the mother at around 120 days' gestation (18–24 weeks if it is the woman's first baby or a little earlier if she has had babies previously). However, jurists were not agreed on whether to sanction or prohibit abortion if performed prior to the quickening phase. Al-Ghazali, one of the great jurists of the twelfth century AD, was of the firm opinion that adultery constitutes a valid reason for abortion prior to quickening. 'If the zygote is the result of adultery, then the allowance of abortion may be envisaged. If it is left until it reaches the stage of animation, then prohibition is certain' (Al-Ghazali 1302 AH).

According to the Hanafi School, a pregnant woman can have an abortion without her husband's permission, provided there are reasonable grounds, such as where the pregnancy poses a threat to the health of the woman or where the pregnancy is a result of rape (Ibn-Abidin 1965); according to the Maliki school, as described by Ibn-Juzayyah (1953), to induce abortion would be tantamount to murder. For some it was permissible on the grounds that no life in the sense of a person existed, and therefore no crime could be committed. This view was based on scientific knowledge and the medical beliefs prevalent at the time, and there is no reason why the moment of quickening should carry any particular ethical significance now, with advanced understanding of foetal development and function. There is no point during embryogenesis or foetal development when a person can be said to have clearly emerged.

A modern Islamic position confers an increasing moral consideration of interest for the embryo and foetus as it develops in the womb (Islamset 2006). In this view the 'crime' of abortion grows more and more serious as the developing conceptus passes from one phase to another, reaching the worst degree when the foetus is born alive. In 1981, the First International Conference on Islamic Medicine was held in Kuwait. As a result, an Islamic Code of Medical Ethics was produced (Islamic Code of Medical Ethics 1982). In contrast to the 'delayed animation' view in traditional Islam the Code regards the human embryo from the moment of conception as a 'complete human being deserving protection'.

Islam allows abortion to save the life of the mother on the general *Shariah* principle of choosing the lesser of two evils. Abortion is a lesser evil because the mother is the 'originator' of the foetus, the mother's life is well-established and has value, the mother has duties and responsibilities and dependents as part of a family, and in any event, allowing the mother to die would most likely kill the foetus too. Although not generally accepted, some modern Islamic opinions and rulings have also accepted prenatal diagnosis and abortion of the foetus if it is found to be so severely abnormal that if born it would suffer profoundly or cause severe suffering for the family (Muslim World League Conference of Jurists 1990).

Most of these arguments do not hold for an embryo conceived and maintained *in vitro*, not least because there is no inherent risk to the life of a mother. However, in IVF treatment several embryos may be transferred to the womb to ensure a successful pregnancy. In the case of a multiple pregnancy, selective reduction of embryos is allowed only if there is a clear danger to the life and health of the mother or if the completion of multiple pregnancy becomes extremely dangerous (Tantawi 1991).

Sex selection was notoriously popular amongst early Arab communities (Gad El-Hak 1992). Islamic jurists issued a cautionary note on sex selection, that it predetermines a secondary status for women in Muslim society. Pre-conceptional sex selection is prohibited in Islam as it infers a challenge to the will of Allah. Neither Qur'an nor Sunnah or Hadith make reference to medically assisted procreation. Instead these affirm the importance of marriage, family formation and procreation. Various Islamic schools of thought prohibit sex selection from an ethical and moral point of view, as it is considered to be an act of discrimination against female embryos and foetuses, discouraging the birth of a female child (Fathalla 2000). Whilst some have advocated sex selection on social grounds of 'family balance' (Kilani 1999), this is not generally supported. In this regard, Islam concurs with Article 14 of the Convention on Human Rights and Biomedicine of the Council of Europe (1996) that the use of techniques of medically assisted procreation 'shall not be allowed for the purpose of choosing a future child's sex, except where serious hereditary sex-related disease is to be avoided'.

Research on human embryos

In the IVF process, embryos are produced that will not be needed for placement in the woman's womb. There are two circumstances when Islam allows research on such embryos or on human embryonic or foetal cells: if the embryos are no longer needed for infertility treatment and would not be placed in a woman's womb, then these are considered as *najus* (impure); similarly, umbilical cord is also considered to be *najus* and can be used to extract stem cells if it is required for medical treatment or research. Such research might seriously harm any resultant offspring if the embryos were subsequently placed in the uterus of a woman (Robertson 1994). This reasoning conforms to the position adopted by Islamic jurists that research on embryos is permissible, provided they are not going to be placed in the womb for further development, and follows the Shari'ah principle of 'purposes and higher causes of the Islamic law' (Islamic Institute 2001). It makes an ethical distinction between embryos for research purposes and those created for reproduction; a distinction between therapeutic and reproductive use. It is also permissible to seek preventative treatment in the form of *najus*.[15] On this basis research on, and the use in treatment of, human embryonic stem cells is judged permissible. It should be clear that this logic does not hold for the creation of human embryos specifically for research or therapeutic purposes, which is held to be contrary to Islamic law and is prohibited in all its forms. Such embryos would not in this case be as a result of IVF for the purpose of procreation, and therefore would not have resulted from a 'higher cause'.

From an Islamic perspective humans are directly charged by God to combat disease and suffering (Qummi 1983). Islamic jurists believe that good is served through assisted reproductive technology in combating infertility. Spare embryos are inevitably created in this process, in which case it is considered a social obligation to use them in research rather than simply killing them. A greater good follows if it leads to better diagnoses, preventions or treatments for genetic, congenital diseases or other diseases, such as cancers, and in devising more effective contraceptive techniques or combating infertility and enhancing reproduction (Ahmad 2003).

Considering embryo research and pre-implantation genetic diagnosis (PGD), the First International Conference on Bioethics in the Muslim World held in Cairo in 1991 (Serour 1992) reached the following conclusions.

1. Cryopreserved pre-implantation embryos may be used for research purposes if there is free and informed consent of the couple.

2. Research conducted on pre-embryos should be limited to therapeutic research. Genetic analysis of pre-embryos to detect specific genetic disorders is permissible. Hence

diagnostic aids should be provided for couples at high risk for selected inherited diseases. The treated embryo may only be implanted into the uterus of the wife who produces the ovum from which it is made, and only during the span of the marriage contract.

3. Any pre-embryos found to be genetically defective may be rejected from transfer into the uterus after proper counselling by a qualified physician.

4. Research aimed at changing the inherited characteristics of pre-embryos (for example, hair and eye colour, intelligence, height), including sex selection, is strictly forbidden.

5. Sex selection is, however, permitted if a particular sex predisposes to a serious genetic condition.

6. The free, informed consent of the couple should be obtained prior to conducting any non-therapeutic research on the pre-implantation embryos. These embryos should not be implanted into the uterus of the wife or that of any other woman.

7. Research of a commercial nature or not related to the health of the mother or child is prohibited.

8. The research should be undertaken in accredited and reputable research facilities. The medical justification for the research proposal must be sound scientifically and conducted by skilled and responsible researchers.

It can be argued that this view of the status of the pre-implantation embryo conflicts with that in the Islamic Code of Medical Ethics adopted in 1981, which regards the human embryo from the moment of conception as a 'complete human being deserving protection'. However, the position adopted currently is an ethical solution to a conflict of moral imperative: Islam approves of IVF because it combats infertility and embryo selection may prevent disease and suffering; but the IVF technique produces more embryos than can be used in procreation. These embryos could be allowed to die without further use, or they may be used where possible to reduce human suffering.

Cloning human embryos

Cloning human embryos as an alternative in human reproduction is unacceptable under Islam because it destroys the basic social concepts of family, married life and parenthood, not least because it interferes with lineage and identity. From an Islamic perspective, a cloned child would be without mother or father. The clone will still be a human being with the rights, dignity, and sacredness of a human being, but (s)he will be a human being without a lineage. Islamic scholars are also concerned that not enough is known of the potential harmful consequences for any offspring produced through cloning techniques. The Islamic Fiqh Council, after consultation with the Organisation of Muslim Doctors, has concluded that human cloning could not be permitted as it would create complex and intractable social and moral problems (Usmani 1999). It leaves open the question of whether it might be permissible in some circumstances if it could be shown to be the only way to combat a hereditary disease; the development of cloned embryos might also be permissible for stem cell research and the potential stem cell therapies to combat diseases or abnormalities (Fischbach and Fischbach 2004).

Islam has not adopted the Roman Catholic position that cloning or other reproductive technologies interfere with the work of God. According to the Qur'an, Allah is the creator of all things: 'He has created everything and has measured it exactly according to its due measurements' (25:2). But Islamic scholars make a distinction between creation in the sense of bringing into being from nothing, and creation in the sense of applying knowledge of how things are. If we make a mark with a pen or build a wall with bricks, then in one sense we are creating these things; the mark or the wall did not exist until we made them, but they were not made from nothing. Only by understanding the nature of things could we create them. Only by understanding the nature of biology can we make anything to combat disease. Only by understanding the 'laws of nature' or, in an Islamic sense, the 'will of Allah' can man create anything with purpose. Islam holds that humans have a duty to apply such understanding in finding new cures for diseases and eliminating suffering. Cloning in this sense does not go against the 'will of Allah' if it is part of this search.

Infertility

Islam is not against the application of modern scientific technological developments to treat infertility,[16] provided it does not contravene the will of God in the process of creating a pregnancy (Eskandarani 1996). Islam encourages infertile couples to seek treatment for infertility and to fulfil their wish of having a baby of their own.

Assisted reproductive technologies and IVF

Assisted reproductive technologies and IVF were not initially permitted by Islamic jurists because third parties were involved in fertilisation procedures (Gad El-Hak 1980; Serour 2005). It was not until the Fatwas from Al-Azhar in 1980 and the Islamic Fiqh Council in Mecca in 1984 that these procedures became permissible. They are now being practised in many Islamic countries with the proviso that the sperm should be of the husband and the ovum that of his wife (Serour 2005) and the fertilised eggs are transferred to the uterus of the wife.

Surrogacy

Surrogacy cannot be supported in Islam. Fertilisation of the ovum of a woman by the sperm of a man who is not her husband is regarded as an 'adulterous union' and considered illegal. Thus sperm donation in assisted reproduction is prohibited if it is not that of the woman's husband, as is ovum donation if it is not that of the male's wife. Any contractual arrangement between a surrogate and a married couple cannot be justified under the Shariah law (Gad El-Hak 1980) and would be considered a *batil* (invalid) contract.

Equally, Islam regards as unacceptable a surrogate carrying in her womb the foetus of another couple. This is so even when the sperm and ovum have been taken from the husband and wife. The surrogacy not only takes place outside the marriage contract but it also splits the genetic from biologic formation, the act of procreation, which Islam considers a unity and part of the bond between husband and wife. Furthermore, if surrogacy involves a commercial agreement with the exchange of money, it is considered dehumanising, as it treats both the surrogate and the offspring as commodities; by so doing it reduces motherhood to a commercial price and ignores the potential emotional trauma for all parties involved, particularly if the pregnancy should fail, the baby be born handicapped or an abortion be considered necessary. The implications are more problematic if a surrogate decides not to relinquish the baby.

The ethical, moral and social issues concerning surrogacy have been discussed for a long period of time and the arguments continue, particularly over whether there are any exceptions to its prohibition. There have been regular debates between eminent Islamic scholars, lawyers and physicians considering the potential of surrogacy in particular situations; for example, how to fulfil the demand of a woman whose uterus has previously been removed because of multiple fibroids. For this reason, the Islamic Research Council held a special meeting in April 2001 and published a statement condemning surrogacy on the basis of third-party involvement in procreation. Nevertheless, unanimous agreement could not be reached on many of the issues raised: 'While the Islamic Fiqh Council of Mecca and the Church of Alexandria previously allowed surrogacy to be performed on the second wife of the same husband or a friend of the family, respectively, both councils soon after denied surrogacy and their guidelines became identical with those of Al-Azhar' (Serour 2001).

On the question of surrogacy (*Nasab*), the Prophet Muhammad (pubh) is reported to have said, 'The child is for the bed' (Al-Bukhari 1996), meaning that the mother is the one who gives birth to it. Therefore, the surrogate is ethically, morally and legally the mother of the child. There are nevertheless some basic objections to surrogacy in Islam. For example, it is maintained that:

1. surrogacy tampers with the Sunnah (ways) of Allah in the normal process of procreation

2. for an unmarried woman to become a surrogate and to 'lease' her womb for monetary benefit undermines the institution of marriage and family life

3. surrogacy may tempt married women to resort to this technique in order to relieve themselves of the pains of pregnancy and childbirth. Islam does not consider pregnancy as a burden but a blessing. If a mother dies during pregnancy or childbirth she is given the status of *shahidah* (martyr)

4. surrogacy encourages the surrogate to claim legal rights to the couple's child she bore. It creates confusion in blood ties and the identity of the potential child.

According to Khamash (2001), the Jordanian scholar, the only case where surrogacy might be permissible is when it is arranged between the wives of the same man, where the surrogate would solve the problem of a second wife who is unable to give birth. (Under Shi'a Islamic law it is permissible to have several wives and it is also permissible to have a temporary marriage with a fixed duration; Sunni Muslims are allowed to have up to four permanent wives but temporary marriages are prohibited.) But the psychological problems still remain, particularly as society might look with disrespect to both women, mainly the surrogate mother who has accepted to hire her womb, even to one of the wives of her husband.

Third-party assisted conception – oocyte and embryo donation

An indication that ethical problems of assisted conception are not insurmountable for Islam has been demonstrated in Iran, where the spiritual leader issued a decree (fatwa) that oocyte donation is not in itself prohibited (Zahedi and Larijani 2006). This decree has paved the way for third-party assisted conception in an Islamic country, and embryo donation to infertile couples was sanctioned by the Iranian parliament in 2003. There are nonetheless still ethical, legal, psychosocial and cultural issues to be resolved. Gamete donation and artificial insemination may create new concepts of kinship, and they still pose difficulty in the area of lineage, so important to Islamic culture and identity. This fatwa nevertheless demonstrates the progressive ethical approach of Islam to reproductive medicine and technology, and in particular to the problem of infertility.

Cryopreservation of sperm, ova and embryos

From an Islamic point of view, cryopreservation of sperm, ova or embryos is permissible, provided there is a valid marriage contract. If the wife gets pregnant with her husband's sperm after his death, then the child would be regarded as illegitimate (Ebrahim 1998).

Similarly, there is no Islamic objection to the preservation of any number of frozen embryos produced through IVF, provided that they remain the property of the couples who have produced them; if they are used subsequently in reproduction, that they are only implanted to the uterus of the woman from whose ovum they were created; that there is a marriage contract, valid at the time of transplantation, with the man who produced the sperm. If the husband has died or if the couple have divorced, these embryos should not be used in reproduction.

Pre-implantation genetic diagnosis (PGD)

From an Islamic perspective, PGD and selection of embryos are acceptable if used to avoid harm to the mother or to prevent a foetal anomaly incompatible with life (Serour and Omran 1992). As in ethical discourse generally, it is unresolved whether PGD should be extended to cover other life-threatening or late onset diseases.

Islam gives great weight to the prevention of genetic disorders or congenital malformations and to the fitness of offspring. The Prophet Muhammad (pubh) and his companions frequently preached on securing normal and healthy babies. The Prophet Muhammad (pubh) said: 'Select your spouses carefully in the interest of your offspring because lineage is a crucial issue.' In another hadith he said: 'Do not marry your close relatives because you will beget weak offspring.' The second Caliph of Islam, Omar ibn El-Khattab, upon noting that a particular tribe intermarried with increased frequency, remarked to them: 'You have weakened your descendants. You should marry strangers (people outside your tribe).'

Conclusions

Islam has a distinct ethical process seeking guidance in the Qur'an, the sayings and actions of the Prophet Muhammad (pubh), and in analogy, reason and consensus. Fertility is a central feature of

Muslim life, and Islam looks favourably on the use of reproductive technologies such as IVF if they are used to produce offspring within the sanctity of marriage. It has also a pragmatic view of contraception if this is used to plan fertility and take account of the fitness of the mother and her offspring. Abortion is acceptable only if there is a great threat to the life of the mother from the pregnancy or if the offspring are likely to be born with a profound handicap; the selection of embryos through PGD is also acceptable where this is used to avoid severe hereditary diseases or malformations affecting the offspring. Sex selection is acceptable in the case of sex-linked genetic disorders. It looks favourably on the use of human embryos in research where these have been produced as a result of the IVF process but are not used in reproduction. Lineage and heredity are an important aspect of identity in Islam and key to the pivotal role of the family in Muslim societies; for this reason reproductive techniques that interfere with lineage, such as surrogacy and sperm donation or reproductive cloning, are considered impermissible.

Notes

1 For example, those which are: a) *haram* – forbidden; b) *makrooh* – reprehensible but permitted, c) *mubah* – legal, natural, permitted; d) *mandoob* – encouraged.

2 Islam does not have a bipolar view of moral right and wrong. There are five categories of human behaviour: obligatory (*wajib*), prohibited (*haram*), recommended (*sunna*), discouraged (*makruh*), and permitted (*mubah*).

3 *Fiqh* literally translated means 'to comprehend and understand'.

4 Sunni Muslims ('people of the tradition') are the largest denomination of Islam. *Sunnah* means in the tradition of the Prophet.

5 Shi'a Muslims believe that specific members of Muhammad's family (the *Imams*) were the best source of knowledge about the Qur'an. *Shi'at Ali* means 'the followers of Ali' or 'the faction of Ali'. Shi'a Muslims believe that Ali, the Prophet's cousin and son-in-law, was the rightful leader of the faith after Muhammad's death. Thus, Shi'as consider the first three ruling caliphs (Abu Bakr, Umar ibn al-Khattab and Uthman ibn Affan) a political imposition and not a matter of faith.

6 A *fatwa* is a legal pronouncement made by a *mufti*, a scholar capable of issuing judgements on Islamic law (*sharia*). These are neither binding nor legally enforceable, but provide invaluable insight when gauging Islamic opinions on a given topic. Fatwas can be published in daily newspapers and periodicals or broadcast on radio or television. Amongst the many important collection of fatwas, there are three volumes which are more commonly recognised; *al-Fatawa al Hindiyya, al-Fatawa al-kubra al-fiqhiyya* and *al-Fatawa al-Islamiya*.

7 The ruling of any one school can never fanatically invalidate the rulings of others, because they, also, are based on sound principles of reasoning (*ijtihad*).

8 In Arabic, '*rahim*' refers to the womb, but it also represents a 'value' based on blood relatives and the tie of compassion that binds them.

9 Islam holds that all humans are born without sin (*fitrah*) and with freedom of will.

10 Qur'an 23: 12–14.

11 Qur'an 22:5.

12 Sperm.

13 A little piece of flesh, shapely and shapeless.

14 Foetus.

15 When the people of Medina were suffering from gastrointestinal disease, the Prophet instructed them to go outside of Medina and to drink from the urine and milk of the camel to protect themselves from the disease.

16 Qur'an Sura 4, Verse 3.

References

Ahmad, N.H. (2003) 'Assisted reproduction – Islamic views on the science of procreation.' *Eubios Journal of Asian and International Bioethics* 13, 59–60.

Al-Ghazali, Ihya' Ulum al-Din, Al Matba al-Azhariyya al-Misriyya (Cairo, 1302 AH).

Alwani, T.J. (1993) 'The ethics of disagreement in Islam: Issues in contemporary Islamic thought.' Virginia: The International Institute of Islamic Thought.

Bukhari, S. al- (1996) *Book of Muslim Morals and Values*. Riyadh, Saudi Arabia: Dar-ul-Salam Publications.

Council of Europe (1996) *Convention for the Protection of Human Rights and Dignity of the Human Being with Regard to the Application of Biology and Medicine*. Strasbourg: Council of Europe.

Daar, A.S. and Khitamy, A.B. (2001) 'Bioethics for clinicians: 21. Islamic bioethics.' *Canadian Medical Association Journal 164*, 1, 60–63.

Ebrahim, A.F.M. (1998) *Biomedical Issues, Islamic Perspective*. Islamic Medical Association of South Africa.

Edge, I. (1996) *Islamic Law and Legal Theory*. Aldershot: Dartmouth.

Eskandarani, H. (1996) *Assisted Reproductive Technology: State of the ART*. Publications of the Islamic Educational Scientific and Cultural Organisation (ISESCO). Saudi Arabia: Al-Wafa Printing.

Faruqi, I.R. al- (2006) *Contraception and Abortion in Islam.* Accessed 14/11/2007 at http://brexmother.blogspot.com/2006/08/contraception-and-abortion-in-islam.html

Fathalla, M.F. (2000) 'The girl child.' *International Journal of Gynaecology and Obstetrics 70*, 7–12.

Fischbach, G.D. and Fischbach, R.L. (2004) 'Stem cells: science, policy, and ethics.' *Journal of Clinical Investigation 114*, 1364–1370.

Gad El-Hak, A.G.H. (1980) '*In vitro* fertilization and test-tube baby.' Cairo, Egypt: *Dar El Iftaa 1225*, 1, 115, 3213–3228.

Gad El-Hak, A. (1992) 'Islam, a religion of ethics.' In G.I. Serour (ed.) *Proceedings of the First International Conference on Bioethics in Human Reproduction in Research in the Muslim World.* Cairo: ICBHRR.

Haleem, A. (1993) 'Medical ethics in Islam.' In A. Grubb (ed.) *Choices and Decisions in Health Care.* London: John Wiley & Son.

Hanooti, M. al- (2003) 'Fatawa: Belief in Qadar and committing sins.' Accessed 3/10/06 at www.islamonline.net/servlet/Satellite?pagename=IslamOnline-English-Ask_Scholar/FatwaE/FatwaE&cid=1119503545040

Ibn-Abidin, al- (1965) *Hadiyyah al-alaiyyah.* Third edition. Damascus.

Ibn-Juzayyah, K. (1953) *Al-qawanin al-Fiqhiyyah.* Fez: Mataba al Nahda.

Irfan, H. (2005) 'What future for Muslim orphans?' Accessed 6/02/08 at www.islamonline.net/servlet/Satellite?c=Article_C&cid=1157365802861&pagename=Zone-English-Family%2FFYELayout

Islamset (2006) 'Islamic ethics: Topics in Islamic medicine.' Accessed 01/11/06 at www.islamset.com/ethics/topics/abort.html

Islamic Code of Medical Ethics (1982) *World Medicine Journal 29*, 5, 78–80.

Islamic Institute (2001) 'A Muslim perspective on embryonic stem cell research.' 11, 3. Accessed 10/06/2006 at www.islamicinstitute.org/i3-stemcell.pdf

Khamash, H. (2001) *The Star.* 41: 12–18.

Kilani, Z. (1999) 'Pre-implantation genetic diagnosis for family balance and sex chromosome aneuploidies.' *Fifth International Annual Conference of the Egyptian Fertility and Sterility Society.* Cairo.

Maguire, D.C. (2003) *Sacred Rights. The Case for Contraception and Abortion in World Religions.* Oxford: Oxford University Press.

Musallam, B.F. (1983) *Sex and Society in Islam.* Cambridge: Cambridge University Press.

Muslim World League Conference of Jurists (1990) *Regarding Termination of Pregnancy for Congenital Abnormalities* [No. 4]. 12th session. Mecca.

Natour, A., Bakri. B. and Rispler-Chaim, V. (2005) 'An Islamic perspective.' In S. Blazer and E.A. Zimmer (eds) *The Embryo: Scientific Discovery and Medical Ethics.* Basel: Karger.

Nicholson, R. (1966) *A Literary History of the Arabs.* Cambridge: Cambridge University Press.

Qaradawi (1994) *The Lawful and Prohibited in Islam.* Plainfield, IN: American Trust Publications. Chapter 4, p.88.

Qummi, A. (1983) *Safinat-u-Bihar* Volume 3. Reprinted by Dar al-Uswah (1995), Iran.

Reinhart, K. (1983) 'Islamic law as Islamic ethics.' *Journal of Religious Ethics 11*, 2, 189.

Robertson, J. (1994) *Children of Choice: Freedom and the New Reproductive Technologies.* Princeton, NJ: Princeton University Press.

Serour, G.I. (1992) 'Guidelines on bioethics in human reproduction research in the Muslim world.' IICPSR, Al-Azhar University, Cairo.

Serour, G.I. (2001) 'Attitudes and cultural perspectives on infertility and its alleviation in the Middle East area.' *WHO Expert Group Meeting on ART.* Geneva. Accessed 27/05/09 at www.who.int/reproductive-health/infertility/8.pdf

Serour, G.I. (2005) 'Religious perspectives of ethical issues in ART: 1. Islamic perspectives of ethical issues in ART.' *Middle East Fertility Society Journal 10,* 3, 185–190.

Serour, G.I. and Omran, A. (1992) 'Ethical guidelines.' In *Proceedings of the First International Conference on Bioethics in Human Reproduction in Research in the Muslim World,* 10–13 December 1991. Cairo: IICPSR.

Tantawi, S. (1991) 'Islamic Sharia and selective fetal reduction.' *Al-Ahram Daily Newspaper 2,* 926. Cairo.

Usmani, T.M. (1999) 'The 1997 Islamic Fiqh Academy.' Accessed 26/06/09 at www.albalagh.net/qa/ifa.shtml

Zahedi, F. and Larijani, B. (2006) 'Considerations of third-party reproduction in Iran.' *Human Reproduction 22,* 902.

4

Hinduism and Reproduction in Contemporary India

Vedic Learnings

Gautam N. Allahbadia, Swati G. Allahbadia and Sulbha Arora

Introduction

When Brahmans know their self, and have risen above the desire for sons, wealth, and [new] worlds, they wander about as mendicants. For a desire for sons is desire for wealth, a desire for wealth is desire for worlds. Both these are indeed desires. (*Brihadaranyaka Upanishad*)

Hinduism is unique among world religions in that it has no founder or date of origin. While most major religions derive from new ideas taught by a charismatic leader, Hinduism is simply the religion of the people of India, which has gradually developed over four thousand years. The origins and authors of its sacred texts are largely unknown. Although today's Hinduism differs significantly from earlier forms of Indian religion, Hinduism's roots date back as far as 2000 BCE, making it one of the oldest surviving religions. Because of its great age, the early history of Hinduism is unclear. The most ancient writings have yet to be deciphered, so for the earliest periods scholars must rely on educated guesses based on archaeology and the study of contemporary texts.

Hindus, like any other religious group, love their children dearly. They believe that their children are gifts from gods and rewards of their previous karma. Many presume that their children were related to them in their past lives or were their close friends. Hindus are very possessive about their children and spend a great deal of their time and energy in bringing them up. Because of orthodox sentiments and moral values, parents are always concerned about their children's welfare and upbringing and expect them not to bring a bad name to themselves or to their families. Hindus are sentimentally and emotionally attached to their children and experience great warmth and intimacy in their relationships. The bond between parents and children remains intact even after the children grow up and get married.

Since a Hindu firmly believes in rebirth (Babb 1989), he or she views his or her own life from an existentially wider perspective that encompasses not just this life but many other lives that preceded it, as well as those that will succeed it, and views individual existence as a part of a great cosmic cycle. Endowed with the belief that relationships repeat themselves and that a person's life is intricately intertwined with many others who share the same destiny, the Hindu acts with a spiritual sense of duty and responsibility towards him or herself and all those who depend upon, or are related to, him or her. Since Hindus sincerely believe in the continuity of life and relationships, they work for the welfare of their family and its financial security through a policy of self-denial and austerity in personal expenditure.

History

Traditional view

Hinduism has a long and complex history. It is a blend of ancient legends, beliefs and customs, which has adapted, blended with and spawned numerous creeds and practices.

1. Prehistoric religion (3000–1000 BCE)

The earliest evidence for elements of the Hindu faith dates back as far as 3000 BCE. Archaeological excavations in the Punjab and Indus valleys have revealed the existence of urban cultures at Harappa, the prehistoric capital of the Punjab (located in modern Pakistan) and at Mohenjodaro on the banks of the River Indus. Archaeological work continues on other sites at Kalibangan, Lothal and Surkotada. The excavations have revealed signs of early rituals and worship. In Mohenjodaro, for example, a large bath has been found, with side rooms and statues, which could be evidence of early purification rites.

Elsewhere, phallic symbols (Figure 4.1) and a large number of statues of goddesses have been discovered, which could suggest the practice of early fertility rites (Bhattacharya 2006). This early Indian culture is sometimes called the Indus Valley Civilisation. The Indus valley communities used to gather at rivers for their religious rituals. They regarded rivers as sacred, and had both male and female gods, although none specifically relating to infertility.

Figure 4.1 Phallic symbol

2. Pre-classical (Vedic) (2000 BCE–1000 CE)

Some time in the second millennium BCE, the Aryan people arrived in northwest India. The Aryans were a nomadic people who
may have come to India from the areas around southern Russia
and the Baltic. They brought with them their language and their
religious traditions. These traditions were also influenced by the
religious practices of the people who were already living in India.
The Aryans gathered around fire for their rituals (Frawley 2000).
The Aryan gods represented the forces of nature: the sun, the moon,
fire, storm and so on. Over time, the different religious practices
tended to blend together. Sacrifices were made to gods such as
Agni, the God of Fire, and Indra, the God of Storms.

Aspects of the Aryan faith began to be written down around
800 BCE in literature known as the Vedas. These developed from

Figure 4.2 A havan

oral and poetic traditions. One can see some of the Vedic traditions in Hindu worship today. Many infertile couples, especially in North India, undergo rituals around the holy fire for begetting children, called 'havans' (Figure 4.2).

Demography

Of the total Hindu population of the world (over 1 billion people) approximately 900 million live in India. Significant numbers of Hindus reside in Bangladesh, Bhutan, Fiji, Guyana, Indonesia, Malaysia, Mauritius, Nepal, Singapore, South Africa, Sri Lanka, Suriname, and Trinidad and Tobago. There are also sizeable Hindu populations in the Middle East, Pakistan, the Philippines, the United Kingdom and United States. In Bali and Nepal, Hinduism is the major religion, and is still reflected in the traditional culture and architecture. (See 'The World Factbook' at www.cia.gov.)

Dharma and karma

Two words that play a crucial role in understanding the Hindu (as well as Buddhist and Jain) attitude towards life are *Dharma* and *Karma*. Dharma and Karma can best be understood by reading *The Mahabharata* (translated as 'the great tale of the Bharata Dynasty'), which is one of the two major Sanskrit epics of ancient India, the other being the *Ramayana*. With more than 74,000 verses, long prose passages, and about 1.8 million words in total, the *Mahabharata* is one of the longest epic poems in the world. It is of immense importance to the culture of India and the Indian subcontinent, and is a major text of Hinduism.

Dharma is essentially duty that must be performed for the sake of social as well as cosmic stability. Failure to do so leads to social anarchy and cosmic chaos. Duty is traditionally defined by one's inherited caste (teacher, protector, provider and servant being the traditional four castes) and by one's stage in life (student, householder, senior citizen, hermit) (Sutton 2000). Hindus being deeply spiritual, a large populace, after fulfilling the Vedic duties of providing for their families, relinquished their homes and family life to become ascetics or '*sadhus*', proceeding towards spiritual colonies along the river Ganges, and spent the rest of their lives meditating away from civilisation or in the service of temples or religious *ashrams* (seminaries). Producing a child is one's biological duty applicable to all human beings. Those who wanted to renounce the world were only allowed to do so after they had fulfilled all worldly duties.

Men who could not fulfil their biological obligations because of impotence or homosexuality were termed rather derogatorily *kliba* or *napunsaka*, the sexually dysfunctional 'non-man'. In the *Manusmriti*, an ancient Hindu law book, such men were debarred from sacred rituals and from inheritance. Only by producing children were a man and woman considered biologically fulfilled. It must be remembered that only after marriage was a man in Hindu society given the right to enjoy worldly pleasures and possess worldly wealth. A king could not be king unless he was married. And an impotent man or a man who could not father a child was not allowed to be king. Hence, in the *Mahabharata*, when the heir to the throne of Hastinapur state – Pandu – learns that he will die the moment he has sex with his wife, he renounces his crown – his inability to father a child debars him from kingship.

Karma means both 'action' and 'fate'. Hindus (as well as Buddhists and Jains) believe that every action leads to a series of reactions. All creatures are obliged to experience the repercussions of their (conscious and unconscious) actions, either in this life or the next. Thus, every event is the result of past actions. If one is barren, it is because of events that occurred in the past, either in this life or in the one before. A folk story based on the *Mahabharata* illustrates this point. At the end of a great war, Queen Gandhari is informed that each of her hundred children is dead. She weeps and seeks a reason for this unfair situation, to which a sage replies, 'In your last life, you sat on a stone under which there were a hundred turtle eggs. The eggs were crushed. So the mother-turtle cursed you that you too would experience the loss of a hundred children.'

A situation is governed by Karma, but one's reaction to it is governed by free will. Astrology helps understand what Karma has in store for us. The result of Karma can be either endured or modified by certain occult rituals incurring the power of holy men, or by the grace of god. This is the reason why childless men in India visit temples, go on pilgrimages, seek the intervention of holy men or perform elaborate rituals.

Childlessness is viewed with great concern within orthodox Hinduism. Women without children experience considerable social discomfort and questioning from friends and relatives. Newly married couples have to deal with a lot of peer pressure if they fail to produce children within a reasonable time after their marriage. Childlessness causes great hardship for both men and women in Hindu families, despite the fact that overpopulation is a major problem of present-day India. While for men it is mostly a subtle stigma against their virility and manhood, for women it is an overt stigma of barrenness, and considered to be very inauspicious.

Shiva

The god Shiva is part of the Hindu Trinity, along with Vishnu and Brahma. In Shiva, the opposites meet. Shiva the destroyer is a necessary part of the trinity because, without destruction, there can be no recreation. His city is Varanasi or Benares in Central India, and any Hindu who dies there is believed to go straight to heaven. Shiva is the source of both good and evil, who combines many contradictory elements. In pictures and sculptures, Shiva is represented as Lord of the Dance who controls the movement of the universe. He is also associated with fertility. Shiva has many consorts, including Kali, often portrayed as wild and violent, Parvati, renowned for her gentleness, and Durga, a powerful goddess created from the combined forces of the anger of several gods.

Lingam or *Linga* (Sanskrit: gender, as in *purusha-linga*: phallus) is used as a symbol for the worship of the Hindu god Shiva (Figure 4.3). The use of this symbol as an object of worship has a timeless tradition in India; mainstream scholars connect the origin of the lingam/linga to the early Indus Valley civilisation (Basham 1959). Interestingly, there is no mention of Lingam in the Vedas; this is held by most scholars to be a significant indication of the different origins of the Aryans with whom the Vedas are associated, and the people of the Indus Valley Civilisation, to whom Shiva and the Lingam were important objects of worship. Notwithstanding its absence from the Vedas, the Shiva Lingam is of pervasive importance in many other major Hindu scriptures, including the Puranas. Hinduism conceptualises Brahma, the supreme power, as having three main roles: that of God the Creator, God the Preserver and God the Destroyer. The deities Brahma, Vishnu and Shiva respectively represent this trinity iconically. Thus, it is Shiva, the destructive form of the Almighty, who is represented by the Lingam or phallus,

Figure 4.3 Shiva Lingam

which is manifestly the creative or generative power of Man. This points to an origin of the tradition of using the Lingam as a divine symbol that is utterly sublime in its philosophical underpinnings.

There is a passage in the Bible in which the Hebrew patriarch Jacob appears to be performing something very similar to a Lingam ceremony, in which a precious substance such as milk or oil is poured on the stone artifice in sacrificial intent: 'And Jacob rose up early in the morning, and took the stone that he had put for his pillow, and set it up for a pillar, and poured oil upon the top of it' (Genesis 28:18). Also: 'And Jacob set up a pillar in the place where he talked with him, even a pillar of stone: and he poured a drink offering thereon, and he poured oil thereon' (Genesis 35:14). It is mentioned in several published articles that the term for oil or drink used in this verse is the Hebrew *shemen afarshimon* (Hamblin and Seely 2007), which appears like the English word *semen* and thus seems to be appropriate to the phallic nature of the Lingam.

The Great Goddess (Mahadevi)

The great Goddess appears as a consort of the principal male gods and encompasses the thousands of local goddesses or *matas*. These can be both beautiful and benign, like Lakshmi, or all-powerful, destructive forces like Kali.

Great Goddess shrines are associated with agriculture and fertility and the female energy, or Shakti, is important in ancient texts known collectively as the Tantras. Shakti is contrasted with Shiva, whose masculine consciousness is powerless without the creative female energy.

The Hindu family

A son is generally preferred because he upholds the family values and ensures the family lineage. A family without a male child is considered less blessed. Male children are preferred for many reasons. Financially a male child is an asset because of the dowry system prevalent in most Hindu communities. Socially he stands for the continuity and the exalted image of the family. Spiritually he helps his parents in their afterlife, by performing their funeral rites when they die and saving them from the hell of 'Punnama' where people without sons are believed to go. Thereafter he performs the 'Shraadh' ceremonies at regular intervals to ensure their well-being in the heavens.

Female children are excluded from participating in funeral ceremonies and are not even allowed to visit the cremation grounds. This is based on the rationale that only the males carry forward the family tree and are eligible to deliver the last rites to their ancestors. If a couple has more than one son, the elder one and the younger one would light the funeral pyres of their father and mother respectively.

In many families female children are subjected to gender bias. Having too many girls in a family is considered a great financial burden, since the parents have to pay large dowries for their marriages. The girls have no right of inheritance and the family's ancestral property invariably goes to the male children. Parents have the right to distribute their own wealth (*Swarjitam*) to their daughters, but generally they do not do so unless they do not have male heirs. According to vedic beliefs, following marriage a woman becomes the 'property' of her husband, although this is taken to mean that she becomes his responsibility, and both vedic and societal customs restrain her from continuing to live in the home of her parents.

While the birth of a son is still welcome in almost every Hindu family, nowadays many educated parents also consider a female child as an auspicious sign, as if a goddess is born in their house, and welcome the birth of a baby girl. A baby girl today is welcomed as Lakshmi, the Goddess of Wealth, and even in contemporary rural India, Lakshmi is one of the commonest names for a baby girl.

In a Hindu family it is an obligatory religious duty of the sons to look after their aged parents and provide them with decent means of living. Many do so. But, as in other societies, aged people are increasingly suffering from problems of alienation, isolation, and their children's indifference and neglect. In contemporary society, daughters are increasingly picking up the 'cultural' responsibilities of a 'son'.

The Hindu family system is undergoing radical transformation. But a great majority of Hindu families still consider their children as products of their past deeds (*Purvajanma Sukrutam*). If a child strays and brings a bad name, they blame it upon themselves and their previous Karma.

The following rites are associated with the birth of a child:

1. Rites performed before the birth of an individual, invoking gods to make a woman of the household conceive.

2. Rites performed during the third month of pregnancy invoking gods for the birth of a male child. (The Aryans were chauvinistic and wanted more male children!).

3. Rites performed at the time of the birth of a child, invoking the gods to create auspicious stars so the baby gets a good horoscope.

4. Rites performed at the time of the name giving ceremony, so that the gods shower strength and longevity on the baby. Usually, Hindus are named after some gods or events in Hindu mythology.

5. Rites performed six months after the birth of the child, so that the child survives the first year of life with glowing health.

6. The hair cutting ceremony (tonsuring ceremony) (Figure 4.4).

7. Rites performed at the time of 'panayana' to make the individual a 'Dvija' or 'twice born'.

Gender relationships and intergenerational issues

Her father protects (her) in childhood, her husband protects (her) in youth, and her sons protect (her) in old age; a woman is never fit for independence. (*Manusmriti* 9.3)

Although women may be classified according to Varna,[1] they are also considered a section of society in their own right. They do not pass through the four stages available to men. Rather the *Manusmriti* talks of three stages for a woman:

Figure 4.4 Hair cutting (tonsuring) ceremony

1. As a child protected by her father. Traditionally, girls did not receive a formal academic education. A woman's role, considered essential in preserving social and cultural values, was learned in the home.

2. As a married woman, protected by her husband. Hinduism places great value on pre-marital chastity and this has significantly influenced practices. Girls were betrothed and married at a very young age. In married life, the wife's roles were centred on the home and she was not burdened with contributing towards the family income. Fulfilling one's responsibility as a loving and available parent was considered paramount.

3. As a widow, protected by the eldest son: if the husband died or took *sanyasa* (became a *sadhu*), then the eldest living son

would look after his widowed mother. Older women were always treated with great respect.

A wife performs four roles for her husband: 1) as his servant (*dasi*) in duty; 2) as his minister (*mantri*) in decision-making; 3) as a mother (*mata*) to his children; and 4) as a lover (*rambha*) in his bed. In ancient times, when a Hindu died, his wife either committed *sati* (ritual self-immolation) on his funeral pyre or retired into a life of social damnation, religious contemplation and perennial solitude. Now the situation has changed. *Sati* is illegal and an anathema.

Hinduism and fables of fertility

Having children has always been important since time immemorial, and the continuity of the family unit has been of major significance in Hindu culture. Infertility is a social stigma even today, and Indian mythology is full of stories about what couples have done in the past to overcome their fertility problems. Ancient tales hold the key to the unconscious desires of a people. They help us appreciate the fears and insecurities of people who visit state-of-the-art infertility clinics. In this chapter, sacred narratives from ancient scriptures are explored to understand the importance of fertility in the Hindu religion.

Debt to ancestors

The following story of the sage Agastya from the great Hindu epic *Mahabharata* tells us why Hindus, in particular, and Indians, in general, are so obsessed with children. Besides social factors like 'someone to take care of me in my old age', it directs our attention to a profound religious demand for a child, especially a male one.

The sage Agastya wanted *moksha*, or liberation, from the endless cycle of rebirths. So he broke all social bonds, went to the forest, meditated and performed austerities. He believed that by refusing to succumb to any desire, by refusing to yield to the illusory pleasures of the material world, his soul would break free from the prison that was his body. He spent years mortifying himself. Liberation eluded him. Then, one night, he had a vision: he saw his ancestors hanging, head down, over a gaping hole. They were crying, 'We are trapped in the land of the dead. And there is no hope of escape.' 'What can I do to help?' asked Agastya. They replied, 'Father children, so that we can be reborn. Help us return to the land of the living so that we too can work towards our *moksha*. Or else, you will land up in the hell known as Put and suffer there for all eternity. Repay the debt you owe your ancestors.' Thus admonished, Agastya returned to his village, got married, fathered children, and only after they had become independent did he return to the forest.

Hindus believe that all men come into this world burdened by a debt – the *pitr-runa* (*pitr* = ancestor; *runa* = debt). The only way to repay this debt is to father a male offspring. During funeral rites, known as *shraadh*, Hindu males are reminded of this debt. Since the birth of a child, preferably a male child, liberates a man from his debt, the Sanskrit word for son is *putra* (deliverer from Put). The daughter or *putri* is also a deliverer from Put, but to a lesser extent.

White seed and red seed

Why a male offspring is more important to a Hindu can be traced to certain beliefs. In the *Mahabharata,* it is said that the soul of a man lies locked in the semen. Semen is the medium through which ancestors slip into the land of the living. The soul in semen is embodied in the womb.

According to ancient Hindu seers known as *rishis*, within the womb is the red seed known as *rajas* (the counterpart of the white male seed known as *shukra*). The *rajas* wraps the soul in flesh and blood. The *shukra*, besides being a medium for the soul, is also the source of bones. Thus all living creatures come into being because of the father's white seed and the mother's red seed. The former generates consciousness and transforms into the skeleton, while the latter creates the flesh.

There is an interesting story in this regard from the *Padma-Purana* (this is one of the major 18 Puranas, a Hindu religious text, which is devided into five parts). A king had two wives but no children. He asked some sages to make a potion that would make his wives pregnant. He died before the potion was ready. The two widowed queens did not want to waste the magic potion. So the elder queen drank it while the younger queen made love to her 'like a man'. In due course, the elder queen gave birth to a child, but it was only a lump of flesh. The sages said, 'Since no white seed was part of the conception, the child had no bones and no consciousness.' They appeased the gods and the child was 'repaired'.

Power of the white seed

Indian men are known for their obsession with virility (Basu and Banerjee 2006). Virility here refers to many things, physical strength, mental agility, sexual energy as well as the ability to father a male child. So when an Indian says, 'I have less strength (*takat kum hai*),' he could be referring either to malaise or lethargy, or to impotence or inability to father a male child. Here again is an ancient belief that physical strength is reflected in the seminal strength (Shrivastava 2005).

The ancient seers believed that food consumed is transformed in the body into sap (plasma), then flesh, then blood, then bone, then marrow, and finally seed (hence the traditional Indian belief that out of a thousand drops of blood comes one drop of semen). The seed can produce a new life or, if retained, can transform into a magical substance called *ojas* that gives a man superhuman strength and occult powers. It also helps man escape from the cycle of rebirths.

In women, the red seed is shed every month. Hence, women are considered to be the weaker sex – they cannot attain 'spiritual' status because they have no access to *ojas*.

Men, on the other hand, can retain their white seed and become 'holy'. This is the reason given to explain the presence of a greater number of holy men than holy women in India. This is also the reason why powerful warrior gods like Hanuman and Ayyappa are associated with both virility and celibacy.

In the *Mahabharata*, it is said that a male child is born when the white seed is stronger than the red seed; or a virile man (one whose semen is strong) fathers only male children. When the red seed is strong, the child is female. The traditional explanation for transexuality and homosexuality was that neither white nor red seed was stronger than the other. This belief perhaps explains why, despite modern genetic data on X and Y chromosomes, it is the woman in India who is 'blamed' for the feminisation of the foetus, and why she is given special diets to make the foetus male. This also explains why men feel angry and ashamed when they father daughters. The sex of the child is linked to their virility, or lack of it.

The fertile period

According to the *Dharmashastras*, though sex for pleasure was per-mitted, greater importance was given to sex for procreation. Men who had to father male offspring were advised not to waste semen. They were advised to have intercourse only when the woman was in 'season'. This period was known as *ritu* and it roughly corresponds to the days in the menstrual cycle when a woman is most likely to conceive. Women were advised to make themselves beautiful and present themselves to their husbands after their periods.

If a woman who was in her fertile period approached a man for sex, he was obliged to have sex with her, the reason being that a fertile period should not be wasted. Every time a fertile period was lost, an ancestor lost his opportunity to be reborn. When a woman menstruated, she was held responsible for the opportunity lost. She was equated with 'death' and hence considered polluted. She was asked to isolate herself during her periods.

A man who turned down a woman who approached him during her fertile period was described as a eunuch and held in disdain. In the *Mahabharata* there are tales of women who approached men who were not their husbands during their fertile period, because their husbands were unavailable. This was legally sanctioned. The sage Aruni was horrified when his guru's wife approached him for sex. However, she explained, 'Your guru has gone on a pilgrimage. Asking you to fulfil his biological obligations is a lesser sin than wasting this fertile period.'

The time when men and women had sex affected the nature of the child conceived. The *Bhagavata Purana* includes the story of Diti, who approached her husband, the sage Kashyapa, for sex in the evening, a time reserved for prayers to ward off malevolent spirits. As a result, she conceived children who were demons. When a man approached a woman, before intercourse he was expected to invoke the gods, especially Vishnu, the God who sustains natural order, and Tvastr or Vishvakarma, the god who makes things. Only through their blessings was it believed that a child could be conceived. This was known as the *Garbhadhana Sanskara*, or the rite of conception.

The infertile man

When a man could not produce a child with his wife, he was given the benefit of the doubt and allowed to marry again, and again. If, despite this, he failed to father a child, it was concluded (but never explicitly stated) that he was sterile. In such circumstances, the *Dharmashastras* suggested that another man be invited to cohabit with the wives. This practice was known as *niyoga*, or levirate. In Hindu families *niyoga* is followed (rather clandestinely) even today, whereby sterile men make their wives cohabit with relatives or with holy men. Though religiously sanctioned, this practice is socially frowned upon and so no one talks about it openly.

In the *Mahabharata*, when king Vichitravirya (*vichitra* = odd; *virya* = virility) died, his mother invited the sage Vyasa to conceive children with her widowed daughters-in-law. Children thus produced were called children of Vichitravirya (their legal father), not the children of Vyasa (their biological father).

The *Kathasaritsagar*, a collection of stories written in the eleventh century AD, contains the story of a king who makes an offering of rice balls to his ancestors. As he is about to throw the offering in the river, three hands reach up – one of a farmer, one of a priest and one of a warrior. The oracles revealed, 'The farmer is the man who married your mother, the priest is the man who made your mother pregnant, and the warrior is the man who took care of you.' The king is advised to give the rice ball to the farmer because scriptures describe him as the true father. Thus was the practice of *niyoga* established.

Artificial insemination

There are tales that suggest that our Indian ancestors were familiar with the 'idea' of artificial insemination. For example, we learn of 'magic potions' being created by sages for queens of childless kings, that make the women pregnant.

One story states that the God Shiva once spurted semen when he saw Vishnu in the form of the celestial enchantress Mohini. Sages collected this semen and gave it to the wind-god Vayu, who poured it into the 'ear' (a common mythical metaphor for the womb) of Anjani, a monkey, who gave birth to Hanuman, the monkey-god. Devoid of the mythical aura, one might say that the tale refers to the practice of artificial insemination: semen is transferred to the womb without sexual intercourse.

Surrogacy

In the *Bhagvata Purana*, there is a story that suggests the practice of surrogacy. Kans, the wicked king of Mathura, had imprisoned his sister Devaki and her husband Vasudeva because oracles had informed him that her child would be his killer. Every time Devaki delivered a child, he smashed its head on the floor. He killed six children. When the seventh child was conceived, the gods intervened. They summoned the goddess Yogamaya and had her transfer the foetus from the womb of Devaki to the womb of Rohini (Vasudeva's other wife who lived with her sister Yashoda across the river Yamuna, in the village of cowherds at Gokul). Thus the child conceived in one womb was incubated in and delivered through the womb of another woman.

Snake worship

In India today, when a couple does not have children, they often visit shrines and pray. Some visit holy men. Others offer cradles and dolls at shrines of mother-goddesses. Still others visit serpent shrines. Serpents in many ancient cultures have been associated with fertility (Enthoven 2003). There are many reasons for this. Probably because the serpent could slough its skin, it was believed to possess the power of rejuvenation. Probably because the serpent lived under the earth, it was believed to be the keeper of the secret that transforms seeds into plants. Farmers in India worship serpents in the hope of having a good harvest. Women worship serpents so that they are fertile and their husbands virile.

Modern India, contemporary Hindu society and assisted reproduction

Hinduism is not a religion, but a set of beliefs and practices. It is not a religion like Christianity or Islam or Buddhism, because it is not founded by any one person, nor does it have an organised controlling body like the Church or an order. Everything is acceptable in Hinduism because there is no single authority or organisation to accept, reject or to oppose it on behalf of Hinduism. Only rarely do Hindus proselytise; most respect the rights of others to their own beliefs. According to the tenets of Hinduism, all philosophies and belief systems are considered to be equally valid paths to salvation, and it is considered inappropriate to judge the choices of others. Exceptions to this attitude are found in politically motivated disturbances, such as the Hindu–Muslim or Hindu–Sikh riots in the twentieth century. Without political exploitation, Hindus live in close harmony with those of all religions. As in most families, Hindu children grow up learning to follow the tenets and customs of their parents. But in adolescence and young adulthood, they are encouraged to make their own choices as to what primary Hindu gods or goddesses they find personally inspiring. Although as adults they will continue to practise many family rituals, they also conduct their own private worship in whatever manner seems most beneficial to them. In order to perform appropriate rituals correctly, they usually rely upon the advice of respected religious teachers and priests. Many do choose to continue to observe the rituals associated with the deity to whom the family has prayed for generations. It is, however, by no means unusual for a son or daughter to realise that his or her needs will be better met by focusing attention on a different deity and its corresponding rituals. In most cases they will still retain the respect and goodwill of those who continue inherited traditions. It is remarkable that as Hindus have modernised and chosen lifestyles that embrace contemporary technologies and occupations, in general their traditional beliefs are not diminished. A neuro-surgeon is just as likely to be devout as a farmer, a nuclear physicist as a craftsperson, and a computer technician as a housewife. Hinduism continues to be one of the most adaptable religions in the world (Weightman 1998).

The editors of *Hinduism: Past and Present* (Michaels 2004), in a compilation of Hindu thought on the issue of cloning, suggested a morally neutral stance, indicating that Hinduism neither 'condones nor condemns' cloning research. 'If done with divine intent and consciousness, it may benefit; if done in the services of selfishness, greed and power, it may bring severe negative karmic experiences.' But research may pose difficulties: Hindus are not allowed to injure sentient beings, so the tradition rejects both animal research and the destruction of embryos.

Hindu creation narratives suggest the world was created with a cloning-like process, and the tradition believes in reincarnation, so there is not the kind of fundamental objection seen in many Christian traditions. But most Hindu scholars say cloning can only be supported if it somehow contributes to the cultivation of spiritual self-awareness, rather than being purely an effort to manipulate the external environment (Palaniswami 1997; Satguru 2003).

Gender selection and the modern Hindu

Approximately 50 million women are 'missing' in the Indian population (Allahbadia 2002). Generally three principal causes are given: female infanticide, better food and health care for boys, and maternal death at childbirth. Prenatal sex determination and the abortion of female foetuses threaten to skew the sex ratio to new highs – with unknown consequences.

Various methods now exist for attempting to choose to have a baby of a desired sex. In the modern Hindu 'male dominated' society such as India, the commonest methods employed by the vast majority of the populace, usually after two female children, is ultrasound-directed foetal sex determination at 13–14 weeks' gestational age, and in more affluent urban areas the chorionic villus sampling technique at 8–9 weeks. Sex selection has become a national crisis in India, where cheap mobile ultrasound clinics travel the countryside, testing pregnant women. Women who discover that their foetus is female often opt for a legal abortion, referred to as 'medical termination of pregnancy'. Among the very affluent Hindu and Jain trader community, whose religious beliefs do not allow medical termination of pregnancy, pressure has grown for the provision of PGD-IVF service to allow the selective transfer of male embryos.

Estimates of the number of female foetuses being destroyed every year in India vary from two million to five million. This practice has reportedly skewed sex ratios from the natural 106 boys to 100 girls to as high as 130 boys to 100 girls. Such results led India to ban ultrasound testing for the purpose of prenatal sex determination on 1 January 1996 (www.csrindia.org), imposing financial penalties and jail terms for doctors, as well as relatives who encourage the test. However, despite exemplary punishment of some medical practitioners found to have breached the law, there is a great deal of public support in India from advocates of sex-selective abortion, who argue that these procedures are the answer to population control in India, that they help families cope with intransigent problems, especially dowry, which represents an enormous burden that often wipes out a family's entire savings, and avoid recourse to more barbaric practices, such as female infanticide (discussed on p.132). Legislation is widely regarded as having driven the practice underground, and now service providers charge a premium, corrupt government officials extort bribes from flourishing sex-selection clinics across the country, and health clinics, buoyed by record profits, aggressively market their wares. One clever economic pitch blares from tens of thousands of billboards through the country: 'Pay five hundred rupees [US$13] now rather than five lakhs [Rs 500,000 or $13,000] later'. Poor families, fearing expensive dowries that can cripple a family, willingly undergo the tests.

Such phenomena are not, of course, of recent origin and attempts to select children's sex have a long history, from the herbal nostrums recommended by traditional healers to more recent therapists' advice about which forms of intercourse are allegedly likely to produce a girl or a boy. The selection of gender has been a quest of couples for as far back as recorded history illustrates. Early drawings from prehistoric times suggest that our earliest ancestors were investigating sex selection efforts. The *Charaka Samhita*, a manual written around 800 BCE in India, advised prospective parents who expressed a preference for sons that they should 'abstain from intercourse for a week, gazing every morning and evening upon a majestic white bull or stallion, being entertained by pleasant tales, and feeding their eyes on men and women of gentle looks.' Mistaking vaginal secretions for semen, ancient Greek, Hebrew and Indian literature stated that both men and women produced semen (Thapar 2002). Sons were born when the male semen was predominant. Masturbation after a period of sexual abstinence usually results in the ejaculation of a greater amount of semen. Based on this observation, sexual abstinence was recommended for men who wanted sons.

A ritual which originated amongst certain of Rajasthan's tribal communities, and which was designed to forestall future problems for families once a baby girl had been born, was the murder of female infants. Such actions were morally cleansed by the reasoning that killing takes place before the ritual bath seven to ten days after birth, which grants an infant 'human status' (Bhatnagar 2005). This is further upheld by superstitions maintaining that the act enhances the chance of the next born being the preferred son.

The killing of infants with physical impairments soon after the birth is also a frequent occurrence in India. The culprits are the *dais* (traditional birth attendants) and old ladies who attend to childbirth in rural communities. They, in their own way, protect the family from the financial expenses and social stigmas associated with bringing up such a child in a country where a lack of social education prevents these unfortunate infants from being rehabilitated and living a full life. The killing of infants with physical impairment has assumed monstrous proportions in just the past two decades. Despite the century-old law prohibiting female infanticide, few Indian states show the political will to enforce it.

Hindus and their leaders have been very tolerant regarding abortion, the development of reproductive technologies and embryo and stem cell research, seeing these as the face of progress in modern India. Ultra-right-wing Hindu leaders and modern-day gurus have appeared time and again on television, advocating all modern assisted conception techniques.

Hindu tolerance of reproductive technologies is perhaps nowhere more strongly evidenced than in relation to its medical tourism industry. Driven by many of the same factors that have led Western businesses to outsource some of their operations to India in recent years, an increasing number of infertile couples from abroad are coming here in search of women who are willing to act as surrogates (Cohen 2006; Jones and Keith 2006). Against concerns that this is yet another example of third-world exploitation, with the poor women in India paying the price, business is reported to be 'booming'. By some estimates, Indian surrogacy is already a $445-million-a-year business (www.southasia.oneworld). At the same time, the Indian Council for Medical Research (ICMR) has formulated National ART Guidelines, for regulating and supervising the functioning of ART clinics and helping to ensure the provision of safe and ethical services (www.icmr.nic.im). According to ICMR estimates, helping both residents and visitors beget children could bloom into a nearly $6-billion-a-year industry by 2015 (www.southasia.oneworld).

Note

1. The varna system, also known as *varnashrama dharma*, is based on principles laid out in the scriptures of the Vedic tradition, which categorise Hindus into four varnas or social classes and prescribe specific duties for each. These are the *brahmanas* (brahmins, serving as priests and teachers), *kshatriyas* (duties of administration, battle and law enforcement), *vaishyas* (customarily agriculture, commerce, and cow-protection) and *shudras* (who provide service to members of the other three varnas). In this system, it is supposedly the brahmins, and not the kings, who command the greatest respect in society despite their relative lack of wealth or political power.

    Manu divided men's life into four distinct stages or *ashramas*: *brahmacharya ashrama* (student life), *grihastha ashrama* (household life), *vanaprastha ashrama* (retiring from social life and living in the forest) and *sannyasa ashrama* (the attainment of freedom).

References

Allahbadia, G.N. (2002) 'The 50 million missing women.' *Journal of Assisted Reproduction and Genetics 19*, 9, 411–416.

Babb, L.A. (1989) 'Redemptive encounters. Three modern styles in the Hindu tradition.' *Asian Folklore Studies 48*, 2, 326–328.

Basham, A.L. (1959) *The Wonder that Was India: A Survey of the Culture of the Indian Sub-Continent before the Coming of the Muslims.* New York: Grove Press, Inc, Evergreen Edition.

Basu, S. and Banerjee, S. (2006) 'The quest for manhood: masculine Hinduism and nation in Bengal.' *Comparative Studies of South Asia, Africa and the Middle East 26*, 3, 476–490.

Bhatnagar, R.D. (2005) *Female Infanticide in India.* New York: SUNY Press.

Bhattacharya, S. (2006) *Marginal Progeny, Modern Technology: a Hindu Bioethics of Assisted Reproductive Technology.* New York: SUNY Press.

Cohen, J. (2006) 'Procreative tourism and reproductive freedom.' *Reproductive Biomedicine Online 13*, 1, 145–146.

Enthoven, R.E. (2003) *Folklore Notes.* Delhi: Asian Educational Services.

Frawley, D. (2000) *Gods, Sages and Kings: Vedic Secrets of Ancient Civilization.* Twin Lakes, WI: Lotus Press.

Hamblin, W. and Seely, D. (2007) *Solomon's Temple: Myth and History.* London: Thames and Hudson.

Jones, C.A. and Keith, L.G. (2006) 'Medical tourism and reproductive outsourcing: the dawning of a new paradigm for healthcare.' *International Journal of Fertility and Women's Medicine 5*, 6, 251–255.

Michaels, A. (2004) *Hinduism: Past and Present* (5th ed.). Princeton, NJ: Princeton University Press.

Palaniswami, P. (1997) 'Cloning: the Hindu Perspective' (editorial). *Hinduism Today*, April Publisher's Desk.

Satguru Sivaya Subramuniyaswami (2003) *Dancing with Siva, Hinduism's Contemporary Catechism.* Kapaa, HI: Himalayan Academy Publications.

Shrivastava, S. (2005) 'Sexual sites, seminal attitudes: sexual masculinities and culture.' *Feminist Theory 6*, 377–378.

Sutton, N. (2000) *Religious Doctrines in the Mahabharata.* New Delhi: Motilal Banarsidass.

Thapar, R. (2002) *Early India: from the Origins to AD 1300.* Berkeley, CA: University of California Press.

Weightman, S. (1998) 'Hinduism.' In J. Hinnells (ed.) *The New Penguin Handbook of Living Religions.* London: Penguin Books.

Related websites

https://www.cia.gov/library/publications/the-world-factbook

www.csrindia.org/PDF/Implementation%20of%20SAARC%20Convention%20Bharti.pdf

http://www.icmr.nic.in/guidelines.htm

http://southasia.oneworld.net/todaysheadlines/surrogacy-law-on-the-anvil-in-india-1

5

Chinese Traditional Belief Systems, Livelihood and Fertility

Geok Ling Lee, Celia Hoi Yan Chan, Elizabeth Wai-Hing Choi Hui and Cecilia Lai Wan Chan

[A] pregnant woman is preparing [for] two births: her baby's and her own rebirth. *(K.P. Chan 2005)*

Chinese people tend to view suffering as a form of virtue, a view well represented in the ancient Chinese characters for body, pregnancy and child (see Figure 5.1).

The original meaning of the Chinese character for body (身 – *shen*) is pregnancy. The ancient character *shen* shows a side view of a pregnant woman, the dot indicating the foetus. The ancient character for pregnancy (孕 – *yun*) gives a pictorial view of a child

(子 – *zi*) being delivered via the mother's vagina. Childbirth is painful, but it simultaneously brings warmth and joy (Ye 2000).

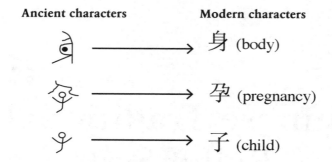

Figure 5.1 Ancient and modern Chinese characters for body, pregnancy and child

Introduction

China is a huge and greatly diverse country, which consists of 23 provinces and 56 ethnic groups (Neile 1995). There are also millions of overseas Chinese distributed in all parts of the world. It would therefore be a mistake to assume that Chinese people are a homogeneous group and share one standard set of folk beliefs and practices. Instead, a rich cultural spectrum of religious beliefs, spiritual practices, rituals and traditions is embraced and practised among the Chinese people, both within China and abroad.

Chinese traditional beliefs basically take two forms: institutionalised (that is, religion) and non-religious (that is, folk culture). These beliefs significantly affect fertility, particularly women's livelihood, in the aspects of reproductive health, potency, family line continuation, lineage connections, marriage, childbearing and childrearing.

Chinese religious belief systems and fertility

Chinese culture adheres strongly to the teachings of Confucianism, Daoism and Buddhism, commonly known as the three traditional Chinese beliefs or, to some, life philosophies. The three leaders of these philosophies – Confucius, Lao Tze, and the Buddha – are treated as gods of worship in many temples in China. For most Chinese people, it is neither possible nor necessary to distinguish between religious beliefs and life philosophies; they form the basis of daily living, in accordance with family traditions and individual choices (Schott and Henley 1996). Following is a discussion of how Confucianism, Daoism and Buddhism articulated behavioural guidelines to increase or limit fertility.

Confucianism

In Confucianism, the foundation of a good man's (*junzi*) morality is filial piety (Rainey 2004). Filial piety has long been practised as a principle governing Chinese patterns of socialisation (Ho 1996). Mencius, the classical Confucian writer, stated, 'There are three vices that violate the principle of filial piety, and the biggest is being without an offspring (*buxiao yousan, wuhou weida*)' (quoted in Qiu 2001, p.77). Thus, men see failure to produce offspring as a disgrace to their ancestors (Chan *et al.* 2002).

As stated in the *Confucian Analects* (*Lun-yu*), 'eat, drink and the man–woman relationship are basic desires of human beings (*yinshi nannü, renzhi dayu cunyan*)' (Nan 2005). Sexual intercourse is a natural part of marriage for the purpose of continuing the family line. Sexual activity outside of marriage is prohibited (Rainey 2004), which may explain why polygamy was commonly practised. It could be seen as an Asian mode of assisted conception.

Confucian philosophy mainly addresses men; women are barely mentioned (Parrinder 1996). In a culture that is dominantly patrilineal and patriarchal, filial piety addressed male actions and the role performance toward fathers, grandfathers and the patrilineal line of ancestors. Yet, interestingly, the chastity of women is greatly emphasised. A woman's virtue is said to consist primarily of 'preserving her virginity before marriage, of modesty and sexual loyalty in marriage, and of continuing loyalty to the memory of her husband in widowhood' (Rainey 2004, p.119).

Daoism

The focus of Daoism is on finding the Way (*Dao,* also known as *Tao*), the ultimate integration with the natural world. The *Dao* is timeless, pervades all things, but is nameless and indescribable. In daily life, people should strive for transcendence from self, harmony, and balance with nature and within their society (Parrinder 1996; Rainey 2004).

Theories developed from the classic *Book of Changes* (*I-Ching*, also known as *Yi-jing*) influence how Chinese view sexual intercourse. The *I-Ching* states, 'the constant intermingling of Heaven and Earth gives shape to all things, and the sexual union of man and woman gives life to all things' and 'the interaction of one *yin* and one *yang* is called *Tao*' (Parrinder 1996, p.80). *Yin* and *yang* are interdependent, like man and woman, and the aim is thus to attain a perfect balance of the *yin* and the *yang*. Sexual intercourse in Daoism is not only for childbearing but also a means to strengthen male energy by absorbing female *yin* essence. However, women can also absorb the male *yang* essence. Daoism sees sex as a necessary part of life and as important for maintaining men's health and longevity. Like Confucianism, Daoism mainly addresses men.

Buddhism

In contrast to the teachings of Confucianism and Daoism, Buddhism is concerned with achieving a state of enlightenment through understanding that life is suffering and that the root of suffering is ignorance, illusion and desire; and with practice of the three principles (wisdom, morality and meditation) (Gross 1994). The Buddhist way to attain enlightenment is monkhood, in contrast to the Chinese traditional attitudes to, and practice of, filial piety. Entering monkhood requires one to renounce marriage, intimacy and family attachments (Nadeau 2001). As in Confucianism, women are considered virtuous when sexually inactive (Rainey 2004).

When Buddhism entered China, it underwent a Chinese transformation and became a 'pro-family' religion (Nadeau 2001). That is, Chinese Buddhism is predominantly home-based and closely related to family in times of great need, such as marriage rites, prayers for sons and funeral rites. Female lay followers in particular are attracted to Buddhism, because their spiritual needs are met with Buddhism's creed of universal compassion (Parrinder 1996). Women often make pilgrimages to temples, sacred mountains, and sacred sites to worship the gods and to pray for sons. One such popular and beloved Buddhist representation among female devotees is Guanyin (Karetzky 2004; Yu 1996), the Bodhisattva of compassion and mercy, who originated in the Mahayana Buddhist tradition in India (Rainey 2004). Guanyin is portrayed as having feminine characteristics, and as a fertility goddess who has the power not only of granting children, especially sons, but also of protecting women and assuring safe childbirth. Therefore, people also call her 'Giver of sons' (*Songzi Guanyin*) (Yu 1996) (see Figure 5.2).

Chinese folk belief systems and fertility

Fertility in Chinese societies is primarily patriarchal, and a woman usually undergoes a transformation culturally, socially and physically after pregnancy (Chan, Chan and Chung 2001). Having a son is the primary concern. After birthing an heir, the mother will be given formal status in the extended family. The importance of children gives rise to many folk beliefs and rituals on fertility.

Figure 5.2 Porcelain figure of Songzi Guanyin, Hong Kong (photographed by Mr Michael Sun, 11 November 2007)

Folklore and fertility

Marriage is perceived primarily as an instrument for reproduction and attainment of prosperity. The first ritual on fertility is in the wedding ceremony. Candles and lamps are lit to secure prosperity for the couple after marriage, especially in childbearing (Doolittle 2002, p.52). The importance of having children is also evident in the Chinese character for family (家 – *jia*), consisting of a pig under a roof (see Figure 5.3). Like pigs, an ideal family should have many children (Ng *et al.* 2004).

宀 + 豕 = 家

(roof) + (pig) = (family)

Figure 5.3 The Chinese character for family

Gender and fertility

Contribution to male potency is the highest priority. Fertility, sexual ability and potency are equated with male strength and energy in life (Chan *et al.* 2002). In Chinese medicine (CM), the function of the kidney[1] is not only urine excretion but also to store *jing* (vital essence), which serves as the source of life, providing vital essence necessary for growth, development, reproduction, and the functional activities of all organs and tissues. The kidney governs the 'fire of the vital gate' (*mingmen zhihuo*), which warms the body, promotes growth, development, and sexual potency, and activates the functioning of all organs.

In Hong Kong there is a popular and sacred place known as the Lovers' Rock, a symbolic representation of fertility and manhood. People associate the shape of the rock with a penis (see Figure 5.4) and believe that it will grant a happy marriage and many offspring to devoted worshippers. Worshippers, hoping to find a good part-

Figure 5.4 Lovers' Rock, Hong Kong (photographed by Mr Michael Sun, 11 November 2007)

Sons are preferred to daughters, as they continue the family name, and only sons can perform the ancestral rites to ensure care for the soul after death (Myers 1997). Sons are also responsible for providing economic support to elderly parents. In contrast, daughters are traditionally regarded as temporary members in their family of birth, because they will be the 'property' of the husband's family. Support from daughters is seen as a last resort and a source of shame (Croll 2004). Hence, efforts will be made to conceive a son when the firstborn is female, even if that requires treatment and technology.

No son: one of the seven grounds for divorcing a wife

A family law called 'Seven grounds for divorcing a wife' (qichu zhi-tiao) originated in the Han Dynasty (206 BCE–220 CE). According to this law, a man could divorce his wife if she committed any of the seven offences: disobedience to her parents-in-law, barrenness, lewdness, jealousy, suffering from a loathsome disease (such as mental illness, a contagious disease like leprosy or being mute, deaf, blind, hunchback, bald or lame), talkativeness, or stealing from the household (Academy of Chinese Studies 2002). The order of importance of the grounds changed, and barrenness was the first reason from the Tang Dynasty (618 CE–907 CE) to the Qing Dynasty (1636 CE–1912 CE). This change reflects the evolved expectation of womanhood and the importance of childbearing in different times. Owing to the consequences of blame and shame, women would seek religious assistance to get pregnant and especially to have a son.

Rituals in pregnancy, childbirth and after childbirth

Two rituals are common among Chinese families when a female member conceives and then bears a child. The first is prayers. Prayers are given at a local temple or ancestral hall when the woman conceives, during childbirth or immediately afterwards, to ensure the health and well-being of both mother and child, and again when the child is one month old.

Careful intake of food is the second ritual. According to Hui (2007), 32.4 per cent of pregnant women in Hong Kong avoid 'cold' (*ying*) food or drinks (for example, crab and watermelon juice), and another 21.1 per cent also avoid 'damp' and 'hot' (*yang*) food (such as mango). They try to keep a balance of *yin* and *yang* food, according to traditional beliefs. Hui's findings (2007) showed that her respondents practise these nutritional and behavioural rituals conscientiously. Table 1 gives other examples of such beliefs and traditional practices.

Acceptance of medical technology such as artificial reproductive technology (including insemination of the husband's sperm, IVF and intracytoplasmic sperm injection (ICSI)) has not been easy in Chinese culture. There is constant negotiation when traditional values and practices are challenged by modern technology. However, modern reproductive technologies are acceptable in traditional Chinese families as long as the child is genetically related to the parents, particularly the father (Qiu 2006). In Hong Kong, the regulation of assisted conception relies on Chinese 'family' values (Ng *et al.* 2004), and only married heterosexual couples can gain access to such services. Surrogacy is also actively discouraged. Similarly, in China, as indicated in the law of the People's Republic of China on Maternal and Infant Health Care (Chapter III, Article 17), only married couples in their childbearing age may consult and seek assistance from medical services on infertility (Laws and Regulations of the People's Republic of China 2001).

Chinese cultural values and assisted conception

Infertility is seen as a physical problem, compounded by sociocultural factors in Chinese societies. To the Chinese, infertility is usually linked to bad luck and even retribution for moral wrongdoing (Qiu 2001). Although it affects men and women emotionally and socially, because both masculinity and femininity are linked with

Table 1 Examples of beliefs and traditions practised during pregnancy, childbirth and the first month after childbirth

During pregnancy

- The furniture in the house should not be rearranged. Neither mirrors nor pictures are to be hung on the wall, because this may result in harelip.

- The mother should not go to a funeral or visit a graveyard, because the baby has no soul yet. This prevents spirits from getting to the baby.

- The mother should not pick fruit from trees, because the tree will die.

- The mother should not start a fire, because the baby will be born with a birthmark on his or her face.

- The mother should not rub her belly too much, or she will spoil the child.

- The mother should not work with glue or adhesives, as this may result in complications during delivery.

During childbirth

- It is believed that drinking special tea during labour helps with the pain.

- Only warm/hot (*yang*) food and beverages are consumed, to keep the balance of *qi* (life force or spiritual energy). No ice should be in the beverages.

During the first month after childbirth

- Eat plenty of chicken, rice, fish cooked with ginger, and/or pig knuckle soup in vinegar or wine is good. It is believed that ginger can drive out excess 'wind' in the body and keep the body 'warm'. ('Wind' in CM has to do with the uncontrollable flow of *qi* inside the body. If it is not driven out of the body, it may cause pain, headache and irritable moods.)

- Avoid salty food because it is believed to hinder milk production for breastfeeding.

- Baths, showers and washing the hair are not allowed. Rather, the mother is advised to take a sponge bath with boiled water and ginger peel. This helps to promote blood circulation and to get rid of the 'wind' inside the body.

- Women are expected to stay indoors and avoid getting ill. Windy, cold areas and outdoor activities are to be avoided.

fertility, women's well-being is more adversely affected than men's. Women tend to bear disproportionate blame for infertility and to be the focus of infertility and infertility-related responsibility. The extended family is likely to blame the woman for not bearing children, which may lead to suicide threats (Scharping 2003, p.11). Women are stigmatised by their social network, suffer from marital turmoil, and are even abandoned by their husbands. Couples who are unable to have children due to male infertility face additional pressure. To protect the husband's self-esteem, the wife rarely reveals the truth to others. Instead, couples seek medical help, to minimise family conflicts and prevent long-term trauma.

Chinese religious belief systems and assisted conception
Chinese religious beliefs may also influence how couples perceive infertility and their decisions about assisted conception. For instance, a key principle in Buddhism is the Law of Karma, which holds that 'the circumstances of rebirth are determined by an individual's moral status at death' (Keown and Keown 1995, p.266). Karma is 'the law of moral retribution, whereby not only does every cause have an effect, but he who puts the cause in action suffers the effect' (Humphreys 1994, p.15). Accordingly, one's life today is the outcome of one's thoughts and actions, including actions done in previous lives. A childless Buddhist couple may accept childlessness as their karma.[3] In fact, a Buddhist sutra (*fahua yishu*, Chap. 6, T. 34, p.0538b) states that childless couples should refocus their attention on cultivating their compassion and compassionate behaviour.

As mentioned in the introduction to this chapter, Chinese people are not a homogeneous group and they embrace and practise a wide spectrum of religious beliefs, spiritual practices, rituals and traditions. One such ethnic group is the *Yi,* whom the first and fourth authors encountered in Sichuan in August 2007. According to Jia (2003), there are more than seven million Yi Chinese living in three provinces (Yunnan, Sichuan and Guizhou), of which 27.1 per cent are in Sichuan. Yi women's practices provide a glimpse of some unique folk religious beliefs among the Chinese.

Yi folk religious beliefs and practices regarding fertility

Yi women protect their fertility by holding onto their jewellery. They believe that the 'spirit of fertility' (*gefei*) is attached to the jewellery, and giving it away may cause female infertility or a high mortality rate among the giver's children (Ba-mo 2004). A local spiritual healer (*bimo*) will be consulted if a prayer for fertility is required. The prayer usually takes place at a tree in full bloom, at a small hut built in front of the tree. The hut houses the ancestors of both husband and wife. Only male family members attend the prayer. Led by the eldest, they will run in order of seniority nine times around the tree. On every round, they will receive grass from the *bimo*. The grass, which is spread with lard, is put inside the men's pockets. The purpose of the prayer is to ask for the blessings of the ancestors for prosperous generations, with many children and grandchildren, like a tree in full bloom (Ba-mo 2004).

The importance of fertility for Yi women can be understood through their practices in marriage, divorce and remarriage after the death of a spouse (Su 1997). Marriage for the Yi Chinese serves mainly an economic function. The role of the wife is to fulfil the husband's sexual needs, bear children to continue the family line, and manage the household chores and food so that the family can become prosperous.

Divorce is rare. A husband can file for divorce on the grounds of infertility or inability to bear a son, as women are seen as the cause of infertility. A wife cannot prevent her husband from marrying another woman. The infertile wife will be given the lowest status in the family and not be allowed to attend auspicious celebrations. When she dies, her name will not be placed beside her deceased husband's on the ancestral tablet. Yet, it is difficult for a wife to initiate a divorce. After the divorce, all the children belong to the husband. The divorced wife will not be given any financial assets, and her husband confiscates her dowry (Su 1997).

Traditionally, when her husband dies, if the widow is still of childbearing age, she will be asked to marry a brother of her deceased husband, even if the brother is married. If the deceased husband has no brothers, the widow may have to marry either someone from the younger generation (such as a nephew) or from the older generation (such as an uncle, or even her father-in-law). The reasons for this practice are economic and it is a manifestation of power and control over women. The wife is seen as an asset, because the family has paid for the marriage and she is seen as a tool for bearing children. Interestingly, the women also view it as shameful if they are not married into the husband's family after the husband's death (Su 1997).

Implications for health care practice, health policies and clinical practice

The government of the People's Republic of China has claimed that women's status has taken a great leap from the old feudal, male dominant, chauvinistic and patriarchal society since the China reformation in 1949 (Chan 1995). Though equality between men and women was advocated and practised during the Maoist era (1949–1978), the recent years of economic reformation have seen the diminished emancipation of women (Chan, Liu and Zhang 1998). Women began to face difficulties in seeking education and employment, were less active in political participation, and faced challenges at home such as divorce, extramarital affairs and violence. One plausible reason could be related to the state's political and administrative control becoming relaxed over the presence of religious institutions. In a more liberal and accepting environment, there may be a revival of religious and cultural practice that promotes male supremacy. The following sections bring the discussion into focus, and suggest ways of putting health care practice, health policies and clinical practice into the Chinese context.

Development of culturally specific health care practice
Health education to increase awareness and knowledge on reproductive health

Religious beliefs and cultural practices may affect intimate relationship in Chinese couples. Chinese men and women have inadequate knowledge about their reproductive organs and sexual functions because of religious beliefs and lack of information (Tang *et al.* 1996). For instance, men lack knowledge about the changes in the mind and body of pregnant women (Tseng 2000). The idea of sacred and asexual motherhood and the goal of preventing miscarriage may explain why most women think they should abstain from sexual intercourse during pregnancy (Cheng 1992). As a culture of shame exists among the Chinese (Holroyd *et al.* 1997), to promote family relationships and reproductive health, culturally specific sexual health education should be developed for parents-to-be. Identification of reproductive health awareness as a dimension of sexual and reproductive health programmes will strengthen the overall quality and effectiveness of these programmes (Pyper 1997).

Pregnancy care using Eastern philosophy

Despite a growing interest in alternative approaches to healing based on Eastern philosophies and religions (such as *qigong, taijiquan*, yoga, acupuncture, herbal medicine, mindfulness and meditation, physical and therapeutic exercises, and body–mind–family wholeness treatment) (Chan 1997a, 1997b; Harold 1994; Lee 1984; Mikulas 2002; Ng 1995; Sheikh and Sheikh 1989; Topley 1978; Yang 1995a, 1995b), little attention has been paid to the spiritual dimension of pregnancy and fertility. It is believed that psychosocial and mindfulness intervention may be the choice of treatment to promote maternal, foetal and infant health. The reason is that the spiritual and psychosocial makeup of a pregnant woman will influence the health of the newborn child. One such proposal was made by Chan (2005), who proposed an Eastern-based model of body–mind–spirit intervention to educate pregnant Chinese women in Hong Kong. The pilot study of four subjects showed that the ideas of the Four Immeasurables of Buddhism (loving kindness, compassion, sympathetic joy and equanimity) and mindfulness practice were easily understood and accepted by Chinese women, Buddhist and non-Buddhist. One plausible reason for this acceptance is the familiarity and influence of Buddhist teachings on Chinese culture and way of life.

Infertility interventions using Eastern body-mind-spirit approach

The growing interest in Eastern philosophies, energy work, body–mind connection and CM can contribute to maternal physical and mental health. Chan and colleagues (2006) published a study on the effectiveness of the Eastern body–mind–spirit approach in working with women prior to their receiving treatment in IVF. The spirituality of the meaning of childbearing and marital intimacy was found to be a core component of intervention that can reduce anxiety and emotional distress. Thus, the religious and spiritual beliefs of the women contribute to their attitude and response to infertility.

Development of health policies: a fundamental change from son preference

Following the introduction of the 'one-child policy' by the China government in 1979, each couple, with few exceptions, is limited to having one child only (Xie 2000). Childbearing couples try various ways to ensure the birth of a son, primarily through prenatal sex selection, using ultrasound, and through termination of female pregnancies (Coale and Banister 1994). Unwanted daughters are abandoned, resulting in an exceedingly high number of female deaths within 24 hours of birth (Li, Zhu and Feldman 2004). The concepts of 'face' and 'face-saving', which are highly emphasised in Chinese society, may explain why a son is preferred. 'Face' is a kind of prestige and reputation achieved through success in life (Bond 1991), and Chinese people will try to save or enhance their own face. A field report by Murphy (2003) states that there remains a strong basis for son preference. A villager without a son is said to feel 'without face' (*meiyou mianzi*), 'without power' (*meiyou shili*) and 'without voice' (*jianghua shengyin meiyou bieren da*) (p.613).

The result of preference for males is an imbalanced gender ratio (Gupta 2005; Murphy 2003). The ratio of males to females in the age group 0–4 increased from 1.19 in 1998 (Chan *et al.* 2002) to 1.23 in 2005 (National Population Census of China 2005). Greater gender disparities will exist due to female babies being aborted, born unregistered, abandoned, or even killed (Banister 2004). Some adult males will be unable to find wives, especially those from poor families in remote villages. Their unmet intimacy needs may cause psychosocial liabilities, possibly ending in social disharmony and instability. For example, because of a shortage of young women, some may be kidnapped and sold into marriage. The rising disparity in the male–female birth ratio, especially in rural areas, may also foster the burgeoning sex industry.

Great effort is required to bring fundamental change in the value systems of Chinese people regarding the unchallenged importance of sons over daughters in performing family and religious obligations, and the perceived temporary relationship of daughters and family of origin (Chan, Blyth and Chan 2006; Croll 2004). The change should be made at two levels. The first level of change is to improve the educational level of the population. As Chan and colleagues (2002) suggest, increasing the educational level of the population may reduce emphasis on preference for sons. At a higher level, the 'one-child policy' which was set almost three decades ago requires a review to prevent long-term catastrophic consequences for women. In brief, there is a genuine need for the Chinese government to take positive affirmative actions or provide resources to rectify the negative impact on women.

Health insurance and health care for females

Li (2004) found that gender inequality and the state's family planning policy significantly affect maternal and childcare utilisation in China. For instance, it was found that a husband's participation in housework and childcare was positively related to the wife receiving prenatal examinations and giving birth under aseptic conditions. However, mothers with female infants were less likely to receive prenatal examinations, stop strenuous work before birth and deliver under aseptic conditions. Female infants with older sisters were found to be least likely to receive immunisations. This illustrates the submissive social position Chinese women have (Croll 1995; Hall 1997). There is clearly a need to provide affordable health insurance and health care for women in need. More proactive measures should be taken to ensure female babies, both before and after birth, receive basic health care.

Development of culturally relevant clinical practice

Traditional religious and cultural beliefs strongly influence the attitudes and behaviours of Chinese people, particularly those who adhere to religious/cultural beliefs and taboos. Some common attitudes and behaviours found among these people include preference to seek help from religious institutions rather than health care professionals, delay in seeking help with health care professionals, low compliance with professional advice if it conflicts with their beliefs and values, and not keeping an appointment instead of clarifying concerns they might have from previous appointments. Professionals thus need to be culturally sensitive, to 'start where the client is'. Chinese clients or patients may react differently to clinical practice that is heavily influenced by Western models. For instance, the Chinese client may think that empowerment and advocacy are inappropriate methods because maintaining a harmonious relationship is of paramount importance, and tolerance and endurance to hardships are preferred virtues.

Conclusion

This chapter describes the influence of Chinese traditional belief systems, based on religion and folk culture. However, Chinese people are greatly diversified. Within mainland China, there are remote areas where traditional religions and folk culture still prevail, whereas in urban areas, Chinese culture is intermingled with Western values. Moreover, there are 56 ethnic groups within mainland China, each having a unique set of cultural practices and spiritual beliefs. In addition, there are modern Chinese societies such as those in Taiwan, Hong Kong and Singapore. In multicultural societies like the United States, the United Kingdom, Canada and Australia, Chinese people are a minority ethnic group. Hence, different types of Chinese communities may interpret traditional belief systems and practices differently.

Most traditional religious beliefs have ancient roots, but the rationale and reasons for them have been largely forgotten or lost over time. Educated people may understand and internalise the values by reading classical Chinese philosophies. However, those who are less educated may be more influenced by traditional folklore, drama and stories.

In conclusion, though some Chinese beliefs and practices may sound different or new in the West, it is our objective to move towards a greater accommodation of differences and develop culturally and ethnically sensitive practices in multicultural countries.

Notes

1   It is important to note that the kidney, according to CM, consists of the reproductive system and urinary system. Hence, the function of the kidney has a physical and a cultural meaning, which is particularly important to men. The kidney has to do with male potency, which in turn gives rise to men's sense of pride in performing sexual activities and in the ability to produce children.

2   The theories of *yin–yang* and five elements were the two commonly used interpretations of natural phenomena in CM (Cheng 1999, p.12). Many things are classified into two contrary components, such as *yin* or *yang*, 'hot' or 'cold'. The idea is to incorporate opposite forces into the principle of *yin* and *yang*, Because of

the fluidity of the interaction between the opposites, any excess in one area must be immediately counterbalanced by the opposite to maintain vital energy, *qi*, which is the source of life and is defined as the energy circulating in the body (Yang 1994). According to the CM model, illness is a result of improper flow of *qi* through the system. Herbs and food are prescribed to treat imbalances of *yin* or *yang* in the body. Similarly, in the theory of the five elements (that is, wood, fire, earth, metal, and water) each category is said to have distinctive properties respectively. For example, the character of fire is heat and earth represents dampness.

3   Karma is neither good nor bad. However, lay followers believe that it is good karma if the child is born well-behaved and brings joy to the family. In contrast, if a child is born to bring trouble and sorrow to the family, it is a bad karma.

References

Academy of Chinese Studies (2002) *Seven Grounds for Divorcing a Wife.* Accessed 30/07/07 at http://hk.chiculture.net/1002/html/b03/1002b03.htm

Ba-mo, A.Y. (2004) *The Yi World of Belief: Field Reports on the Religious Life of the Yi of Liangshan.* Guangxi: Guangxi Renmin Publisher. [In Chinese]

Banister, J. (2004) 'Shortage of girls in China today.' *Journal of Population Research 21,* 19–45.

Bond, M.H. (1991) *Beyond the Chinese Face: Insights from Psychology.* Hong Kong: Oxford University Press.

Chan, C. (1997a) 'The application of Eastern philosophy in cancer counselling.' Paper presented at the 14th Asian Cancer Conference and 4th Hong Kong International Cancer Congress, Hong Kong.

Chan, C. (1997b) 'Chinese values and group counselling.' Paper presented at the Third International Conference of Social Work Education in Chinese Societies, Taiwan.

Chan, C.L.W. (1995) 'Gender issues in market socialism.' In L. Wong and S. MacPherson (eds) *Social Change and Social Policy in Contemporary China.* Aldershot: Avebury.

Chan, C.L.W., Blyth, E. and Chan, C.H.Y. (2006) 'Attitudes to and practices regarding sex selection in China.' *Prenatal Diagnosis 26,* 610–613.

Chan, C.L.W., Chan, Y. and Chung, M.M.L. (2001) *Women, Sex and Reproductive Health Training Manual.* Hong Kong: Department of Social Work and Social Administration, The University of Hong Kong. [In Chinese]

Chan, C.L.W., Liu, M. and Zhang, Y.L. (1998) 'End of women's emancipation?' In J.Y.S. Cheng (ed.) *China in the post-Deng Era.* Hong Kong: The Chinese University Press.

Chan, C.L.W., Yip, P.S.F., Ng, E.H.Y., Ho, P.C., Chan, C.H. and Au, J.A.K. (2002) 'Gender selection in China: Its meanings and implications.' *Journal of Assisted Reproduction and Genetics 19,* 9, 426–430.

Chan, C.H.Y., Ng, E.H.Y., Chan, C.L.W., Ho, P.C. and Chan, T.H.Y. (2006) 'Effectiveness of psychosocial group intervention for reducing anxiety in women undergoing *in vitro* fertilization: A randomized controlled study.' *Fertility and Sterility 85,* 2, 339–346.

Chan, K.P. (2005) 'Spirituality and psycho-education of pregnant Chinese women: An evaluation of the effect of an Eastern-based model of mind-body-spirit intervention on maternal and fetal health status.' Unpublished manuscript presented at a research meeting at the Centre on Behavioral Health, The University of Hong Kong.

Cheng, M. (1992) 'A survey of pregnant women's knowledge, attitude and behaviour toward sexual activity during pregnancy.' *Journal of Nursing 39*, 77–88. [In Chinese]

Cheng, X.N. (ed.) (1999) *Chinese Acupuncture and Moxibustion*. Rev. ed. Beijing: Foreign Languages Press.

Coale, A.J. and Banister, J. (1994) 'Five decades of missing females in China.' *Demography 31*, 459–479.

Croll, E. (2004) 'Sex ratios at birth in China: An international perspective.' In *Background Paper prepared for Workshop on Ethical, Legal and Social Issues of Sex Ratio Imbalance (0–4) in China*. Beijing, June 2–28.

Croll, E. (1995) *Changing Identities of Chinese Women: Rhetoric, Experience and Self-perception in Twentieth-century China*. Hong Kong: Hong Kong University Press.

Doolittle, J. (2002) *Social Life of the Chinese*. London: Kegan Paul.

fahua yishu, Chap. 6 in *Da Zheng Cang*, T. 34, p.0538b. [In Chinese]

Gross, R.M. (1994) 'Buddhism.' In J. Holm (ed.) *Women in Religion*. London: Pinter Publishers.

Gupta, M.D. (2005) 'Explaining Asia's "missing women": A new look at the data.' *Population and Development Review 31*, 3, 529–535.

Hall, C. (1997) *Daughter of the Dragon: Women's Lives in Contemporary China*. London: Scarlet Press.

Harold, E. (1994) *Know Yourself, Heal Yourself: A Complete Guide to Natural Healing*. Victoria, Australia: Penguin.

Ho, D.Y.F. (1996) 'Filial piety and its psychological consequences.' In M.H. Bond (ed.) *Handbook of Chinese Psychology*. Hong Kong: Oxford University Press.

Holroyd, E., Fung, K.L., Lam, S.C. and Ha, S.W. (1997) 'Doing the month: An exploration of postpartum practices in Chinese women.' *Journal of Health Care for Women International 18*, 301–315.

Hui, C.W.H. (2007) 'The transition to motherhood for Chinese women.' Unpublished doctoral dissertation. Hong Kong: The University of Hong Kong.

Humphreys, C. (1994) *Karma and Rebirth*. Richmond, Surrey: Curzon Press.

Jia, Y.Z. (2003) *The Tourism Culture of the Yizu, China*. Chengdu: Sichuan Minzu Publisher. [In Chinese]

Karetzky, P.E. (2004) *Guanyin*. New York: Oxford University Press.

Keown, D. and Keown, J. (1995) 'Killing, karma and caring: Euthanasia in Buddhism and Christianity.' *Journal of Medical Ethics 21*, 5, 265–269.

Laws and Regulations of the People's Republic of China (2001) Beijing: China Legal Publishing House.

Lee, R. (1984) 'Chinese and western health care systems: Professional stratification in a modernizing society.' In A. King and R. Lee (eds) *Social Life and Development in Hong Kong*. Hong Kong: Chinese University of Hong Kong.

Li, J. (2004) 'Gender inequality, family planning, and maternal and child care in a rural Chinese county.' *Social Science and Medicine 59*, 4, 695–708.

Li, S., Zhu, C. and Feldman, M.W. (2004) 'Gender differences in child survival in contemporary rural China: A county study.' *Journal of Biosocial Science 36*, 1, 83–109.

Mikulas, W.L. (2002) *The Integrative Helper: Convergence of Eastern and Western Traditions*. Pacific Grove, CA: Brooks/Cole-Thomson Learning.

Murphy, R. (2003) 'Fertility and distorted sex ratios in a rural Chinese county: Culture, state, and policy.' *Population and Development Review 29*, 4, 595–626.

Myers, J.H. (1997) 'Birth-planning policy in rural China: The cultural imbalance between innovation and tradition.' *Journal of International and Area Studies 7*, 22–31.

Nadeau, R.L. (2001) 'Harmonizing family and cosmos: Shamanic women in Chinese religions.' In N.A. Falk and R.M. Gross (eds) *Unspoken Worlds: Women's Religious Lives* (3rd ed.). Australia: Wadsworth Thomson Learning.

Nan, H. (2005) *Lunyu Biezai* (8th ed.). China: Fudan University Publisher. [In Chinese]

National Population Census of China. (2005) Accessed 08/09/07 at www.stats.gov.cn/tjsj/ndsj/2006/indexch.htm

Neile, E. (1995) 'The maternity needs of the Chinese community.' *Midwifery 91*, 1, 34–35.

Ng, H.Y. (1995) 'Healing in the Chinese temples: A challenge to clinical social work practice.' *Hong Kong Journal of Social Work 24*, 2, 10–17.

Ng, E.H.Y., Liu, A., Chan, C.H.Y. and Chan, C.L.W. (2004) 'Hong Kong: A social, legal and clinical overview.' In E. Blyth and R. Landau (eds) *Third-Party Assisted Conception across Cultures: Social, Legal and Ethical Perspectives.* London: Jessica Kingsley Publishers.

Parrinder, G. (1996) *Sexual Morality in the World's Religions.* Oxford: Oneworld Publications.

Pyper, C. (1997) 'Reproductive health awareness: An important dimension to be integrated into existing sexual and reproductive health programs.' *Advances in Contraception 12*, 2–3, 331–338.

Qiu, R. (2001) 'Sociocultural dimensions of infertility and assisted reproduction in the Far East.' In E. Vayena, P.J. Rowe and P.D. Griffin (eds) *Current Practices and Controversies in Assisted Reproduction.* Report of a meeting on Medical, Ethical and Social Aspects of Assisted Reproduction, WHO Headquarters, Geneva, Switzerland, September 17–21.

Qiu, R. (2006) 'Bioethics: A search for moral diversity.' *Eastern Mediterranean Health Journal 12* (suppl. 1), S21–S29.

Rainey, L.D. (2004) 'Women in the Chinese traditions.' In L.M. Anderson and P.D. Young (eds) *Women and Religious Traditions.* Don Mills, ON: Oxford University Press.

Scharping, T. (2003) *Birth Control in China, 1949–2000: Population Policy and Demographic Development.* London and New York: Routledge Curzon.

Schott, J. and Henley, A. (1996) *Culture, Religion and Childbearing in a Multiracial Society: A Handbook for Health Professionals.* Oxford: Butterworth-Heinemann.

Sheikh, A.A. and Sheikh, K.S. (eds) (1989) *Eastern and Western Approaches to Healing: Ancient Wisdom and Modern Knowledge.* New York: John Wiley & Sons.

Su, K.M. (1997) *The Research on the Moral Values of Liangshan Yizu.* Chengdu: Sichuan University Publisher. [In Chinese]

Tang, C., Siu, B.N., Lai, F. and Chen, T. (1996) 'Heterosexual Chinese women's sexual adjustment after gynecologic cancer.' *Journal of Sex Research 33*, 189–197.

Topley, M. (1978) 'Chinese and western medicine in Hong Kong.' In A. Kleinman (ed.) *Culture and Healing in Asian Society.* Cambridge, MA: Schenkman.

Tseng, Y. (2000) 'A study on expectant fathers' sexual knowledge, attitude and behaviour and related factors.' *Nursing Research (China) 8*, 3, 275–288. [In Chinese]

Xie, Z. (2000) 'Population policy and the family-planning programme.' In X. Peng and Z. Guo (eds) *The Changing Population of China.* Oxford: Blackwell.

Yang, J. (1994) *Chinese Qigong Massage.* Jamaica Plain, MA: Yang's Martial Arts Association.

Yang, K.A. (1995a) *Buddhism and Health.* Heilongjiang: Heilongjiang Xinhua Books. [In Chinese]

Yang, K.A. (1995b) *Taoism and Health.* Heilongjiang: Heilongjiang Xinhua Books. [In Chinese]

Ye, J.C. (2000) *The Changes of Han Characters* (2nd ed.). Hong Kong: Ming Pao Publishers. [In Chinese]

Yu, C.F. (1996) 'A sutra promoting the white-robed Guanyin as giver of sons.' In D.S. Lopez (ed.) *Religions of China in Practice.* Princeton, NJ: Princeton University Press.

6

Buddhist Family Values

Fertility and Technological Intervention in the Quest for Enlightenment

Michael G. Barnhart

Discussing the realm of what is usually thought of as 'the family' and 'private' from the perspective of any version of Buddhism is an especial challenge. Traditionally, Buddhism has been preoccupied with the quest for individual enlightenment and so has demanded of its committed practitioners a monkish abandonment of family life that echoes the Buddha's own in his effort to exterminate what may loosely be translated as suffering in the world.[1] However, it is also true that Buddhism has adapted itself to different times and needs as they have developed over the course of human history. This seems hardly surprising when we reflect on the fact that, although it originally arose in response to tensions in ancient Vedic[2] religious practices, it spread throughout Asia over the course of its 2500 year history and now is popular in both Western Europe and the US. It has died out in places such as India, only to re-emerge in the nineteenth century largely as a movement to bring social justice to the *dalit* castes (untouchables). In the United States it has offered a religious alternative to disillusioned Christians, especially. And though still relatively small by the standards of the major religions, it is a world religion and, by some estimates, can count nearly 350 million practitioners.[3] So, given contemporary angst over the changing nature of the family, especially in modern, developed societies, it is perhaps not inappropriate to re-ask the question: are there family values that are inherently Buddhist? And, if so, then what kind of family structure and what forms of its perpetuation are appropriate from a Buddhist point of view?

'Re-ask' because, in fact, Buddhism has in its early past once confronted the demand to say something enlightening about the nature of family life. In the Indian Pali Canon, the earliest source of Buddhist literature,[4] we find at least one work devoted to a dialogue between the Buddha himself and the layman Sigala on the question of proper conduct in family relationships. This rather well-known text will motivate much of what emerges in the chapter and my comparisons to common arguments over private decision-making and reproductive rights in a western, biomedical context. First, however, a few words about the particular conception of Buddhism on which this discussion revolves.

Buddhism

Buddhists generally aim to emulate the example of the historical Buddha and his achievement of enlightened triumph over existential suffering. 'Buddha' simply means 'enlightened one' in the ancient Indian languages of Pali and Sanskrit and was the honorific traditionally attached to a North Indian prince, Siddhartha Gautama, who is believed to have lived around the period of the sixth century BCE. There are at least three major, recognised branches of Buddhism, roughly corresponding to different periods in the expansion of Buddhism within India and its spread throughout much of Asia. Between these branches are deep doctrinal and philosophical differences, and given Buddhism's spread throughout the very culturally diverse regions of Asia and now Europe and the United States, many scholars as well as Buddhists themselves question the possibility of talking about Buddhism as a unified or single phenomenon. For example, Buddhists who take their primary inspiration from the texts and traditions of the earliest forms in India, typically regard the historical Buddha as the one and only Buddha, the model for all to follow. Later 'greater vehicle' or Mahayana Buddhists accept that the Buddha has been reincarnated, or better re-manifested, in many different individuals over the eons and will continue to be so.

However, because there are elements both basic to and shared by Buddhism in all its myriad forms, and because these elements do tend to determine the limits of a Buddhist perspective, at least in the sense of ruling out some actions and beliefs, I will focus on these in discussing what Buddhism means and what Buddhists believe and do. Besides the Buddha, two other 'treasures' or 'jewels' are held sacred by all Buddhists: the *dharma* or law and the *sangha* or monastic community.[5] Though each of these has many different interpretations throughout the world of Buddhism, in regard to *dharma*, certain texts and concepts are universally accepted, and in regard to the *sangha*, it has never been entirely exclusive of lay practitioners. Additionally, *dharma* prescribes certain rules and practices for the *sangha*, and these have often been a rich source for understanding Buddhist ethics. Beyond that, all Buddhists, lay or monk, accept five basic precepts (The Five Precepts) the first of which prohibits taking life, while the others prohibit variously stealing, engaging in improper sexual relations, lying, and consuming intoxicants.

Principally, what Buddhists revere in the life of the Buddha is his resolve to confront the reality of suffering (*dukkha*) and his achievement of an enlightened form of life that uproots it entirely. Not only this, but his achievement is repeatable, a model that any individual may successfully follow if with sincerity and in good conscience. The elements of doctrine that are also universally accepted – the Four Noble Truths, the Eightfold Path, and the Doctrine of Dependent Origination (*pratitya samutpada* in Sanskrit) – closely parallel this reverence for the life of the historical Buddha. The Four Noble Truths and Eightfold Path come from the purported First Sermon of the Buddha and claim that: 1) all life is suffering; 2) suffering has a root which is 'grasping', 'craving', or 'attachment' (some translations prefer 'inappropriate desire'); 3) extirpating the root through the achievement of *nirvana* destroys suffering; 4) destroying the root requires treading the Eightfold Path of right views, right resolve, right speech, right action, right livelihood, right effort, right mindfulness, and right concentration. Extirpating the root or overcoming craving and attachment requires insight into the twelve-fold chain of mutual dependence or origination (co-arising) – that craving arises ultimately through a perceptual apprehension of the world that mistakes things as real, shall we say, 'possessables'.[6] Furthermore, this apprehension drives the process whereby we construct a 'self' that is equally fictive but nonetheless a genuine source of existential misery. This latter doctrine, that of 'no-self' (*anatta* or *anatman*), represents another continuity within all forms of Buddhism where the concept of a continuously existing or even a permanent self is replaced with a nominalist concept of a composite of disparate elements, *skhandas* in Sanskrit.[7] In other words, neither things nor selves are independently existing elements but arise in conjunction with a grasping, perceptual apprehension of the world. The key is, then, to root out this apprehension through the practice of the Eightfold Path. Right views undermine our sense that the self and its objects of conquest are real or meaningful, right resolve keeps us focused on the overcoming of suffering, right speech and right action enmesh us in a fundamentally different form of life from that of suffering, as does right livelihood, and right effort, mindfulness, and concentration complete the reorientation of individual personality away from the life of craving.

All of which raises the question as to just what a Buddhist form of life is actually like. What kind of 'rightness' permeates right speech or right livelihood? Historically, two different sorts of answers have been given to this question. On the one hand, particularly the more traditional Buddhists, the Theravadins, have answered with lists of dispositional qualities that emerge within the personality of the committed 'stream entrant'.[8] Following Keown (1995), I believe we can condense what is sometimes a fairly extensive list into three: life, wisdom, and friendship. Life because of the commitment to non-injury of all living things, wisdom in the sense of both an understanding of the nature of reality, but also deep compassion for all living beings as a full aspect of wisdom, and finally friendship because of the importance of non-self-centred living and the consequent importance of such traditional Buddhist values as giving and loving kindness. On the other hand, Mahayana Buddhists, in particular, have emphasised the importance of the Bodhisattva's vow to bring all sentient beings to enlightenment (*nirvana*) through the employment of skilful means (*upaya*) before final attainment for him- (or her-) self. This latter option has traditionally embodied ideals of flexibility and improvisation in one's practical dealings with others, and hence often a criticism of specific codes and rules of behaviour as soteriologically counterproductive.[9] Perhaps the Japanese Zen traditions (Chinese Ch'an) represent the most extreme form of such an approach with their emphasis on the most austere forms of meditation – *zazen*, or 'just sitting' meditation and *ko'an* practice ('What was your original face before you were born?').[10] From the Mahayana viewpoint, the Theravadin emphasis on specific values is somewhat misplaced, as it is either too formulaic or, because of its emphasis on dispositional cultivation, inconsistent with the Buddha's focus on right mindfulness and concentration, both of which require a self-reflective capacity that habituation tends to discourage. Mahayana tends to celebrate unexpected and paradoxical responses to the varieties of suffering in the world, as well as critical responses to Buddhist doctrines themselves that are meant to drive one to a greater depth of Buddhist insight.[11]

Clearly, Buddhist values and ethics are a diverse and sometimes inconsistent lot. However, despite the differences, Buddhist practices across the various traditions tend to exhibit a fair degree of similarity. All emphasise benevolence and nonviolence, an interest in helping others, often to the point of provision of social services to the poor or activism on their behalf, and a strong element of meditational practice aimed at unseating dogmatic or selfish tendencies within the individual personality. All view the world as transient and inherently unreal at a basic level, deeply inflected with the psychology of the individual mind within it, and hence the self and its role as at the root of existential suffering. And finally, all exhibit some flexibility about the extensiveness of the Buddhist community. Though *sangha* literally means 'noble ones', what that covers exactly in the way of actual human communities is not particularly prescriptive. The term has always embraced the communities of monks who choose a Buddhist path, but it has never entirely excluded the layperson, the 'householder', which has led some to ask whether it could extend as far as the family unit as well (Hershock 2000). That is, could we regard the family as a *sangha* where individuals can pursue the path of Buddhist enlightenment or a community that fosters the conditions of achieving *nirvana*?

While an interesting and perhaps important claim, the point is no doubt highly controversial. However, it is certainly clear that Buddhist values need not be confined to the insides of monasteries. Besides, there is at least one text among the oldest and most authentic pieces of the tradition that suggests a set of possible Buddhist 'family values', the *Sigalavada Sutra*, or 'Discourse to the [Layman] Sigala'.[12] In this text, a young layman, Sigala, in the midst of carrying out his dying father's instructions to 'pay homage to the [six, cardinal] directions' encounters the Buddha early in the morning. The Buddha questions the boy, and upon learning what he is attempting to do, immediately proceeds to enlighten him as to the true meaning of honouring the six directions. What emerges includes a picture of proper family relations as taught by the Buddha and in ways that coincide with what I have described as core Buddhist values.

Buddhist family values

According to Sigala, 'honouring the six directions' means saluting the compass points as well as the nadir and zenith. That is, Sigala takes his father's injunction literally. Direction just means spatial orientation. However, the Buddha suggests otherwise. First, he claims that one should 'abandon the four defilements of action', that is, obey the first four of the Five Precepts (not to kill and injure, lie, steal, or have improper sexual relations). In addition, one should avoid the 'six causes that waste a person's wealth'. Thus, the 'fourteen evils'[13] are also vanquished and 'by covering the six directions, he [the observant one] practices in order to attain both worlds'. The Buddha then goes on to elaborate in rather exquisite detail exactly how Sigala is to put this advice into practice and correlatively how to distinguish a true from a false friend, which is the key to the sort of associations that do not 'waste a person's wealth'. If one follows this prescription, according to the Buddha, then one will be in a position actually to honour the true six directions in an appropriate manner because the six directions are in fact the sum of one's social relations with others, particularly the family, which constitutes both the eastern and western directions as well as, depending upon how one defines the household, the nadir.

And how is leading a life informed by Buddhist values – following the Five Precepts and not indulging in wasteful or wanton actions, for example drunkenness – the same as honouring family and others? The Buddha suggests that if Sigala does as advised, he 'collects wealth like a bee flies about gathering honey / The wealth one accumulates rises up like an anthill' (Holder 2006, p.198). Of course, though this sounds like reasonable advice, perhaps somewhat Pollyannaish, one might wonder what it has to do with Buddhism and enlightenment, traditionally non-materialistic notions. However, the Buddha goes on to add that one is providing for the clan, and 'the wealth should be divided in four ways / So one binds oneself to one's friends' (Holder 2006, p.198). In other words, the point of following a Buddhist path for a layperson is, at least in part, to enjoy a degree of material success. Wealth allows one to provide for the needs of family and friends – one's dependents, and wealth is most successfully accumulated by doing as the Buddha prescribes. Providing in this fashion, because families and dependents require material support, is key to honouring the 'true' six directions fully, which are:

> One's mother and father should be known as the eastern direction; teachers should be known as the southern direction; one's children and wife should be known as the western direction; one's friends and companions should be known as the northern direction; servants, workers, and helpers should be known as the nadir; and religious wanderers and Brahmins should be known as the zenith. (Holder 2006, p.198)

Honouring these six directions is, therefore, paying respect to these respective dimensions along which a layperson's life unfolds, and that in turn requires honouring those who make up each direction. To honour one's father and mother is to 'perform duties for them, keep the family tradition', at the time of their deaths to 'offer gifts to their honour'. If the child honours the parents in this manner, then, supposes the Buddha, the parents will respond in a reciprocally caring manner 'by encouraging the child to do good, by training the child in a craft, by marrying the child to a suitable spouse', and so on.

With regard to each of the remaining directions, a similar degree of reciprocity is called for in the dealings one has with those in question. In the southern direction, 'students should minister to their teachers' by 'giving them service' and 'by thoroughly learning the teachers' arts', for example. And crucially for the family, 'a husband should minister to his wife…by showing her respect, by not showing her disrespect, by not being unfaithful, by relinquishing authority to her, and by providing her with sufficient adornments'. Correspondingly, 'his wife will respond showing compassion to her husband by performing her work well', for example 'by keeping the servants well-organized…by guarding their stored goods, and by being skilful and diligent in all of her duties' (Holder 2006, p.199).

Obviously, discharging such duties requires some degree of material means, and so acquiring those means a lay duty. Hence, it would be a mistake to read the initial emphasis on the practical or financial benefits of adhering to Buddhist principles as an entirely venal argument for persuading a layperson to take the Buddhist path. Yes, a layperson will give 'practical' considerations more weight than a wandering monk or ascetic, and so citing them will provide an incentive for such a person to tread the Buddhist path. However, it is also the case that the material benefits attending a well-regulated life may be harnessed in the direction of creating relationships with others that are honourable. And from a Buddhist point of view, honourable relations are those that exemplify such values as compassion and giving. In fact, the three core values identified by Keown (1995) – life, wisdom, and friendship – are arguably more fully advanced the more one tends to live in the sort of way the Buddha prescribes to Sigala. For example, Sigala is counselled to 'be a helper', a 'refuge when one is frightened', to protect others' property, to 'not abandon one in misfortune', and so on.

More specifically, and in regard to one's wife and children on the one hand and parents on the other hand, the Buddha instructs Sigala that there are five ways to cover the directions in regard to both. First, with regard to one's parents,

> I will support those who brought me up...I will perform their duties for them, keep the family tradition, and make myself worthy of my inheritance, and at the time of their deaths I will offer gifts in their honor. (Holder 2006, p.199)

In turn, they will 'respond showing the child compassion, by restraining the child from doing evil...by training the child in a craft...by handing over the child's inheritance at the right time'. This direction, the text adds, is thus 'peaceful and free from fear'.

Second, and in regard to one's wife, there are also 'five ways that a husband should minister to his wife in the western direction':

> ...by showing her respect, by not showing her disrespect, by not being unfaithful, by relinquishing authority to her, and by providing her with sufficient adornments. So, when a husband ministers to his wife in these five ways...his wife will respond showing compassion to her husband by performing her work well, by keeping servants well-organized, by being faithful, by guarding their stored goods. (Holder 2006, p.199)

So, to honour especially these 'family' directions is to achieve a cooperative and reciprocal relationship with others that exhibits compassion and is sustained by peace and freedom from fear. To do this requires a degree of material success in the world that is then conserved and utilised to create and sustain what the Buddha interestingly describes as circumstances for 'showing compassion' toward parents, children, spouse, and even household servants.

Even more interestingly, such compassion is displayed in terms of practical accomplishment, performing one's work well, or refraining from doing evil. To do Buddhist good in the world therefore requires, at least of laymen, that they not abandon the household and their worldly obligations but rather seek to undertake them in a way that fosters mutual benefit, as measured by the presence of friendship and compassionate regard.

In other words, the Sigala discourse suggests a Buddhist vision of a world of social harmony where all play their socially evolved roles in ways that generate Buddhist values. Just as the text emphasises reciprocity and harmony between people, so it suggests a more abstract reciprocity between the social goods and Buddhist values. Pursuing Buddhist values secures the recognised means to a good and materially successful life (though not venally successful), and correlatively achieving those goods leads to the fostering of the very values that Buddhism proclaims. In fact, the Buddha suggests as much in the closing refrains of the text:

> Being impartial to each person
> According to what is fitting,
> These are the four forms of kindly behavior in the world
> Like the axle pin of a chariot that is moving. (Holder
> 2006, p.201)

Family and fertility issues

It is quite clear what sort of family issues and concerns lie within the purview of the Sigala Discourse and what it aims to discourage in the way of morally problematic behaviours. The emphasis on not being unfaithful, not beating the servants, honouring wandering religious ascetics, giving children their rightful inheritances, and so on – these are the concerns within the Discourse. However, though some of these remain perennial issues for most or all families in contemporary society (for example, child and spousal abuse), there are a host of others with which contemporary societies wrestle, largely undreamed of at the time of the Buddha. Especially in regard to the economically developed world, a number of factors impact on the family and raise significant ethical issues. The first is the erosion of traditional authority and growing embrace of personal freedom as an ideal.[14] The second is the growth of technology and our ability to exercise control over what we traditionally thought of as 'the hand that nature dealt us'. For example, assisted conception has enabled the previously infertile to bear children, and recombinant DNA technology offers the possibility of excising heritable illnesses from our collective future. So, as individuals assert more individual autonomy in their choices regarding with whom and for how long they enter into family relationships, and families come into increasing control over whether and what children they will have, we find that the range of socially contentious issues that fall under the category 'family' and 'private' has grown immensely since the time of the Buddha.

Should an infertile couple be able to use donated eggs or sperm? Should they have access to technologies such as *in vitro* fertilisation? Is the use of contraception, especially abortifacient contraception, permissible? May unwanted children be aborted, especially if they pose no risk to the mother's health, or suffer no serious deformities or ailments themselves? Do families have a responsibility to procreate in the first place? Are parents becoming too permissive in regard to their children's behaviour? Is corporal punishment, for example spanking, a form of child abuse? What exactly is a family? Does it require two parents of opposite sexes to count as a true family? Technology and the elevated status of individual choice have introduced a broad range of concerns undreamed of in the Buddha's discourse to Sigala and in terms that arguably neither the Buddha nor Sigala would meaningfully relate to.

In the interests of simplifying the discussion to some extent, perhaps we can distil the former list under a few fairly general-purpose headings: family structure and lines of authority on the one hand, fertility control and what count as its acceptable methods on the other. At the risk of oversimplification, contemporary debate and discussion of such issues usually revolve around the conflict between individual choice and the demands of tradition. As societies increasingly liberalise, which is not to say that most are, individuals and individual families assert a right to exercise control over whom they marry, whether to marry, whether to have children, how many, and even their genetic make-up (Inglehart 1997). Almost inevitably, because such practices have become deeply sedimented in the customs of a culture, this sets up a debate between those who conceive themselves to be guardians and conservators of their people's customs and those who assert such rights of self-determination. Ideas such as procreative rights, alternative families, single-parenting, and the like have raised challenges to the traditional conceptions of family and parental role, especially in the west but increasingly in more developed nations in Asia and elsewhere.

Drawing on the Sigala Discourse, it is clear that these are not the terms in which basic Buddhism would address the issues. The emphasis, as noted, tends to be on reciprocity in the family relations and emphasis on those aspects of traditional roles that lead to health and well-being. Husbands are supposed to 'show respect' and not be unfaithful; the wife is supposed to 'perform her work well', and so forth. Little in the surface of the text suggests that individuals have certain inherent rights to make associational decisions in the formation of a family, or procreative decisions, including whether to have children in the first place. The conception of family in the text is clearly a traditional one in many respects – that people are in families insofar as they mean to have children. There is no discussion as to how such children are conceived, nor of the meaning of such terms as 'husband' or 'wife', but one imagines that these terms are understood in the traditional sense. Thus, it might be tempting to imagine that the sorts of concerns and objections that cultural traditionalists raise towards the exercise of personal and unconventional choice in regard to family matters would be familiar and accepted within the ambit of traditional Buddhism as well.

However, the picture is more complicated. The philosophical rationale for an overall traditionalist approach in, for example, Roman Catholicism, depends very heavily on a conception of what is 'natural', hence God-given, and known by the application of reason to the question of what is the essential nature of human beings. Indeed, any traditionalism, even if it rejects the idea of a universal human essence, embraces the idea of a historically given conception that defines both what it is to be human and what the good life therefore is. Such conceptions, consequently, place limits on the meaningfulness of those choices that violate our natural roles. In essence, this constitutes the major argument advanced by philosophers such as Kass (1985) against everything from assisted conception to cloning, and justifies an ongoing suspicion of all technological interventions that expand the range of individual choice in family and reproductive matters (Kass 1997). However, a close examination of the Sigala Discourse reveals no such dominant conception of the natural or normal. It tends to focus more on the specific virtues that are associated with living 'compassionately' within the various general 'directions' along which life is oriented.

Take, for example, the manner in which the 'six directions' are introduced. In the text, the Buddha lists each of these directions: parent–child, teacher–student, husband–wife, friend–friend, master–servant, household–religious wanderer, and clearly they correspond to the traditional interactions that define individual life in his time. However, at no point does the Buddha insist that these are exclusive of other roles or are eternal and grounded in a human essence, God-given or otherwise. That these roles persist even into the present day is no more than a contingent fact as portrayed in the text, though it is difficult to conceive a good life in which all of these were absent.

The emphasis in the discourse is rather on the overall manner in which one should conduct oneself in living according to these directions. And there the stress is on reciprocity. Of course, the conception of role in each direction is fairly traditional – for example, children offering gifts to their parents or keeping 'the family tradition', while parents are to marry 'the child to a suitable spouse'. But the result is compassionate responsiveness back and forth between those who constitute the dimension: 'When the child ministers to his or her mother and father in these five ways as the eastern direction, the parents will respond showing the child compassion...so that it is peaceful and free from fear.' In other words, reciprocity in compassionate execution of one's established social obligations to others, especially in the context of family, represents a further avenue for securing that freedom from suffering that is the focus of the Four Noble Truths and the Eightfold Path.

Family relations are therefore to be judged not according to whether they conform to some pre-ordained conception or ideal image. Rather they are to be judged in light of the degree of compassionately motivated reciprocity resulting in a freedom from suffering: 'When a husband ministers to his wife in these five ways as the western direction, his wife will respond showing compassion to her husband...so that it [the western direction] is peaceful and free of fear.' Again, the image 'kindly behavior in the world / Like the axle pin of a chariot that is moving' (Holder 2006, p.201) suggests our concern should be on what actions bring out kindness and avoidance of suffering in the various turnings of the wheel of existence. In fact, much of the later Mahayana tradition emphasises an even more radical conception of adapting to circumstance in the ideal of *upaya* or expedient means. Practising expedient means can go so far as repudiating traditional Buddhist formulae where doing so furthers the cause of enlightenment and encourages compassion. In other words and in a very real sense, it is not uncommon for Buddhism to treat little as sacred in the cause of advancing its core mission of combating *dukkha*.

Consequently, I can see little that suggests a 'traditional' definition of the family. If families no longer always feature a parental male–female relationship, so be it. The question is not whether this is a proper family, or even whether it is a family at all. Perhaps it simply constitutes a new 'direction' that emerges in the world. The question is whether it affords an opportunity for compassionate reciprocity and hence the possibility of deliverance from fear; that is, can it be a peaceable form of existence. Of course, it is something of an open question whether certain kinds of relationship are such that violence and fear are an intrinsic aspect of their make-up. But I think Buddhist teaching gives us little reason to believe that this can be judged *a priori* or by reference to what is natural or even traditional. So, in regard to family structure, gender relationships, and 'alternative' families, there is no basis for moral condemnation in Buddhism. There is nothing that represents the 'six directions' as timeless universals. In fact, one might even argue that the Sigala suggests a reciprocity in husband–wife relations that is somewhat 'liberal'. The husband, remember, is to 'relinquish authority to her [his wife]' and work to inspire a compassionate response to him on her part. If anything, that suggests a kind of gender equality in the context of marital role that sounds more like J.S. Mill or some versions of modern feminism.

The issues of fertility control and technological intervention in the procreative process present a more difficult task of reconstructive interpretation. To begin with, though fertility has always been within human discretion to some extent, including methods that today sport modern sounding acronyms – DI (donor insemination) for example – the range of technologically sophisticated forms of intervention and their precision is tremendously greater. Furthermore, a modern method such as IVF offers the possibility of side-stepping certain moral concerns such as the use of donated tissue and consequent violation of the sexual exclusivity of marriage. Abortion, though still a rather crude method, at least in the early stages avoids some of the horrors of infanticide. However, it is not as though these older methods, especially infanticide, were not practised. So, the relative silence of Buddhist authorities on such practices is interesting and perhaps instructive. Indeed, even in a place such as Japan, where Buddhism was deeply rooted, infanticide as a response to periods of famine and in the interests of preserving the family, *mabiki* as it was called, was rarely condemned by Buddhist authorities.[15] Similarly, there is little reason to think such practices were unknown at the time of the Sigala Discourse in India. However, there is nothing in the text that specifically addresses the issue of measures to control the number of children within a family.

In fact, the structure of the Sigala is rather curious if practices aimed at controlling fertility were a target of Buddhist ethical concern. The issue of reciprocity between parent and child is addressed to the child and at a point where he or she is capable of social interaction. Sigala is told to 'perform duties for them', the result of which is that 'the child's parents will respond showing the child compassion'. Nothing is said that would suggest a parental duty to bring anyone into the world or to avoid action that would prevent conception or birth. And when the husband's and wife's family duties are discussed, the issue is again reciprocity in sharing authority. When specifics are discussed, they extend to matters such as the wife's adornments or her duty to keep 'the servants well-organised', matters that some might regard as trivial or even venial.

Given relative silence on fertility practices that are typically more overtly violent than what is currently practised, it is hard to imagine that traditional Buddhism would suddenly take a larger interest in such subjects. However, a number of scholars regard such silence as at best, simply a matter of focus, and at worst, a question of moral consistency – especially Keown, who has argued strenuously that traditional Buddhism condemns abortion for reasons not unlike those of the Roman Catholic Church. That is, he argues, Buddhism is committed to an understanding of human life that pegs its inception to the moment of fertilisation and, given the first of the Five Precepts forbidding killing, a firm moral argument against practices that imperil such life. One could also extend this condemnation to practices such as IVF, as he has in *Buddhism and Bioethics* (1995, pp.135–138), on the grounds that fertilised embryos, and hence life in the morally relevant sense, are being intentionally destroyed or are likely to be destroyed in the process.[16] In other words, the relative silence of ancient texts is not necessarily indicative of what Buddhism in general should think, or what contemporary Buddhism with a traditional flavour should think.

Indeed, Buddhism is famously adaptive, not only culturally, given its spread throughout much of Asia and now the US and western Europe, but historically in its persistence through many periods of ancient and modern history. So, historical precedent is of limited value in determining what Buddhist ethics demand. However, a more 'liberal' approach to assisted reproduction and fertility control is also possible from a Buddhist perspective. The philosophical weak point in an argument such as Keown's is the relevant definition of life. There are many reasons, both philosophical and sociological, to believe that there is no such consensus within Buddhism. The famous 'no-self' doctrine, standard in all versions of Buddhism, regards the individual as a composite of various elements, all of which must be present to constitute the self, consciousness being an especially important one. Thus, if a Buddhist happens to believe, and there is no strong Buddhist reason not to, that at the moment of conception consciousness is lacking, then there is no reason to regard embryo destruction as an instance of 'killing' a fully human being or ending a fully developed life.[17] Furthermore, if one considers the Japanese concept of *mizuku kuyo*, 'water child', around which an entire set of Buddhist rituals have grown, the clear-cut view of life's origins advanced by Keown and similar commentators grows very muddy. Buddhist scholar LaFleur (1992) points out that this concept involves the idea of life as an emergent phenomenon that solidifies gradually, hence suggesting that what a foetus or even perhaps an early infant represents is not so much a fully formed life but a more intermediate, 'liquid' stage that is reversible without prejudice to the possibility of reforming and re-emerging at a later time. Again, it is difficult to see anything in Buddhist philosophical views that conceptually disqualifies such a notion. Thus, Buddhist rituals offering the chance for parents to 'apologise' for abortions, that is to apologise for reversing the solidifying of a life and the return of the child to its more liquid state, do not notionally violate any standard Buddhist ethical teachings.[18]

In other words, Buddhists are relatively free to determine what sorts of rites and socially sanctioned relationships with others, especially within the family, support the injunction in the Sigala to honour the directions along which life is lived in a way that promotes peace and freedom from fear through compassionate reciprocity. In this vein, the sorts of reasons that people generally give for engaging in the various practices we normally associate with fertility control, even those technologically advanced practices such as IVF, to 'have a child of one's own', do not necessarily violate deep Buddhist principles. Of course, people can seek the aid of such practices for selfish reasons, but that is true for the 'natural' form of procreation as well; and Buddhism never suggests sex itself should be prohibited or discouraged because of such a possibility – only sexual indiscretion is prohibited within the Five Precepts, and that presumably because its motivation is typically selfish. However, if by 'one's own' one means not a possession of one's own but an opportunity to live one's life in a way that draws out compassionate reciprocity between parents and child and spouses – not that one needs a marriage licence to qualify as a spouse – then technologically assisted fertility does not pose special moral problems for Buddhism.

In sum, the important problem is not if this or that practice is specifically prohibited, but rather if it affords a pathway along those human life-directions whereby peace and freedom from fear may be achieved in acts that inspire reciprocal compassion. Arguably, the more complicated the range of alternatives, the more readily they may be tailored to the specifics of an individual family situation, and hence the more important the role of informed individual judgment in determining one's way along the six directions.

Notes

1   The Pali term for this is *dukkha* (*duhkha* in Sanskrit), which is variously translated as 'suffering, pain, sorrow, unsatisfactoriness, unhappiness, being out of balance', and so forth. Clearly, the problem is the lack of an exact English equivalent. Generally, I will stick with 'suffering' as it suggests the general and existential flavour of the original word.

2   The term 'Vedic' refers to the dominant religious tradition of ancient India, probably originating with Aryan, nomad invaders sometime in the second millennium BCE. The term refers to the corpus of religious texts, originally oral, known as the Vedas, that recounted the mythological, ritual, and spiritual basis of what came to be known as Hinduism.

3   Most such estimates are found on the internet and are of undetermined reliability. They range from a low of 150–200 million (Encarta.msn.com) to a high of 760 million (faithandmedia.com). Many web-based figures seem to rely on adherents. com, which puts the number at 376 million. The website of the Interdisciplinary Centre for the Study of Religions and World Views at the University of Leuven says 371 million (kuleuven.be/icrid/religies/religions_xurvey.htm).

4   Holder (2006) has a fine discussion of the Pali Canon, especially those sections labelled Sutta Pitaka or 'Discourse Baskets' (see pp.vii–xxiii). Another very accessible, though older and less available, selection from these same materials can be found in Henry Clarke Warren's *Buddhism, in Translations* (New York: Atheneum, 1974; originally published by Harvard University Press, 1896).

5   Careful readers will note that I sometimes slip between the Pali and the Sanskrit versions of Buddhist terms. Generally, where the Sanskrit version of a key term is more familiar to readers, or even a borrowed term in English now, I will use the Sanskrit. So, *dharma* (Sanskrit) for the Pali, *dhamma*.

6   I admit this is a somewhat unconventional way of expressing the familiar Buddhist doctrine of the 'emptiness of things', *sunyata*. My point is an attempt to convey the view that seeing a thing as 'substantial' (*svabhava* or 'self-existent' in Sanskrit) is a function of our craving for it. Its substantiality does not arise in the context of *nirvana*.

7   These are: form/body, feeling, thought, character or disposition, and consciousness or perception. We designate their contingent association by the conventional term self or atta/atman.

8   See Harvey's discussion (2000), pp.37–41.

9   For a particularly vivid example, see Suzuki's enlightenment story concerning Shen Kuang's amputation of his own arm in achieving satori under Bodhidharma (Suzuki 1955, p.15).

10   I discuss the moral issues surrounding these practices in Barnhart (2006).

11   The Vimilakirti Sutra is the classic reference. Hershock (1999) has dubbed this strategy 'dramatic improvisation'.

12   Found in Holder (2006) pp.191–201. In the Pali Canon, the *sutta* (generally the oldest texts of the Pali Canon containing expositions of doctrine) is in Digha Nikaya 3, pp.180–193.

13   These consist of the abovementioned four defilements, the four bases actions based of such defilements (i.e. desire, hatred, delusion, and fear), and the six causes of wasting wealth.

14   See Inglehart (1997), whose World Values surveys seem to indicate a growing trend in this direction across all societies.

15   See LaFleur (1992), especially his discussion of Japanese family structure in Chapter 11.

16   One could make the same argument in regard to stem-cell research as well, as that typically involves therapeutic cloning and eventual destruction of the embryo.

17   Singer makes a similar point in *Practical Ethics* (1979) and Steinbock in *Life Before Birth* (1992).

18   LaFleur (1992) notes that this is a complicated discussion, while many Japanese feel uneasy with the practice and consider it at the margins of what is compassionate. See especially Chapter 10, 'Moral Swamps'.

References

Barnhart, M. (2006) 'Rootlessness and terror: Violence and morality from a Zen perspective.' In D. Allen (ed.) *Comparative Philosophy and Religion in Times of Terror.* Lanham, MD: Lexington Books.

Harvey, P. (2000) *An Introduction to Buddhist Ethics.* Cambridge: Cambridge University Press.

Hershock, P. (1999) *Reinventing the Wheel.* Albany, NY: State University of New York Press.

Hershock, P. (2000) 'Family matters: Dramatic interdependence and the intimate realization of Buddhist liberation.' *Journal of Buddhist Ethics* 7, 86–104.

Holder, J. (2006) *Early Buddhist Discourses.* Indianapolis/Cambridge: Hackett Publishing Company.

Inglehart, R. (1997) *Modernization and Postmodernization: Cultural, Economic, and Political Change in 43 Societies.* Princeton, NJ: Princeton University Press.

Kass, L. (1985) *Towards a More Natural Science.* New York: Free Press.

Kass, L. (1997) 'The wisdom of repugnance.' *The New Republic 2,* June.

Keown, D. (1995) *Buddhism and Bioethics.* New York: St. Martin's Press.

LaFleur, W. (1992) *Liquid Life: Abortion and Buddhism in Japan.* Princeton, NJ: Princeton University Press.

Singer, P. (1979) *Practical Ethics.* Cambridge: Cambridge University Press.

Steinbock, B. (1992) *Life Before Birth: The Moral and Legal Status of Embryos and Foetuses.* Oxford: Oxford University Press.

Suzuki, D.T. (1955) *Studies in Zen.* New York: Dell Publishing.

7

'Broken Calabashes'

Yoruba Traditional Faith

Titilayo O. Aderibigbe

Introduction

This chapter will focus on the Yoruba traditional religion (YTR) of south-western Nigeria. Africa consists of 56 different countries practising different faiths and religions. From Egypt in the north to Namibia in the south, African traditional religions (ATR) are as varied as the estimated 800 million people who inhabit the continent. What is common to all African traditional religions, however, is their common belief in a supreme, omnipotent and omniscient creator (that is, a God called by different names) and the fact that ATR believers' method of worshipping him is similar. Almost all ATRs worship the supreme deity through lesser gods who, they believe, intercede between man and the supreme God. They all share a common belief in spirits, divinities and ancestors who form a link between the present and the past. They all practise divinations, magic and medicine in their worship (Idowu 1973; Thomas 2005).

I focus on the Yoruba traditional religion (YTR) of Nigeria because its adherents are spread across a wide geographical area through western parts of Africa and even far beyond the African continent to the United States of America, Cuba, Haiti and the West Indies.

Yoruba traditional religion

The YTR religion is typical of most ATR and its adherents are mainly of the Yoruba ethnic group or their descendants. Nigeria is situated in the West Africa sub-region and is the most populous black nation on earth, with an estimated population of 140 million people (UNO 2005). The Yoruba-speaking people predominate in south-western Nigeria and are one of the major ethnic groups in the country. The word 'Yoruba' is a generic ethnic and linguistic description that refers to the people, their culture and beliefs as well as their language. The Yoruba trace their ancestry to a common progenitor called Oduduwa. Daryll Forde (1969) says there are about 200 sub-groups of the Yoruba people. The language belongs to the dialectic cluster of the Kwa languages of the Sudanic family. The Kwa language is derived from the Nok culture and historians have said that 'between 500 and 200 BCE the Nok culture, in what is today's Nigeria, was one of the richest and most advanced ancient civilizations in west Africa' (Francoeur 1997, p.3).

Origin of the Yoruba religion

The Yoruba trace their origin and belief to the beginning of creation. Yoruba theology derives from the religion of Kemet, the first religious system which originated in ancient Egypt (Lucas 1996). They believe that their religion was already highly developed thousands of years even before the Hebrew religion (Idowu 1994). According to Yoruba mythology, Ile-Ife is the holy city and place where creation begins. Ile-Ife literarily means 'the land that spreads or is wide'. A German scholar, on visiting Ile-Ife, was so impressed by the city that he concluded that it must be the lost Atlantis and the Yoruba the descendants of the lost kingdom (Idowu 1994). All human life must pass through it at the point of entry from this earth. Ile-Ife is therefore a passage to life and death (Thomas 2005). The Yoruba creation story states that God, called 'Olodumare' (which literally means 'the creator of the world'), and the giver of life, created Earth in four days and on the fifth day Olodumare rested from his work (Thomas 2005). Having been satisfied with his work, Olodumare sent his arch divinity Orisa-nla (the biggest deity) to go down and replenish Earth, while another divinity, Orunmila, was sent to accompany him as an adviser. Olodumare gave Orisa-nla four trees to plant and use as food: the palm tree, the silk rubber tree, whitewood and dodo. Olodumare created the hen and pigeons along with the trees, which provided the inhabitants with food and drink. At the beginning there was close communion and communication with Olodumare until the humans became disobedient and wanted to find out the secret of life. As a result, Olodumare removed his dwelling place from the reach of humans. The role ascribed to Orisa-nla is also ascribed to Oduduwa, who is said to be the acknowledged founder of the Yoruba people.

The other version of the creation story as told by the custodian of Ife traditional history, called 'Oba Ejio', through personal interview is slightly different. Oba Ejio resides in the traditional King's palace. The king is called the 'Ooni of Ile-Ife'. The Oba Ejio states that after the flood (as in the Biblical Noah's ark story) Olodumare sent Oduduwa down to earth with a chain tied round his waist holding him to heaven. The chain would be used to pull him up if the flood had not receded. Oduduwa held a dove in one of his hands, which he sent out to search if the water had receded. In the other hand he held a gourd containing earth, which he was to pour on the water of the flood to form land. Oduduwa also took a three-toed cockerel that was to spread the earth across the water, and a chameleon which used its weight to firmly sink the earth as he poured it on the water and which later became Ile-Ife. Olodumare is worshipped through several minor or lesser gods who intercede on behalf of the people.

The geographical distribution of the Yoruba religion spread far beyond Nigeria itself. Though no statistical data on the exact geographical spread are available, its followers are found in many parts of the world. As far back as the early nineteenth century Clapperton, the British explorer, gave accounts of his contacts with followers of the YTR. Yoruba traditional followers are found in many parts of Africa through trade interactions in Dahomey, Togo and the Republic of Benin (Ojo 1971; Sudarkasa 1991). YTR followers are also found in Haiti, Cuba, the West Indies and the United States of America; slaves took the religion to these countries, where it is still followed today. The YTR is highly sophisticated and is intricately interwoven into every facet of the culture of the Yoruba people with no indication of extraneous influence which, according to Parrinder (1954), shows the culture and religion were not borrowed from Christian or Muslim beliefs.

Yoruba traditional religion: gender relationships and intergenerational association

The Yoruba socio-cultural relationship is hierarchical and defers to chronological age. The younger generation are expected to respect and defer to their elders irrespective of any blood relationship. There is a great desire for children, and there exists a strong bond between parents and their children. There are 'many specific institutions concerned with rights over children and over women's childbearing powers' (Goody 1982, p.250). The Yoruba are preoccupied with problems of fertility of humans and crops, so much that all forms of worship, ceremonies and rites incorporate supplication for fertility of children or replenishment of the land. Traditionally, while a child belongs to his or her parents, the whole community helps in the discipline and raising of the child.

Rites are performed for male and female children once they attain puberty, which is seen as a transition from childhood to adulthood. Female children are closely monitored both before and during puberty, thereby restricting unmonitored social interactions between males and females in order to preserve female virginity and prevent premarital sex, although male children are not so restricted. Accounts by Bascom (1969), Fadipe (1970), Adedokun (1983) and Barber (1991) show female sexuality, procreation and motherhood are traditionally determined and Bascom (1969) and Aderibigbe (2006) state further that almost 90 per cent of female brides were virgins on their wedding nights. A young bride who failed this social expectation was seen as a disgrace to the entire family and could spoil the chances of her other sisters finding suitors once their family is stigmatised for her indiscretion. Social relationships and association were based along gender lines; both men and women across the generational lines had equal but distinct social groups. Polygamy is the traditional marriage institution, which is seen as beneficial to husbands and wives, because the co-wives could share the household chores and farming (since most families were farmers). Polygamy also gave women a greater measure of independence because they could engage in independent trade, which enabled them to acquire personal property independent of their husbands (Isichei 1983). There are no reports, however, of gender imbalances in the population; war and disease may be possible reasons for this. Gender relationships were such that each gender knew the traditional roles they were expected to play within the home and community. Nigerian traditional society has evolved customs and moral values that accord women recognition and respect for their fertility because they are believed to hold the secret of creation in their wombs. Mystical rituals and rites acknowledge women's superiority over men in this regard (Zahan 1979).

In pre-colonial times, Nigerian women were keenly aware of their sexuality and society accorded them equal respect with men. At that time respectability and recognition within society were based on seniority and not gender (Van Allen 2005). But Nigerian society is patriarchal (Federal Republic of Nigeria 1977, Sections 5.3 and 5.3.1), and despite the recognition and respect accorded women in traditional times, nineteenth-century colonialism eroded this because the British enforced on their colonies contemporary British societal values at a time when British women were denied the franchise and equal recognition with their men. In Nigeria of the twenty-first century, men still dominate in all other spheres of life and have sought to subdue and coerce women (Mba 1997; Van Allen 2005). Everything, including the woman herself, belongs to the man; she was considered part of his chattel and decisions were made on her behalf, sometimes without reference to her (Oputa 1989). Because the traditional belief is that children belong to men, this has often been interpreted to mean that men can also control women's reproduction and all aspects of their fertility, as I shall discuss below.

Gender imbalance between men and women is largely due to Nigeria's developing status. Women face a myriad of socio-cultural problems that keep them subservient to men and make it difficult to escape poverty, despite the development status of women in developed countries. Problems Nigerian women face encompass several factors that include poverty, religion (where the three religions of Christianity, Islam and African Traditional teach that women are subservient to men), and poor educational status of women (where, given a choice, families would rather educate male children than females). Traditional property rights and inheritance practices also make it difficult for women to break free of the cycle of poverty and male domination.

Fertility control

Voluntary termination of pregnancy

Traditionally it was not acceptable for married women to attempt to prevent conception because it was the belief that women must give birth to all the children in their womb as their Creator predestined them. In a recent study on reproductive rights of women carried out in south-western Nigeria, which is dominated by the Yoruba ethnic group (Aderibigbe 2006, p.188), a 65-year-old female trader with no formal education confirmed this when she said:

> In Nigerian traditional society, abortion in any form for any reason is an abomination. Those who do so do it secretly and never openly. She does not have the right to terminate the pregnancy since she is a married woman and if it happens that she got pregnant she must deliver it, since it is her husband who is responsible.

In the same study, out of a total of 700 females and 622 males of different ages responding to the question 'are you aware of the existence of abortion in traditional society?', approximately 38 per cent of female respondents said they were aware that abortion took place in traditional society; 24 per cent said they were not; 11 per cent answered 'I don't know', while 26 per cent said it was difficult to say because it was 'before their time'. Among the male respondents, 21 per cent said they were aware abortion took place in traditional society while 39 per cent said they were not; 22 per cent answered 'I don't know', while the remaining 22 per cent did not respond to the question.

While the variation between male and female respondents is narrow, owing to the small population sample, these percentages appear to show that women would carry out abortion without necessarily letting their men know about it when it became expedient. A 39-year-old female respondent said: 'The belief of people then was that a woman had many children in her womb and failure to give birth to all of them may bring problems to the woman as it is against the wish of God' (Aderibigbe 2006, p.184).

It was generally believed that even the choice of abortion was not to be taken by the woman but by her husband. This perception was the same, regardless of the educational level of the people, as can be seen in the two responses given by respondents in the research by Aderibigbe (2006, p.188): 'A married woman belongs to a man, and the man is responsible for all that comes within the marriage if it belongs to him' (36-year-old male bus driver with no formal education). 'I believe in Nigerian traditional culture a married woman is supposed to bear as many children as her husband wants. Therefore, termination of her pregnancy is her husband's decision, not her own. I think it is a taboo for the African woman folk' (34-year-old male university student).

The reasons why traditional society formalised control over women's reproduction were mainly economic. Children were needed to cultivate the land, and the wealth of a man and his social status were measured by the size of his household. The authors Bewley, Cook and Kane (1977) have stated that it is a common feature of agrarian society to value women for their procreative ability because of the value of the work that children contribute to the economic growth of the population. Children were regarded as a blessing and termination of a pregnancy was abhorred, such that a myth existed that any woman who terminated a pregnancy would bring the wrath of the gods on the entire community. This is not unusual in that, with limited knowledge of medical care, there were high infant death rates, which would balance the population and compensate for high birth rates. Women who practised voluntary termination of a pregnancy that did not pose a danger to their health were regarded as prostitutes or witches. It was the belief, therefore, that elaborate rituals would be needed to cleanse the community of the supposed heresy committed by the woman who has had an abortion. Such rituals consisted of shaving off the woman's hair and marking symbols on her body with white chalk while she tied a white cloth around her body. The village priest would appease the gods and take the woman to the river to cleanse the community of the supposed curse.

Another reason given why abortion was socially unacceptable is that attempting to have an abortion could adversely affect the woman's health or even result in her death. Also, the belief is that once conception took place the foetus already had its own pre-ordained destiny, which no woman had a right to destroy. The traditional societal perception is that the primary purpose of marriage is procreation, so a woman should not attempt abortion unless her health would be adversely affected. In this way, through the use of fear, abortion was made socially unacceptable. It was unacceptable because the traditional social construct that embraced a communal way of life could absorb any number of children the community had, and because a child was seen as the responsibility of the entire community and not necessarily of the particular family to which he or she belonged. There was, therefore, no overriding need to encourage termination of pregnancies because the community had the capacity and the structural social set-up to absorb all children.

This is not to assume that traditional women in Nigeria did not practise voluntary reproductive control; it was simply a closely guarded secret that was made available to married couples only. To further buttress the existence of some form of reproductive regulation by women in traditional society, many female respondents in Aderibigbe's study (2006) confirmed that there existed traditional means of inducing abortion. They stated that traditional women often used potash called 'kaun' mixed with lemon juice and native gin called 'ogogoro' to induce abortion. If the women could not go to the herbalist, others believed in the efficacy of special rings with herbal adornments and incantations produced by the herbalist to induce or prevent reproduction. Another form of abortifacient practised by women in traditional days was to tie a thick cloth called 'oja' (which was customarily used to hold a baby in place on its mother's back) round their womb and engage in intense physical exercise, such as pounding food with a pestle in a mortar, in conjunction with the combination of strong drinks and herbs to induce abortion. Olusanya (1975) and Otoide, Oransaye and Okonofua (2001) have documented the use of this type of herbal preparation as one of the forms of traditional family planning among the Yorubas of western Nigeria. This showed that regardless of the effectiveness of the methods adopted, Yoruba traditional women practised some voluntary contraceptive methods to take control of their reproduction. Greer (1984) has also shown that the use of herbs as abortifacients is almost universal and is a practice known in most traditional cultures.

Protection of the unborn

Despite the high regard placed on children in Nigeria, between mother and foetus the concern traditionally is always for the preservation of the life of the mother above that of the unborn child. Aderibigbe (2006), in her study, asked respondents for their responses to circumstances when a woman should have access to abortion. Out of a total of 698 respondents, nearly two-thirds opposed abortion 'when the woman does not want children for whatever reason' and nearly 80 per cent opposed abortion 'when the gender of the baby is not the one desired by the couple'. On the other hand, nearly 80 per cent accepted that abortion would be justified if the life of the mother would be put at risk by continuation of the pregnancy (if medical complications were likely); approximately 56 per cent accepted that abortion would be justified if the life of the mother would be affected by continuation of the pregnancy (for example, where a pregnant girl may face social stigma, expulsion from school or disownment by parents or family), and there was also strong measure of support for abortion where pregnancy was the result of rape (69 per cent), while support for abortion where pregnancy had resulted from incest was more evenly balanced, with 45 per cent in favour and 40 per cent opposed.

Among the Yoruba it is common, when a woman has a miscarriage, or loses a child at birth, to console her with the words, 'It is better for the water to pour away than for the water-pot to be broken' (Aderibigbe 2006, p.297). What the proverb means is that a woman who survives childbirth can always try to have another child if the previous one dies, but if the woman dies, such hope is lost forever. The proverb encapsulates societal belief in the preservation of a woman's life above that of the unborn in order to maintain her role of childbearing. While we can argue that such concern could be due to the utilitarian purpose mothers serve as 'bearers of foetuses' (Johnsen 1985–1986, p.599), the fact remains that the recognition is always for the preservation of the mother's life before that of her unborn child. This is because ultimately the foetus is neither a patient nor a person and, using McCullough and Chervenak's (1994) argument, I believe Nigerian traditional and contemporary society appreciates that the interest of the mother is of greater value to society than the yet-to-accrue interest of the foetus. However, the Yoruba believe that they do have a right to preserve the yet-to-accrue interest of the foetus as far as possible, which accounts for the present stringent law against abortion in Nigeria. This contrasts with the Western view on the rights of the foetus as expressed by McCullough and Chervenack (1994), that:

> the foetus cannot be thought to possess subjective interest…[it] has no values and beliefs that form the basis of such interests… Hence there can be no autonomous-based obligations to the foetus. Hence, also there can be no meaningful talk of foetal rights, the foetus's right to life in part, in the sense that the foetus itself generates rights.

The traditional Yoruba and all ethnic groups in Nigeria accord respect for the foetus depending on its gestational age at the time of the expulsion from the mother's womb. A full-term foetus is given the same burial rights among the Yoruba as a dead baby. When a woman has repeated stillborn babies they are often scarified with incisions on their bodies by the priest before burial, because it is believed that it is the same child who keeps being born to hurt its mother. Scarification would, therefore, prevent the foetus from being born to the mother again. Such children are called '*Abiku*' in Yoruba, which means a child who is born to die repeatedly. The social belief is common to all ethnic groups in Nigeria and each group has a specific name for such children.

Involuntary childlessness

While voluntary contraception was not too widespread in traditional Yoruba society, childlessness was regarded as a curse inflicted by the ancestors. Childlessness is often a sufficient reason for divorce, though in traditional Yoruba society polygamy is the ideal, and research by Olusanya (1975) shows that marital stability is not affected much by female infertility because the husband can always marry other wives who will bear children for him. Voluntary childlessness is almost alien to the Yoruba culture, which means that Yoruba people will do all within their power to find a solution to involuntary childlessness.

Among the Yoruba and all ethnic groups in Nigeria, children are regarded as blessings from God. A Yoruba proverb states that 'a marriage without children is like a pot of soup without salt'. Traditionally, women's procreative ability was acknowledged by society as a mark of their uniqueness. Mystical rituals and rites acknowledge women's superiority over men in this regard because 'they held the secret of creation in their womb' (Barber 1991), a uniqueness given only to women by the Creator, which makes them superior to men. Infertility is often regarded as a reproductive health problem such that its social and psychological effect on women, especially, did not receive much attention from social scientists until recent times. Infertility was not seen as a social problem, but simply a medical disease. Obono (2004) states that infertility comes across as an inverted blessing, within neo-Malthusian positivist discourse especially, because of concerns about over-population, high population growth and high infertility among Africans. Nigeria has a high population growth rate and the average number of children per woman is five (Olawoye, Olarinde and Aderibigbe 1998; Aderibigbe 2002), although there is a growing trend among the younger generation of Nigerians of wanting fewer children (two or three) (Aderibigbe 2002).

The socio-cultural set-up of the Yoruba people and all ethnic groups in Nigeria is interwoven around children. Traditionally children take up the trade of their parents and in the traditional society specific trades or crafts are known to be the preserve of certain families. Names of families usually depict the trade or craft they are known for, or the deity worshipped by the family. For example, blacksmiths are called '*agbede*', which means 'blacksmith', 'Ogun', the name for the Yoruba god of thunder, is a prefix to the names of families who are Ogun worshippers, as in the name 'Ogungbemi' which means 'Ogun saves me'. It is important, therefore, that children are procreated to continue the family name and profession. In the traditionally agrarian Yoruba society, children were the farmhands and a large household determined the size of a family's farm and consequently their wealth. Children are also seen as a link between the present and the ancestors. Sometimes, a family will name a child after a cherished deceased ancestor. A son may be called 'Babatunde', or daughter 'Yetunde', which mean, respectively, 'father (or mother) has come again'. It is believed that ancestors don't die, but are constantly present through their descendants. The traditional view of children as insurance for old age (because they will care for their parents) is perpetuated in contemporary Nigerian society that as yet has no formalised social security system.

Among the Yoruba, children play a pivotal role in everyday social interactions. The Yoruba socio-cultural set-up is such that childlessness is seen as an aberration because almost all social gatherings or interactions make references to and incorporate children. Whenever adult Yoruba strangers meet, the customary greeting is to ask after the health of the spouse and children, simply because it is taken for granted that all adults have children. During festive periods children have specific roles to play, and every couple would want his/her child represented in communal activities such as the masquerade parade, dance of maidens and other communal activities. Couples (and especially women) who do not have children are in this way stigmatised and ostracised from communal activities.

Childlessness is a social problem that is often blamed on the woman by her in-laws and society, even without knowing the cause of a couple's infertility or which of the couple has a reproductive impairment. The pressure from family members becomes acute if a wife does not become pregnant within a year of marriage. The social pressure and stigma is often felt more by women than men, as shown by Dyer *et al.* (2002). Research shows that the most important function of women in traditional society is bearing children (Aderibigbe 2006). A barren woman is referred to as a 'broken calabash'. In the traditional Yoruba society calabashes of varying sizes are useful objects used as containers for almost anything, such as fetching water, keeping objects, serving food and drinks and decorating the house. It is customary for every household to grow a calabash tree within the compound. A barren woman is therefore seen as being as useless as a broken calabash that is replaced, once broken. Because of the polygamous nature of traditional Yoruba society, a husband in a childless marriage is often encouraged to marry other women.

Live childbirth is the culmination of a woman's rite of passage to adult womanhood among the Yoruba, as in all ethnic groups in Nigeria. Until then, a married woman occupies a liminal status in the larger family, where she is regarded as neither man nor fully woman, according to Obono (2004). This cultural belief cuts across all ethnic groups, and elaborate cultural ceremonies were performed for women who were able to meet this societal expectation (Fapohunda 1983). A fertile woman had more land to farm than other wives, was given pride of place at lineage meetings and treated with reverence by her in-laws, and special names such as 'iya ewe' (meaning 'precious mother') were given to her. Women's fertility also gave them the right to remain in their husband's house if he predeceased them. A childless woman is usually married to the deceased husband's closest male relation in a form of levirate marriage. If she chooses not to marry any of them she may be allowed to remain in her husband's house, if she is considered to be of good character by her late husband's family; otherwise she would be required to return to her father's house (Nwogugu 1974).

A childless woman had no status and no voice in the community. Barber (1991, p.109) observes: '…marriage or rather motherhood [that] was expected… A woman without children would be a more unhappy being even than a man without a wife; she would have no voice, no influence and no respect.' Childlessness has often been the cause of separation and divorce between couples in traditional and contemporary Nigeria (Onah 1992; Smith 1954). For traditional Nigerian women, therefore, their womb remains their greatest asset socially.

Among most ethnic groups, only women with children traditionally inherited from their deceased husbands, through their children. However, several Nigerian court cases show that this type of inheritance is only available to women married under customary law; but as children in their father's house all Yoruba children inherit equally, regardless of their gender (Salami v. Salami 1957; Baretto v. Oniga 1961). Under Islamic law, An Na'im (2002) states that only male children had an equal share of an inheritance, while female children received only half of what male children did, and this has been endorsed by the Nigerian Supreme Court in Salami v. Salami [1957], Baretto v. Oniga [1961] and Yinusa v. Adesubukola [1970].

During the course of an earlier research study on the reproductive rights of women in southwest Nigeria (Aderibigbe 2006)

I interviewed several women. Three of them, Amina, Funmi and Lola (not their real names), spoke about how their childless state affected them personally.

Amina's story

Amina is a beautiful, assertive woman in her early forties with a university education. She has been married for 18 years without a child. She is a government official with the economic capacity to maintain herself independently of her husband. Her husband Bala is a physician and has been supportive in trying to solve their problem, through orthodox medicine. She has had fibroids removed from her uterus, and undergone IVF twice. She was told at the hospital that, due to her age, her chances of conceiving are 50 per cent and that the rate diminishes as she gets older. While trying to have a child over the years she has been to several Faith Clinics – hospitals that promise solutions through prayer and which are privately owned clinics (opened sometimes by qualified orthodox medical practitioners or those with a medical background) that provide both traditional and modern health care. Though a devout Moslem, without her husband's knowledge Amina has been to herbalists who have asked her to drink a mixture of herbal extracts combined with some of the afterbirth of a woman recently delivered of a baby. The herbalists told her the drink would induce the spirit of fertility to come to her aid and allow her to conceive also. All these have been to no avail. Her mother-in-law has encouraged her husband to try and have children by other women, in case God did not destine her and Bala to have children together. As a Moslem, he can marry up to four wives, provided he loves them all equally. Amina is sure Bala has tried his mother's suggestion without success; otherwise he would have brought the new woman and child into their home. It is hard for her mother-in-law to understand that either or both of them could have a fertility problem.

Amina seldom goes out to social gatherings after official functions and has become a recluse. Both Amina and Bala seldom travel home to their village during festive periods as is customary, because the villagers would ask her about their children. Despite his education and the respect it accords him, Bala would find it difficult to talk at gatherings of men at village meetings, because he is regarded as not responsible. The communal perception is that without the experience of maintaining a proper family of his own, how can he advise others? The gap between Amina and her old friends with children has widened, because they have little in common. She still has faith that a miracle will happen and that she will someday have a child, but deep down she thinks it may be too late for her.

Funmi's story

Funmi and Tolani are both in their late forties and have known each other since they were university undergraduates. Funmi is a matron in a government hospital, while Tolani is a university professor. They have been married for over twenty years and have tried without success to have children. It is assumed by her husband's family that Funmi is the cause of their childlessness, in the belief that, since she was so popular during their undergraduate years, she must have had many abortions. It is rumoured among the family that she washed away the quota of children God had destined her to have through repeated abortions as an undergraduate. The other wives in the family have called her a 'dry well' behind her back.

After a bitter quarrel with her mother-in-law over her childless state, Funmi had to tell her that the doctors have said that Tolani's low sperm count and the mobility of his sperm are the reasons for their childlessness. The family met secretly to encourage Funmi to allow Tolani's younger brother to father children for them, as was done in the traditional days. This she refused. After spending much money on treatment at different specialist hospitals across the country, and with the years passing them both by, they decided to adopt children secretly within Nigeria from an orphanage outside the state where they live. Funmi travelled out of the country for a year and came back with a baby daughter. Two years later she travelled out again and came back with a baby son. On both occasions they took care to ensure that the physical characteristics of the children were as close as possible to their own. Both of them decided it was better to pretend that Funmi got pregnant and had the children with the help of fertility treatment outside Nigeria, rather than admit that both children are adopted. Now they are both fulfilled, accepted within society, and no longer feel awkward at social gatherings. Life is more meaningful for them.

Lola's story

Lola and Uche are both in their early thirties and have been married for five years without children. There has been a lot of pressure from both their parents, who are anxious to be grandparents since both of them are the first-born of both their families. Despite her education, Lola did not turn to orthodox medicine at first because Uche insisted there was nothing wrong with him, that childlessness is 'a woman's problem' and that she should be the one to find a solution to it. He therefore refused to accompany her to hospital for any tests. She went on her own and was told nothing was wrong with her. She turned to her church for prayer and fasting. After a lot of persuasion from Uche's younger brother, Uche finally decided to go for treatment with Lola at the hospital. The first time they had an appointment at the hospital together, Uche did not show up. He had gone to a church retreat to pray for a solution instead. At the next appointment Uche almost left the hospital because he said the nurses, doctors and other patients were looking at him in a 'funny way'. After a lot of persuasion from the hospital workers he agreed to undergo treatment along with Lola, provided no member of his family other than his brother knew about it.

Social effect of childlessness

While further studies will be necessary on the social imperative of childlessness on interpersonal relations within the immediate and larger Nigerian families, what can be drawn from the stories of Amina, Funmi and Lola is that society is not understanding about the psychological problem that childless couples and especially women go through. While they may be treated with compassion, it is often out of pity in the belief that their life is not complete, and tends to isolate them. Childless women are encouraged more to find solutions to the problem within the confines of the immediate family, through traditional practices. Lola was asked to sleep with her brother-in-law, while Amina's husband was encouraged to marry another wife. It seems adoption is not yet an accepted and favoured option, and a lot of couples who choose this option tend to do so secretly.

Within the Yoruba socio-cultural belief and in Nigeria generally, it is most unlikely that any man or woman would voluntarily decide not to have children. In traditional society, children were seen as a link between the ancestors and the present generation. It was mandatory, therefore, for every man or woman to have children, to enable them to replace the population. Involuntary childlessness was looked upon with pity and was often considered to be a curse resulting from something the person or their ancestors must have done, or as a result of the woman's loose way of life before marriage. In traditional days very elaborate rituals were often performed to appease the ancestors to remove the curse from the woman. Traditional Yoruba society petitions and offers sacrifices to appease or appeal to specific gods or deities to intercede on their behalf to the Supreme God, who is given the ultimate praise, to solve any kind of problem. In the case of infertility problems, the deity Yemoja, the mother deity of all rivers and fishes, who is identified with having innumerable children, would be consulted and appeased by a childless woman or couple (Ojo 1971).

Traditional views on assisted conception

When all efforts failed for a woman or man to produce children, the Yoruba had their own way of assisted conception through surrogacy. Surrogacy was traditionally practised depending on whether it was male or female related. While solutions for female infertility were found through traditional forms of surrogacy, which were open, male-related infertility was often kept a closely guarded secret within the family.

In traditional Yoruba society (and most other ethnic groups in Nigeria) it was socially and culturally acceptable for a barren woman to 'marry' a younger woman as a 'wife' for her husband. That is, she would perform all the traditional marriage rites for the younger woman and pay her bride price. The younger woman would bear children on her behalf through sexual intercourse with the older woman's husband. The children born through this conception would be regarded as the children of the older, barren woman and not necessarily of the younger woman. The barren woman would care for all the needs of the younger woman, who was expected to defer to her and accept that the children she bore belonged to the older woman. When the desired number of children had been born, the younger woman might decide to stay in the household and would be regarded as a wife, or she might decide to marry her own husband, leaving behind the children to whom she gave birth with no claim to them, since they belonged to the barren woman who married her for that purpose specifically. These children would inherit what would be due to the barren woman as if they were her biological offspring.

The relationship of the younger woman to the husband is like that of a second wife, but all concerned recognise that she is there as a surrogate, mainly to bear children for the barren wife. While the barren woman would naturally consult her husband before such a decision was made, he would not object, because it was socio-culturally accepted by the traditional society. Children born under this arrangement are not aware of the identity of their birth mother until they become adults, especially if she has left to form a relationship elsewhere. Sometimes, at the time of the child's marriage, or if a medical or spiritual problem happens to the child, he or she is informed of the true identity of the birth mother.

In the case of infertile men, the nearest male relation (usually a brother) would often be the one to father children for him through sexual intercourse with the infertile man's wife. This type of assisted conception was known and accepted by Yoruba society, but it was not something the people discussed openly within the family or community. Many of the children born through this type of traditional surrogacy might never know who their biological fathers were. They would also inherit normally as biological children of the infertile man. However, many of the traditionally accepted social practices are now dying out through the incursion of other faiths into the Yoruba traditional religion.

Christianity, along with the Arab–Islam religion, has contributed to erosion of the traditional Yoruba religion and beliefs and their communal nature of social interactions which had been acceptable to them for thousands of years. This is also seen in other African societies. Africans accepted the new faiths of Islam and Christianity because they believed it would free them from slavery and oppression. During the Arab jihadist Othman Dan Fodio's Islamic invasion and conquest of the central and western African regions, including northern parts of Nigeria, during the eighth to sixteenth centuries, acceptance of Islam was seen as beneficial to those who accepted the new faith, the impression being that such believers were unlikely to be sold into slavery in Europe by the Arab slave traders. The same was believed to be true of conversion from traditional religion to Christianity by the Europeans whose incursion into the southern parts of Nigeria started Nigeria from the sixteenth to the nineteenth century. Converted Nigerians educated by the British were the ones who collaborated, formed alliances and helped the rule of Britain within Nigeria.[1]

Family creation and diversity

Marriage was considered one of the three important social rites a person must perform during his existence on earth, in the traditional Yoruba society and in all Nigerian ethnic groups – the other two being birth and death. Partners were chosen with care, often through consultation with the ancestors through the priests who consulted the oracle known as 'Ifa'. Marriage was used as a way of creating relationships between families and communities. Young women, who had to be virgins, were often given away as brides to friends or other communities to cement friendships or create filial links. In this way family diversity was ensured and maintained through the patriarchal system of marriage whereby a man could marry as many wives as he could maintain. Children were important to the community, as I stated earlier, so efforts were made to protect the unborn.

Conclusion

The social consequences of infertility, such as stigma, male denial, loss of social status, ostracism, spousal abuse and divorce (Bergstroem 1992, Dyer *et al.* 2002a; Sundby 1997) and depression are common in Nigeria, Africa and other developing countries (Dyer *et al.* 2002b; Obono 2004). There is a need to pay more attention to the social effects of infertility on the individual in relation to their productivity, on the part of policy makers in Nigeria.

Contemporary Yoruba believers do not seem to find a clash between their belief and their search for a solution to infertility problems from orthodox Western medicine concomitantly with solutions given by Yoruba traditional faith healers. This has also been identified in the findings of Dyer *et al.* (2004) in relation to South Africa. Further research will be needed to identify women's treatment-seeking behaviour with specific regard to Yoruba believers experiencing fertility problems. My initial findings show that while orthodox medical practitioners try to dissuade their patients from attending faith healers while receiving treatment for themselves, the patients themselves would rather patronise them but keep this a secret from their physicians. This shows that there is a need to integrate faith healers into the health care system in Nigeria. This becomes more apparent with the emergence of 'faith clinics' in Nigeria and the patronage they get from couples seeking solutions to fertility and other reproductive health problems. Patients' patronage does not seem to be restricted to a particular social or educational class, though this is not a conclusive finding. Yoruba healers attribute fertility problems to causes such as ancestral 'curse' with a need to appease the ancestors, as well as with witchcraft, karma, past misdeed in earlier life, or lifestyle and incompatibility of the partners as destined by their ancestors. Yoruba traditional healers use a combination of herbs, specific food items and Yoruba cosmology to treat their patients. Orthodox medical practitioners, on the other hand, would find explanation in modern bioscience. There is an urgent need for a government policy on collaboration between orthodox and traditional healers to better facilitate the referral of infertile clients to the formal health care system, as also advocated by Sundby (1997).

Faith is the central point of the very existence of the Yoruba and all Africans. While Christianity and colonialism may be seen to have eroded many traditionally accepted norms and beliefs, ATR has been able to withstand their incursion. Somé (1999) states, however, that the acceptance of the new religion did not mean a 'turning away' from traditional African beliefs. To Africans their belief encompasses the very essence of their whole being. On the contrary, several aspects of traditional African forms of worship have been incorporated into the mode of worship in Christianity and Islam. African religion and faith is culturally and racially placed. According to Thomas (2005) you must be born into a faith, as the religion addresses peculiarly specific African problems and provides them with a 'particular axiological grid that looks at the world much differently from the European construct' (p.93). Neither Christianity nor Islam, which have been in Africa for 200 years and 400 years respectively, has so far succeeded in eroding the ATR. As its acceptance spreads through a new awareness and need to self-discover among Africans in the diaspora, such as in Cuba, Brazil, the West Indies, the Americas and Europe, the death knell of ATR, and of Yoruba traditional religion in particular, may well continue indefinitely.

Note

1   The Europeans met a number of empires in Africa when they first landed there in the sixteenth century. In Nigeria different kingdoms existed, which the British conquered and put under their rule. It was Lord Lugard's wife (then the Governor-General of the then Southern Protectorate) who gave the area ruled by the British the name 'Nigeria', meaning 'Niger are' (after the river Niger that flows through Nigeria, which has its source in the River Nile in Egypt).

References

Adedokun, L. (1983) 'Marital Sexuality and Birth-Spacing among the Yoruba.' In C. Oppong (ed.) *Females and Males in West Africa*. London: George Allen and Unwin.

Aderibigbe, T.O. (2002) *Will and Will Making among Public Servants: A Case Study of the Nigerian Institute of Social and Economic Research (NISER)*. Ibadan Nigeria: Nigerian Institute of Social and Economic Research.

Aderibigbe, T.O. (2006) '"My Womb Is Tired": A Socio-Legal Perception of the Reproductive Rights of Women in South-West Nigeria with a Focus on Abortion'. PhD Thesis, University of Kent, Canterbury.

An Na'im, A. (ed.) (2002) *Islamic Family Law in a Changing World: A Global Resource Book*. London: Zed Press.

Barber, K. (1991) *I Could Speak until Tomorrow: Oriki Women and the Past in a Yoruba Town*. Edinburgh: Edinburgh University Press.

Baretto v. Oniga [1961] *Western Region of Nigeria Law Report* (WRNLR), 112.

Bascom, W. (1969) *The Yoruba of Southwest Nigeria*. New York: Holt, Rinehart and Winston Inc.

Bergstroem, S. (1992) 'Reproductive failure as a health priority in the third world: a review.' *East African Medical Journal 69*, 174–180.

Bewley, B., Cook, J. and Kane, P. (1977) *Choice not Chance: A Handbook of Fertility Behaviour*. Cardiff: University College Cardiff Press.

Dyer, S.J., Abrahams, N., Hoffman, M. and van der Spuy, Z.M. (2002a) '"Men leave me as I cannot have children." Women's experiences with involuntary childlessness.' *Human Reproduction 17*, 6, 1663–1668.

Dyer, S.J., Abrahams, N., Hoffman, M. and van der Spuy, Z.M. (2002b) 'Infertility in South Africa: women's reproductive health knowledge and treatment-seeking behaviour for involuntary childlessness.' *Human Reproduction 17*, 6, 1657–1662.

Dyer, S., Abrahams, N., Mokoena, N. and van der Spuy, Z. (2004) '"You are a man because you have children": experiences, reproductive health knowledge and treatment-seeking behaviour among men suffering from couple infertility in South Africa.' *Human Reproduction 19*, 960–967.

Fapohunda, E.R. (1983) 'Female and Male Work Profile.' In C. Oppong (ed.) *Females and Males in West Africa*. London: George Allen and Unwin.

Fadipe, N.A. (1970) *The Sociology of the Yoruba*. Nigeria: Ibadan University Press.

Federal Republic of Nigeria (1977) *National Policy on Population for Development, Unity, Progress and Self-Reliance*. Lagos: Federal Government Press.

Forde, D. (1969) *The Yoruba-Speaking Peoples of South-Western Nigeria*. London: International African Institute.

Francoeur, R.T. (ed) (1997–2001) *The International Encyclopaedia of Sexuality Volume I – IV*. New York: The Continuum Publishing Company. Accessed 27/11/05 at www2.hu-berlin.de/sexology/IES/index.html.

Goody, E.N. (1982) *Parenthood and Social Reproduction. Fostering and Occupational Roles in West Africa*. Cambridge: Cambridge University Press.

Greer, G. (1984) *Sex and Destiny: The Politics of Human Fertility*. London: Secker and Warburg.

Idowu, E. Bolaji (1973) *African Traditional Religion. A Definition*. London: SCM Press Ltd.

Idowu, E. Bolaji (1994) *Olodumare: God in Yoruba Belief* (Memorial Edn). New York: Wazobia.

Isichei, E. (1983) *A History of Nigeria*. London and Lagos: Longman Group Limited.

Johnsen, D.E. (1985–1986) 'The creation of fetal rights: Conflict with women's constitutional rights to liberty. Privacy and equal protection.' *Yale Law Journal 95*, 599–625.

Lucas, J.O. (1996) *The Religion of the Yorubas: being an Account of the Religious Beliefs and Practice of the Yoruba People of Southern Nigeria, especially in Relation to the Religion of Ancient Egypt*. New York: Athelia Henrietta Press. (Originally published in 1948.)

Mba, N.E. (1997) *Nigerian Women Mobilized: Women's Political Activity in Southern Nigeria, 1900–1965. International and Area Studies (IAS)*. University of California at Berkeley, CA and Nigeria: Crucible Publishers Limited.

McCullough, L.B. and Chervenack, F.A. (1994) *Ethics in Obstetrics and Gynaecology*. Oxford: Oxford University Press.

Nwogugu, E.I. (1974) *Family Law in Nigeria*. Ibadan: Heinemann Educational Books.

Obono, O. (2004) 'Life histories of infertile women in Ugep, Southern Nigeria.' *African Population Studies 19*, 2, 63–88.

Ojo, A.G.J. (1971) *Yoruba Culture: A Geographical Analysis. Ile-Ife*. London: University of Ife and University of London Press Ltd.

Olawoye, J.E., Olarinde, E.S. and Aderibigbe, T.O. (1998) *Women and Menopause in Nigeria*. Ibadan, Nigeria: The Social Sciences and Reproductive Health Research Network.

Olusanya, P.O. (1975) 'Cultural Barriers to Family Planning among the Yorubas'. In J.C. Caldwell, N.O. Addo, A. Igun, A.K. Gaise and P.O. Olusanya (eds) *Population Growth and Socioeconomic Change in West Africa*. New York and London: Columbia University Press.

Onah, B.N. (1992) 'The Socio-Cultural Perception of Childless in Anambra State'. In M.N. Kesekka (ed.) *Women's Health Issues in Nigeria*. Lagos: Tamazara Press.

Oputa, C. (1989) 'Women and Children as Disempowered Groups.' In Ajibola, B. (ed.) *Women and Children under Nigerian Law*. Lagos, Nigeria: Federal Ministry of Justice Law Review Series, Federal Ministry of Justice.

Otoide, V.O., Oransaye, F. and Okonofua, F.E. (2001) 'Why Nigerian adolescents seek abortion rather than contraception: Evidence from focus-group discussions.' *International Family Planning Perspectives 27*, 2, 77–81.

Parrinder, E.G.S. (1954) *African Traditional Religion*. Hutchinson House Ltd: London.

Salami v. Salami [1957] *Western Region of Nigeria Law Report* (WRNLR), 10.

Smith, M.F. (1954) *Baba of Karo, a Woman of the Muslim Hausa*. (Autobiography recorded.) London: Faber and Faber.

Somé, M.P. (1999) *The Healing Wisdom of Africa: Finding Life Purpose through Nature, Ritual, and Community*. New York: Tarcher/Putnam.

Sudarkasa, N. (1991) *Commercial Migration in West Africa, with Special Reference to the Yoruba Women in Ghana*. USA: African Studies Center, Michigan State University.

Sundby, J. (1997) 'Infertility in the Gambia: traditional and modern healthcare.' *Patient, Education and Counselling 31*, 29–37.

Thomas, D.E. (2005) *African Traditional Religion in the Modern World*. Jefferson, NC and London: McFarlands and Company, Inc. Publishers.

United Nations Organization (2005) Nigeria's Population.' Accessed 19/10/05 at http://esa.un.org/esa/publications/abortion/doc/nigeria.doc.

Van Allen, J. (2005) '"Sitting on a Man": Colonialism and the Lost Political Institutions of Igbo Women.' In R.R. Grinker and C.B. Steiner (eds) *Perspectives on Africa. A Reader in Culture, History and Representation*. Oxford: Blackwell Publishing.

Yinusa v. Adesubukola [1970] *Journal of African Law 14*.

Zahan, D. (1979) *The Religion, Spirituality, and Thought of Traditional Africa*. Chicago, IL and London: University of Chicago Press.

8

'Give me Children or else I am Dead'

Orthodox Jewish Perspectives on Fertility

Gideon Weitzman

Orthodox Judaism

Orthodox Judaism should really be called Traditional Judaism, since all other branches of Judaism derived from Orthodox Judaism at the end of the nineteenth century.[1] Orthodox Jews may account for some 33–45 per cent of all the 15 million Jews in the world, and some have claimed that the percentage of those who are associated with Orthodox Judaism by extension may be nearer 70 per cent (Elazar 1991).

Orthodox Judaism incorporates a great variety of strands and subsets, but these can broadly be divided into some major groups.

Modern Orthodoxy[2] combines traditional Jewish learning with a more modern perspective, while Charedi Judaism, literally meaning 'the tremblers', rejects modern study and to a certain degree interaction with the outside world. Charedi Judaism can be further broken down into the Chassidim, who stress spirituality in addition to pure study and are organised around a central Rebbe or spiritual leader, and the Missnagdim, the opponents of Chassidut, for whom pure study is the epitome of Jewish expression.[3]

What binds all these strands together and differentiates them from other branches of Judaism is a commitment to following and acting according to halachah.

Halachah – meaning and methods

Halachah[4] is the system of law that guides the actions of the Orthodox Jew. The halachah comprises the Written Law, the Five Books of Moses that are believed to have been given to Mankind by God, and the Oral Law, that is the interpretation of the law according to a set of rules that govern the methods of explanation. The ongoing continuous explanation gives rise to the definitive halachic decision, called *p'sak*, that then becomes normative religious behaviour.

In the past, an organised and recognised body of sages, the Sanhedrin, acted as the definer of *p'sak*, but in the absence of such a central body each rabbi has the ability to participate in the halachic debate and contribute opinion. However, there is an informal hierarchy of senior rabbis who have been accepted by their congregants and beyond as the bearers of this tradition, and they are often referred to as *poskim*, those who can give *p'sak*. While their decisions are not necessarily binding, and they do not always agree, their words carry great weight and later authorities cannot ignore their halachic decisions without halachic proof to the contrary.

The common denominator of all *p'sak* is that it must be founded in earlier halachic precedent, ideally from the Torah or Talmud. An ethic or suggested behaviour that is not strongly founded in halachic precedent will be immediately rejected as having no basis and so being invalid. The halachic debate is rich with interpretations and adaptations of previous decisions and the examination of new situations as they relate to these earlier cases and decisions.

Fertility and infertility in the Jewish tradition

Jewish tradition places great importance on having and raising children; not only is the first commandment of the Torah 'be fruitful and multiply' (Genesis 1:28), but the Torah does not record a specific commandment to learn Torah, an activity that is held to have prime importance within Judaism, other than within the context of teaching one's children Torah (Deuteronomy 6:7).

The Torah records that all of the patriarchs and matriarchs had to face long periods of infertility. Abraham and Sarah had no children until God promised them a son, Isaac (Genesis 18). Isaac and Rivkah suffered from infertility, until eventually they had twin boys (Genesis 25:21–24). Finally, Rachel suffered from infertility for many years, until she eventually bore two sons and died in childbirth (Genesis 35:16–19). Rachel declares the strong but familiar statement of infertile women, 'Give me children, or else I am dead' (Genesis 30:1), and from this the rabbis deduced that someone without children is considered as though they are dead (Babylonian Talmud, Tractate Nedarim 64b) and should be treated carefully and sensitively accordingly.

In addition the halachah recognises the existential and psychological needs of couples to have children. Indeed many halachic authorities view infertile couples as ill and the halachah tends to leniency in such cases (Weitzman 2005: notes 54 and 56).

Judaism lays great importance on the physical relationship between husband and wife, this is part of the marriage agreement

(Exodus 21:10), the *ketubah*, and a couple who cannot engage in sexual activity must divorce (Even HaEzer 76:9). Still the emphasis is on having children, and after ten years of infertility a couple must separate (Yevamot 64a) in order for the husband to fulfil his obligation to bear children.[5]

Three types of questions

The religious Jew suffering from infertility is faced with three different challenges and asks questions in three distinct areas:

1. halachah

2. social

3. theological.

I will look at each of these issues in turn.

Halachic questions
Fertility testing in the halachah

Each stage of fertility testing and treatment raises a variety of halachic questions that have been discussed by the authorities. It is refreshing to see that the religious experts made great efforts to be lenient and to find relevant solutions for all these questions. For example, a semen analysis stands in opposition to the prohibition of wasting seed.[6] However, instead of an automatic prohibition the rabbis strove to find a way to permit performing a semen analysis. Most *poskim* would require performing a postcoital test (PCT), and only when this indicates a male-factor problem would they suggest proceeding to a regular semen analysis. The preferred method of obtaining the sample is using a sheath that can be worn during intercourse.[7] In cases when this is unavailable or inappropriate, a halachic authority should be consulted and may suggest another alternative, such as producing a sample through masturbation (which may be permitted in certain circumstances).

It is interesting to note that the Talmud (Yevamot 76a) itself already discussed a case of testing ejaculation by placing warm barley bread[8] in the rectum, which would cause spontaneous ejaculation. This is similar in physiology to electro-ejaculation and may be an alternative in certain cases.

Another issue to be addressed in both fertility analysis and later treatment is the topic of *niddah*. A woman who sees uteral bleeding is rendered *niddah*, which means that she is not allowed to have any physical contact with her husband. She must wait a minimum of five days and then check herself to ensure that the bleeding has ceased. She then counts seven clean days in which she does not see any bleeding, and then immerses herself in the *mikvah*, a special ritual bath. This allows the husband and wife to resume normal physical and sexual contact.

While bleeding from an abrasion does not render the woman *niddah*, widening the cervix beyond a minimum value does, and therefore any exploration inside the uterus could potentially render a woman *niddah* and bar husband and wife from having family relations. Any medical procedure that involves widening the cervix or causes bleeding from the uterus, or even parts of the cervix, needs to be carefully examined by the couple's rabbi to ensure that it does not cause the wife to be a *niddah*. In our experience an open line of communication between doctor and rabbi is essential to ensure that the correct information is imparted and the correct *p'sak* is given.

The types of treatment that may raise questions range from a hysterosalpingogram (HSG), a Papanicolaou test (PAP) smear or an endometrial biopsy to a hysteroscopy or even a simple vaginal ultrasound. While there are differences of opinions regarding each of these procedures, the doctor has to be careful how he guides the couple, and the couple have to maintain ongoing contact with both the doctor and their halachic expert to ensure that they receive the correct treatment within the confines of the halachah.

Fertility treatments
The commandment to procreate

In addition to all the questions raised by fertility testing, fertility treatments present a variety of questions, both specific to each treatment and related to the permissibility of the various treatments themselves.

While the commandment to 'be fruitful and multiply' is of foremost importance, there is a question raised as to whether this requirement is fulfilled by having children or by fathering them in the regular 'natural' way, in which case having children born through artificial insemination or *in vitro* fertilisation (IVF) would not be a fulfilment of this halachic requirement. This question of whether one fulfils the obligation to 'be fruitful and multiply' through intrauterine insemination (IUI) or IVF has been debated widely by different *poskim*, and one fascinating source has been presented which seems to shed light on this matter.

The Talmud (Chagigah 14b–15a) presents the case of four scholars who were exposed to a great spiritual experience. One of them, Ben Zoma, went mad and his students utilised the opportunity to pose to him all sorts of unusual but fascinating questions. One of these questions was whether a High Priest[9] can marry a pregnant virgin. The Talmud examines this strange question and asks how is it possible that this woman will be both pregnant and a virgin, and presents two possibilities: either that she had intercourse in a way that did not break the hymen, or she became pregnant in the bathtub. The commentators on this passage of the Talmud explain that this refers to a case where a man first entered the bath and ejaculated there, later a woman immersed in the bathtub and the sperm entered into her and she became pregnant (commentary of Rabbi Shlomo Yitzchaki *ad loc.* s.v. 'BeAmbati'). While this may seem incredible,[10] later halachic authorities debate the status of such a child born through fertilisation without intercourse. Some hold that this is not considered the fulfilment of the mitzvah of procreation, while others claim that this child is legitimate and the father who ejaculated in the bathtub has fulfilled his halachic obligation of fathering children. To support this they quote a Midrashic source that the prophet Jeremiah 'fathered' a child in this way and he considered the son to be his and learnt Torah together with him. This son was the oft-quoted sage Ben Sira, and indeed the numerical value of the name Ben Sira is equivalent of the son of Jeremiah.

Until recently it was at the least a rarity, and more probably miraculous, that there could be such a pregnancy without sexual intercourse; however, since the advent of artificial insemination and *in vitro* fertilisation this is an everyday reality. *Poskim* of recent years have renewed this ancient debate and examined whether we can say that a child born from IUI or IVF is a fulfilment of the commandment to 'be fruitful and multiply' or whether we hold that only children conceived in the regular way, 'in the way of all the earth' are a *bona fide* fulfilment of procreation.

While many *poskim* do accept that we can learn from the Talmudic case that any child born through IUI or IVF fulfils the obligation of having children, there is an interesting opinion of Rabbi Jacob Breisch (c1960) that not only does the couple not fulfil their obligation to have children, but the wife is considered childless, and even if she were to have several children through IUI or IVF, were the husband to die she would be required to undergo levirate marriage (Deuteronomy 25:5–10), like any childless woman.

It is clear, though, that most couples do not have children simply to fulfil their halachic obligation, but also have an existential need to have children, and as previously stated this is of supreme importance when counselling couples in this area.

As previously mentioned, fertility treatments may affect the laws of family purity because they may render a woman *niddah*, and each treatment must be examined individually to ascertain the exact procedure and the relevance to these laws. Generally an IUI should not present a problem of *niddah*, as the catheter used is extremely narrow and should not cause uteral bleeding. Egg pickup should also not present any problems, as the needle is placed through the vaginal wall and no uteral bleeding should occur. These procedures are rarely accompanied by uteral bleeding, but if this does occur it requires specific rabbinic treatment.

Fertility treatment on the Sabbath[11]

The keeping of the laws of Shabbat, the Jewish Sabbath, is one of the cardinal elements of Orthodox Judaism, and the Jew who observes these laws bears witness that God created the world and rules over it. During the Shabbat the Jew is not allowed to do any creative work, such as turning on electricity or driving a car. He is not allowed to draw blood or to write. It will be clear that these prohibitions often appear to stand in the way of fertility treatments, and this has been discussed by the *poskim* at length. While it is true that all the prohibitions of the Shabbat are suspended in the case of a danger to life, not all illness is necessarily considered life-threatening. There is an intermediate level of illness which is not life-threatening but requires treatment, and in this case, while the Jew is prevented from breaking the laws of Shabbat, there are some things that he can ask a gentile to do for him.

The definition of this intermediate level is a matter of debate, and there is a discussion whether it includes stress as a *bona fide* category, whether the 'ill' person needs to be in a situation where they are confined to bed in order to be considered ill, and whether Rachel's statement about the unbearable pain of childlessness elevates infertility to a special level.

This is fascinating both in light of the rather lame definition of the World Health Organization (1948) that has remained unchanged but greatly challenged since 1948, namely 'a state of complete physical, mental and social well-being and not merely the absence of disease or infirmity'. And also when compared with a similar discussion of the definition of infertility as expressed in the following letter that appeared in one of the most respected journals in the field.

The mistaken idea that infertility is a disease is commonplace among not only academicians and clinicians but also among third-party payers and the general public and is one of the reasons that infertility is not covered by most insurance plans. The facts are that infertility and its frequent companion, anovulation, are not diseases; they are symptoms of underlying, sometimes serious disease in one or both marital partners. One result of considering infertility and anovulation as diseases rather than symptoms is that unnecessarily powerful and expensive treatments may be used to obtain an immediate pregnancy, whereas chronic disease that may affect lifelong health is overlooked. (Dickey *et al.* 2000, p.398)

For practical purposes, whenever a case arises that needs to be treated on Shabbat, a competent halachic authority should be consulted.

Testicular biopsy

Testicular biopsy is today a common treatment that has great ramifications in halachic terms. The Torah states 'a castrated man and a eunuch cannot enter the congregation of God' (Deuteronomy 23:2), and the Talmudic sources explain that this disqualifies a castrated man from marrying and having children.

The rabbis discussed what is the exact definition of a 'castrated man', in the words of the Mishnah, 'Who is considered castrated? One who has damaged testicles, even if only one of them' (Yevamot 8:1), and the Talmud expands this definition and brings a fascinating example.

The Rabbis taught: Who is castrated? One whose testicles are damaged and even one of them. Even if it was punctured or shriveled or missing. Rabbi Yishmael the son of Rabbi Yochanan ben Broka said, 'I heard from the Elders in Kerem B'Yavneh, anyone who only has one testicle is castrated by the Sun and is kosher.' How is it possible that he can be castrated by the Sun? Rather, it is considered as though he was castrated by the Sun and he is kosher. One who has punctured testicles cannot father children? There was a case of a man who went up a palm tree and a frond punctured his testicle and fluid came out, and afterwards he fathered children. Shmuel sent a message to Rav saying that they need to check out his children to see where they came from. (Yevamot 75a–b)

This passage raises a number of points. First, any puncturing, even of one of the testicles, renders a man unable to marry or even to remain married to his wife. Second, it introduces a new category, namely a man 'castrated by the Sun' who was born that way.[12] He is allowed to marry. The third point raised in this Talmudic passage is the assumption that a castrated man cannot father children, hence, the poor man who fell out of the palm tree was considered castrated and could not father children.

A close reading of these passages will suggest that a testicular biopsy, while enabling the infertile man to become fertile, may in fact render him halachically castrated, and therefore disqualified from marrying or remaining married. This question was examined by several leading *poskim* at the end of the twentieth century and three of them allowed it, but for different reasons. One (Rabbi Breisch, section Even HaEzer 62) allowed it, since the Torah only disqualified a man whose testicles were damaged in a destructive manner, as clearly seen from the example cited in the Talmud. However, when a procedure is performed in a hospital operating room setting, the results are significantly different, and therefore it is permitted. Another reason (Rabbi Weiss 1961, 3:108) why he may not be disqualified is that a man is considered castrated only when an actual hole remains, but when the incision heals and the testicle is healthy he cannot be classified as castrated, and therefore in the case of the testicular biopsy or other such procedures the man is not disqualified from marrying.

Rabbi Moshe Feinstein (Responsa Igrot Moshe, Even HaEzer Volume II, 3), one of the leading authorities of the late twentieth century, takes a completely different approach. He claims that the Talmud clearly suggests that being castrated is synonymous with being infertile, and so if a man became fertile as a result of undergoing such a procedure, then *ipso facto* he could not be considered castrated.[13]

These three responses actually present two distinct models for looking at this question. The first two answers focused on the damage caused to the testicle, whereas the last answer focused on the ability to have children regardless of the damage to the testicle.[14]

It could be claimed (Weitzman and Lieman 2007) that these two approaches can be used in determining the preferred method of testicular sperm extraction. Today there are a number of different possibilities; testicular biopsy (TESE), fine needle aspiration (TEFNA) and microdissection (microTESE) (Practice Committee of the American Society of Reproductive Medicine (ASRM) 2004). If the reason for allowing the individual to enter the congregation is the lack of 'real' damage to the testicle, then the least invasive method would be preferred. However, if the reason to allow the procedure is that he will ultimately be able to father children, then we may prefer the method with the best results for pregnancies and take-home-baby rates.

Third-party assisted conception
Egg donation
The possibility of egg donation has sparked a great debate among the halachic authorities as to the permissibility of such treatments, and more specifically the question of the definition of motherhood. Each side brings proof to support their own position and some of the sources are fascinating within themselves.

One classic source that is used to lend weight to the birth mother being defined as the mother is founded again in the story of Rachel and Leah. The Talmud (Berachot 60b) tells us that Leah, pregnant with her seventh baby, prayed that the child should become a girl so as not to undermine the position of her sister and co-wife, Rachel. However, this Talmudic passage stands in direct contradiction to another passage (Niddah 31a) that states that the gender of the child is determined by which of the parents 'gave seed' first.[15] If the father gives seed first then the child will be a girl, and if the wife, then the child will be a boy. The Talmud states that this was originally an axiom until a verse was found that supported this: 'These are the sons of Leah who gave birth to them for Ya'akov in Padan Aram, and Dina his daughter' (Genesis 46:15), in which the boys are connected to their mother and the girl to her father.

But if indeed Leah prayed and the child turned into a girl, then this verse proves nothing, since Dina was a boy at conception and only later became a girl. Rabbi Shmuel Eliezer HaLevi Idels, writing in the sixteenth century, suggested a possible explanation which has huge ramifications for our question of the definition of maternity. He writes, 'However, the explanation of Dina changing into a girl is that the male foetus in Leah's womb went into the womb of Rachel and the female foetus in the womb of Rachel went into the womb of Leah. Then it makes sense that at conception Dina was a girl.' And since it is clear that Dina was the daughter of Leah, even though she was genetically the daughter of Rachel, it has been argued that the mother is the birth mother and not the genetic mother.

The opposing position quotes other sources such as the Talmud's (Niddah 31a) position that 'there are three partners in the creation of man; God, his father and mother. The father gives the white substance that from here comes the bones, the sinews, fingernails, the brain and the white of the eye. The mother gives the red substance that gives rise to the skin, flesh, hair and the pupil of the eye. God gives the spirit and the soul, and his facial countenance.' From here it seems clear that motherhood is defined by donating genetic material, called here 'the red substance'.

This debate has yet to be fully decided and many authorities hold positions that take both opinions into account, such that if the donor is not Jewish, some require that the child undergo a semi-conversion. On the other hand, many authorities do not require this, but do prefer that the donor is a single Jewish woman where possible.

Sperm donation

The questions of paternity are not relevant when dealing with sperm donation, since the only definition of paternity is that the father is the person who donates the genetic material. Many authorities do not allow sperm donation for this reason, since there is a concern that the donor's 'children' may marry each other. However, two halachic leaders of the previous generation, in the 1980s (Rabbi Moshe Feinstein and Rabbi Shlomo Zalman Auerbach), did allow sperm donation if the donor was not Jewish, since Jewish status is defined by the mother (that is, one who has a Jewish mother is Jewish despite the father being a gentile), and in this case there is no halachic prohibition against these two children marrying each other. It should be noted that there are many opinions that do not accept these arguments, and that since the onset of intracytoplasmic sperm injection (ICSI) the cases in which one needs to rely on a sperm donor are considerably fewer than they were at the time when these responses were authored.

Halachic supervision

Many halachic authorities initially forbade IVF because of concern that mistakes would be made in the laboratory, creating a chaotic situation where no one would be able to vouch for the lineage of the resultant children. Some well publicised incidents of such mistakes failed to provide the necessary reassurance.

The Puah Institute instigated an extensive programme of halachic supervision in which specially trained individuals supervised fertility treatments to ensure that no mistakes would be made (Grazi 2005: 391–403). These supervisors provided the security for the community and the couple that any subsequent halachic questions raised in connection to the child's valid claim to inheritance of the parents would be answered.

Since this programme has been instigated throughout the world, many *poskim* who previously condemned fertility treatments have adopted more lenient positions when supervision is used. This is nothing short of a revolution for the couples concerned, and supervision is a win–win situation both for the laboratories and for their Jewish patients.

The status of the embryo

The Talmud (Yevamot 69b) already clearly stated that the embryo is considered like water until it is 40 days old in utero. This does not mean that one can freely allow abortions until the 40-day mark, as any embryo in the uterus, if left, will potentially grow to reach birth, but it does permit the destruction of unwanted and unneeded embryos stored in clinics (Techumin XI: 272), and seems to permit using these embryos for clinical research and for growing stem cells. This would also suggest a basis for allowing pre-implantation genetic diagnosis (PGD) to prevent disease and may even allow elective PGD for sex selection.[16] In a recent fascinating case a Cohen, a member of the priestly caste, was found to be azoospermic and needed to rely on those authorities that permitted sperm donation (Wolowelsky *et al.* 2007).

However, since the Cohen status would not be conferred on such a child (and were it to be a boy this would become obvious when the child became of age and started to perform his religious duties in the public eye), the Cohen requested permission to undergo PGD to ensure that the child would be female. While some authorities were strict and did not consider this a serious consideration that would override the potential halachic prohibitions, some authorities allowed it, and cited his mental anguish at the thought of his fertility status becoming public knowledge as sufficient to permit this elective procedure.

Even though until now we have only discussed halachic considerations, it will be clear that while the laws of family purity are of interest and peculiar to the Orthodox Jewish patient, the other subjects discussed have an ethical message for the medical community and the ethicists dealing with reproductive medicine as well.

The definition of maternity, the definition of illness, the relationship between child and parents after IUI and IVF, which method is preferred when operating on the testicle to obtain sperm and the status of the embryo are of general interest and, as we have seen, the Jewish tradition has a lot to teach us in these areas.

But it is truly in the more universal questions that Judaism has a strong message for humanity, for the Talmudic sages did not ignore the social and theological questions raised by couples faced with infertility. Indeed the rabbinic literature faces the challenge of the infertile couple and presents a comprehensive philosophical and theological approach to this crisis.

Social questions

The Talmud explained the previously mentioned verse 'Give me children, or else I am dead' (Genesis 30:1) by stating that there are four people who are considered as though they are dead. 'Four are considered dead: the poor person,[17] the leper, the blind person and one who has no children' (Nedarim 64b). The common denominator of these four is that all of them are out of sync with society. The rich man who became poor is distanced from his former friends and colleagues, the leper is to be sent out of the camp of Israel, the blind person is estranged from his surroundings, and this is also the case with the childless couple.

So many of our communal activities are child-based or centre on ceremonies around childbearing and raising: we celebrate circumcisions, baby namings, bar and bat mitzvahs, and so on. We have children's services in our synagogues and children's activities in our communal centres. It is easy and sometimes natural for the childless couple to feel disconnected from the community and this is a double tragedy for them and for the community.

The word religion is related to the Latin word *ligare* meaning 'to bind' or 'be connected'. Religion is supposed to bind us together as a worshipping community, and if our communal activities exclude certain members of the potential community from participating, it is the task of the religious leaders to attempt to be as inclusive as possible within the confines of normative halachic behaviour.

I would suggest that each community that has a child-centred celebration should hold a parallel adult-only event that is open and inclusive of those couples who do not have children. This is good practice, and there is a religious obligation not to exclude such unfortunate individuals, and to try as much as possible to empathise with them and to feel their pain.

Theological questions

Perhaps the most difficult questions that the religious infertile couple raises are those related to their relationship with God in light of their infertility. Religion is supposed to bind us to community, but primarily it is to connect us to God as well. The Talmud states that there are three partners in the creation of a human being, father, mother and God (Niddah 31a).[18] If I am not fertile, what does that imply about my relationship with God? Does my neighbour with the large family have a greater partnership and connection with God than me?

The voluminous rabbinic literature examines this question as well. Taking the lead from Rachel's aforementioned cry, 'Give me children or else I am dead', and Jacob's somewhat troubling response: 'And Jacob got angry with Rachel and said, "Am I in the place of God who has prevented you from having children?"' (Genesis 30:2), one of the medieval commentators, Rabbi Isaac

Arama[19] (1420–1494), explains Jacob's annoyance at his wife's perfectly valid pain. Rabbi Arama explains that Jacob was not ignoring her plight, but rather took offence at her implication that a woman with no children is as good as dead and is worthless:

'A woman has two names; woman like man, to understand and become intelligent, and the other is the name Eve, to bear children and to raise them. When a woman cannot fulfill the second smaller aim, she can still retain the first, like a man who cannot bear children. Therefore Jacob got angry with Rachel.' While it is true that infertility robs a woman of part of her God-given task in life, she still retains another task, no less important and no less connected to God. A woman who cannot produce life can still be a successful, productive and fulfilled human being.

This is a valid attempt to connect the infertile to God and His world. However, there is a wonderful story told of Nechama Leibowitz (1905–1997), the famed Bible scholar who herself went through unspeakable torture during the Nazi Holocaust and had no children. On many occasions she taught this passage from Rabbi Arama, and on one such occasion a close student asked her whether this answer related to her own life. He relates that she replied that with all due respect to Rabbi Isaac Arama, the truth is that Jacob did not understand Rachel at all, and neither did Rabbi Isaac Arama; they could not start to understand what is a woman. With all the best intentions in the world this answer is not close to a definitive solution to the theological questions of the infertile woman.

In another source the Talmud presents another response to the theological quest for a connection with God despite the inability to bear children. The sages stated 'Why were our forefathers barren? Because God seeks the prayers of the righteous' (Yevamot 64a). The Talmud suggests that infertility is far from being a punishment, but rather still connects the couple to the Almighty, not through procreation but through a legitimate alternative.

Whether the infertile couple accepts or rejects this answer, the fact that the talmudic sages gave any answer to the theological questions of the couple is in itself significant. The Talmud did not shy away from difficult questions, but rather attempted to supply answers and to empathise, even in places where there were no complete answers.

Conclusion

We have presented a brief look at the interaction between Judaism and fertility. We have seen that since the questions are not confined to the legal arena, so the answers cover legal, social and theological questions posed by the couple. Since Judaism is more of a way of life than a religion, it is perfectly in keeping that the talmudic sages and the halachic authorities and spiritual leaders throughout the ages have given voice to the infertile couple and given them solutions and answers on all fronts.

Far from there being a clash between two opposing worlds, there is a great synthesis between the religious requirements for procreation, the medical assistance in this commandment and this existential desire of all human beings. Through Jewish organisations such as the Puah Institute that have promoted greater dialogue between the rabbinic and the medical professionals and communities, solutions have been presented that are acceptable to all, such that no one should claim that the reason that they do not have children is that Judaism does not allow a specific treatment. Our prayers are that as we come closer to solving all fertility problems, we should be blessed with the blessing that the Torah affords to those who follow the commandments: 'there will not be among you an infertile man or woman' (Deuteronomy 7:14).

Notes

1   This is obvious and is acknowledged by such diverse authorities as the Orthodox thinker and Chief Rabbi of the British Commonwealth, Rabbi Jonathan Sacks (see *Traditional Alternatives* (1989) Chapter 2), and the Reform historian and thinker, Michael Meyer (see *Response to Modernity* (1995) Chapter 1).

2   Another version of Modern Orthodoxy is Religious Zionism, which is more common in Israel and which holds the settling of the Land of Israel to be a religious imperative equivalent to Torah study and other religious commandments.

3   Of course these are very broad brushstrokes and some of the boundaries tend to blur or expand according to time and region, but this is a basic breakdown of the various groups involved.

4   Literally meaning 'to go' or 'way'.

5   There is a debate today regarding the relevance of this law, since we have fertility treatment and many authorities now hold that infertility is not a clause for divorce.

6   Some hold that this prohibition is related to the *coitus interruptus* practised by Onan and the subsequent punishment, see Genesis 38:9–10, but others relate it to the prohibition against adultery or even murder. The classic code of the Jewish law, the Shulchan Aruch, records that wasting seed is one of the most serious prohibitions of the Torah; see Even HaEzer 23:1.

7   Most authorities require that the condom be perforated so that theoretically some of the sperm cells can traverse the condom and enter the vagina, as this would comply with the prohibition of wasting seed. For a full discussion of this and many other issues related to Judaism and fertility see R. Grazi, ed. (2005: 230–236) regarding semen procurement for a semen analysis.

8   This is presumably since barley bread was a cheaper staple food and would be less wasteful than using wheat bread; however, it may be that barley bread retains heat more than the wheat counterpart.

9   The High Priest, Cohen Gadol, can only marry a woman who is a virgin; see Leviticus 21:13. The question posed to Ben Zoma is based on the dilemma whether she must be physically a virgin, i.e. the hymen must be intact, or whether she cannot have had sexual intercourse. If the latter, then (even if her hymen is intact), if pregnant, she is disqualified from marriage to the Cohen Gadol.

10   Indeed, some commentaries refer to this as a miraculous situation which can be considered impossible; see e.g. commentary of Rabbeinu Chananel *ad loc.*

11   For a full description of this subject see Weitzman (2005).

12   This could also be used to refer to someone who had to undergo life-saving surgery to remove a testicle, and so was castrated 'by the Sun' or by a power greater than his own will and not by a voluntary removal of his testicle. This is utilised when dealing with men with testicular cancer who need to undergo surgery that involves removing the testicle. He is allowed to marry or to remain married to his wife.

13   It is worthwhile noting Maimonides, writing in the twelfth century, already alluded to this in his *Guide to the Perplexed* where he writes (3:49) that the Torah disqualified the castrated man because sexual intercourse with such a person is meaningless.

14   It is pertinent to note that all three of these response were authored prior to the invention of intracytoplasmic sperm injection (ICSI) and discussed a simply

exploratory biopsy, and not one that attempted to yield even single sperm cells to be used for ICSI fertilisation.

15 We do not really have a good medical explanation of this term, but it may refer to which partner reaches orgasm first. When it is the female and the secretions are more present in the vagina, then the male sperm that are naturally quick but vulnerable have a greater chance of reaching the egg first, but this is conjecture.

16 See *Tradition 40*,1 for a variety of articles on this subject.

17 In context this actually refers to a person who was rich and became poor.

18 And as previously noted, there are the different elements that each of the partners contributes.

19 Rabbi Arama was not spared pain in his personal life; he lost a son-in-law soon after his daughter's marriage. He was expelled from Spain together with all the Jews in 1492, and died some two years later.

References

Auerbach, Rabbi Shlomo Zalman Noam I, p.159.

Breisch, Rabbi Jacob Responsa Chelkat Yaakov Even HaEzer 62.

Dickey, R. P., Taylor, S. N., Rye, P. H., Lu, P. Y. and Sartor, B. M. (2000) 'Infertility is a symptom, not a disease.' *Fertility and Sterility* 74: 398.

Elazar, D. J. (1991) *How Strong is Orthodox Judaism – Really? The Demographics of Jewish Religious Identification.* Jerusalem Center for Public Affairs. Accessed 20/05/09 at www.jcpa.org/dje/articles2/demographics.htm.

Feinstein, Rabbi Moshe Responsa Igrot Moshe, Even HaEzer I 71.

Grazi, R. (ed.) (2005) *Overcoming Infertility.* New Milford: Toby.

Idels, Rabbi Shmuel Eliezer HaLevi Gloss of the Maharasha on Berachot 60b.

Meyer, M. (1995) *Response to Modernity.* Detroit, MI: Wayne State University Press.

Practice Committee of the ASRM (2004) 'New techniques for sperm acquisition in obstructive azoospermia.' *Fertility and Sterility* 82: 186–193.

Sacks, J. (1989) *Traditional Alternatives.* London: Jews' College Publications.

Weiss, Rabbi Yitzchak Yaakov (1961) Responsa Minchat Yitzchak. Jerusalem.

Weitzman, G. A. (2005) 'Fertility treatment on the Shabbat and Festivals.' In R. Grazi (ed.) *Overcoming Infertility.* New Milford: Toby.

Weitzman, G. A. and Lieman, H. J. (2007) 'Is testicular sperm extraction permitted by Jewish Law (Halacha)?' *Fertility and Sterility* 88: S393.

Wolowelsky, J. B., Grazi, R. V., Brander, K., Freundel, B., Friedman, M., Goldberg, J., Greenberger, B., Kaplan, F., Reichman, E. and Zimmerman, D. R. 'Sex selection and halakhic ethics: a contemporary discussion.' *Tradition* 40, 1. Accessed 20/05/09 at www.traditiononline.org/news/article.cfm?id=100900.

World Health Organization (1948) 'Preamble' to the Constitution. Official Records of the World Health Organization. No. 2, p.100.

Yitzchaki, Rabbi Shlomo Commentary on the Talmud, Tractate Chagigah 15a s.v. 'BeAmbati'.

9

Faith and Fertility in Reform Jewish Thought

Mark Washofsky

Reform Judaism and the discourse of Jewish tradition

A discussion of the teachings of Reform Judaism on any issue of religious practice must begin with a consideration of the complex relationship between Reform Judaism and the Jewish religious tradition. By 'Reform Judaism' I have in mind the religious outlook of the contemporary Jewish groupings that trace their origins to the movement for Jewish religious reform that began in central Europe during the late eighteenth and early nineteenth centuries.[1] These groupings, which explicitly describe their Judaism as 'Reform,' 'Liberal,' or 'Progressive,' exist in many different countries. In this chapter, I shall focus upon the teachings and statements issued by the institutional branches of the Reform movement in North America, which, at an estimated 1.5 million members, is by far the largest of these groupings (URJ 2007). By 'Jewish religious tradition' I mean 'Torah,' an ongoing literary discourse that begins with the Hebrew Scriptures (especially the first five books of the Bible, known as the 'Torah of Moses') and extends through the vast corpus of the rabbinic literature. The central compendium of the rabbinic literature is the Babylonian Talmud, which comprises texts and sources that express the doctrines, teachings, and interpretations of the 'rabbis' or the 'sages' who flourished in the land of Israel and in Mesopotamia during (roughly) the first seven centuries CE. That literature has determined the accepted interpretation of the Bible and set the parameters for the religious life of virtually all Jewish communities ever since. Jewish 'tradition' is therefore the study of these texts, the approaches that Jews have developed over the centuries for reading, interpreting, and arguing out their meaning and significance. It is an intellectual activity pursued by Jews in an unbroken chain that stretches from late antiquity to the present. Much of this tradition is included under the rubric of *halachah*, a word that can loosely be translated as 'Jewish law.' Halachic discourse, like other forms of legal discourse, expresses itself through the close reading of the sacred texts and analogical reasoning to precedential sources, and it is by means of this discourse that Jews have historically arrived at their religious decisions and constructed their religious world.

Reform Judaism's relationship to this tradition is, as I have indicated, complex. On the one hand the movement's thinkers, stressing Reform's deep commitment to 'informed choice' and the religious autonomy of the individual, have long rejected the notion that *halachah* exercises binding authority over the life of the Reform Jew.[2] On the other hand, *halachah* does retain enormous influence (if not binding authority) upon Reform religious practice. Even if Jewish law *per se* does not automatically determine the correct standard of Reform observance, the shape and substance of that observance follows halachic models. Most Reform Jewish statements and teachings concerning practice, from the growing body of Reform responsa (rabbinical opinions on specific questions of praxis)[3] to the various treatises that the movement has published concerning Jewish religious observance, are steeped in halachic tradition and draw their support from the halachic literary sources.[4] Reform Judaism, in other words, has produced a considerable halachic literature of its own. And like all halachic literature, these writings are based firmly in the interpretation of the traditional Jewish legal sources.

What is special about Reform halachic literature is that it proceeds from a self-consciously Reform perspective, informed by values and affirmations that have come to characterize the Reform Jewish sensibility. Part of this perspective, as we shall see, is the readiness to diverge from some long-standing interpretations of the traditional sources, let alone from some of the decisions that contemporary Orthodox rabbis pronounce in the name of *halachah*. It is characteristic of Reform halachic thought, however, to explain such divergences as themselves part of the *halachah*, the legal tradition taken as a whole, as much as are the traditional or the 'Orthodox' opinions that they displace.

Gender relationships, family diversity, and the mitzvah of procreation

The interaction of which I speak between traditional legal sources and explicitly Reform values is quite noticeable in the movement's understanding of the *mitzvah* ('commandment' or 'religious obligation'; plural *mitzvot*) of procreation, 'be fruitful and multiply' (Genesis 1:28), the 'first' commandment issued in the Torah.[5] Reform Judaism recognizes the fundamental importance of this *mitzvah*, but it also accepts that the nature of the family unit — that is, the structure of interpersonal relationships within which childbearing takes place – is capable of change over time. For example, the movement rejects any suggestion of patriarchal authority within families. The commitment to gender equality is a *sine qua non* in Reform belief and practice: women and men share equally in any duties and obligations that flow from Jewish religious tradition. Thus, Reform Judaism declares that 'it is a *mitzvah* for a man and a woman, recognizing the sanctity of life and the sanctity of the marriage partnership, to bring children into the world' (Maslin 1979, p.11), departing from the traditional halachic view that procreation is a duty more incumbent upon males than upon females.[6] And while the Reform rabbinate has stated that 'heterosexual, monogamous, procreative marriage is the ideal human relationship for the perpetuation of the species, covenantal fulfillment, and the preservation of the Jewish people' (CCAR Report 1990), it has also affirmed the right of same-gender couples to establish long-term relationships, to form households, and to build families (CCAR Resolution 2000; CCAR Responsum 1996; CCAR Responsum 1998a). From these statements it follows that Reform Judaism does not regard single parenthood as 'ideal.' On the other hand, the movement has never formally discouraged single individuals from having children, though it counsels singles (and couples, for that matter) contemplating childbirth to give careful thought as to whether they will be physically and emotionally capable of caring for offspring.

Fertility control and pregnancy termination

Jewish tradition, as we have seen, teaches that it is a *mitzvah* to have children, and though this duty is technically fulfilled by the birth of two children – a son and a daughter – some opinions prefer large families over small ones: one should bring as many children into the world as is practical or feasible.[7] The tradition recognizes, however, that there are times when couples are justifiably not prepared to have children or to increase the size of their families. It also acknowledges that sexual intercourse within marriage is a positive good, quite apart from the matter of procreation.[8] Accordingly, Jewish law under these circumstances permits the use of birth control, including artificial methods of contraception.[9] Reform Judaism respects the right of couples to determine how many children they will have. At the same time, it urges them to consider in their family planning the issue of Jewish continuity, particularly in an age when, after the Holocaust, the world's Jewish population has been so drastically reduced (Maslin 1979, p.11).

Abortion is a hotly contested issue in Jewish law, as it is in Western culture generally. All opinions concur that abortion is permitted – indeed, it is *required* – when, during a difficult birth, the procedure is necessary to save the life of the woman. This warrant to sacrifice the fetus holds until 'the major part of it' has emerged from the womb; at that point, 'it may not be harmed.'[10] There is fundamental disagreement, however, over the justification for this favouring of the mother over the fetus prior to parturition. Some authorities hold that the mother's life takes precedence because the fetus is acting as a 'pursuer' who threatens the life of another. Like all such pursuers, the fetus forfeits the protection of the law. Others explain that the foetus is not yet a legal person (*nefesh*), a status it acquires only upon birth. Since the mother *is* a legal person, her life takes precedence over that of the fetus until it has emerged, when it, too, is a *nefesh* and enjoys a legal status equal to that of the mother.

The practical difference between these rationales is significant. If one follows the 'pursuer' analogy, one is likely to conclude that abortion is permitted only in cases where the woman's life is at stake. If, on the other hand, the warrant for abortion is grounded in the fetus's inferior legal status, that warrant might be extended to circumstances where the pregnancy and the birth do not involve mortal danger to the woman. Some leading halachic authorities, adopting this latter viewpoint, permit abortion for the sake of the woman's 'healing,' even when her life is not threatened by the birth of the fetus. By 'healing' they also mean psychological healing; thus abortion can be permitted in order to spare the mother severe emotional distress that would ensue from the birth, as well as to prevent against damage to her physical health (Feldman 1968, p.251*ff*; Schiff 2000). Reform teaching supports this wider view, both as the more persuasive interpretation of the halachic sources and as a superior expression of moral principle: that is, the concept of 'healing' can and ought to cover a range of circumstances extending beyond mortal danger. In theory, Reform's doctrine on abortion is a nuanced one that holds the procedure to be both *morally serious* and *morally justifiable*. Abortion is morally serious in that it should not be undertaken without good and sufficient cause. 'Healing' is a standard that implies substance, boundaries, and limits; it is not a synonym for abortion 'on demand.' Abortion is morally justifiable because, in that comparatively wide range of circumstances, the standard of 'healing' *can* be met. In practice, therefore, Reform Judaism tends to oppose government action to limit the right of a woman to decide just when a decision for abortion is religiously and morally justifiable. That decision must be made by the woman herself, in the context of her own life and religious commitment, rather than by police, courts, and politicians (Washofsky 2001, pp.242–245 and 449–451).

The embryo and medical research

The above suggests that the fetus – the human embryo *in utero* – possesses a claim to protection under Jewish law, though that claim is superseded for the 'good and sufficient cause' of the mother's 'healing.' This claim decreases substantially for an embryo *in vitro*, the human zygote or blastocyst prior to its implantation in the womb. Even those authorities who rule stringently on abortion agree that the embryo enjoys protection precisely because it is a fetus, that is, a *potential* legal person (*nefesh*). This consideration does not apply to the embryo *in vitro* when its implantation is not contemplated;[11] in fact, halachic authorities have concluded that there exists no actual Jewish legal prohibition against the destruction of such an embryo.[12] It follows that 'spare' embryos created as part of the process of *in vitro* fertilization may be discarded when there is no intention of implanting them. Given that Judaism defines the practice of medicine as an act of *pikuach nefesh*, the saving of human life, arguably[13] the supreme Judaic moral value, it also follows that there is no prohibition against utilizing these embryos in vital medical research. Thus, Reform Judaism has joined with Judaism's other streams in granting broad approval to the extraction of embryonic stem cells from the *in vitro* human embryo (blastocyst) for the purpose of medical research, even though extraction results in the death of the embryo. Some voices within the movement go further, approving the use of therapeutic cloning, the creation of embryos through somatic cell nuclear transfer technology, for the purpose of extracting stem cells from them (CCAR Responsum 2001; URJ Resolution 2003).

Saviour siblings

The Reform movement to date has made no official statement concerning the permissibility of 'saviour siblings,' children conceived with the intention that they serve as donors of life-saving organs or tissue for biological relatives. Any such statement would perforce have to consider two primary ethical issues: the extraction of tissue and organs from a minor incapable of giving informed consent to the procedure, and the very conception of a child for that express purpose. Orthodox discussions of these issues focus upon the question of the level of danger to the paediatric donor. That is to say, if the surgery necessary to extract the tissue or the organ is deemed significantly dangerous to the child, the procedure is prohibited. On the other hand, if that surgery does not pose a significant level of danger, the parents are entitled to consent to the donation on the child's behalf (Bleich 1995, pp.296–309). From this, it might follow that there is no prohibition against conceiving a child expressly for this purpose, provided that the child 'is loved and cherished in [its] own right' (Breitowitz 2003, p.2). I know of no reason why a Reform approach to the question of saviour siblings would necessarily depart from these lines. The potential for saving human life would most likely be the overriding consideration. Nonetheless, parents would have to ask themselves some hard questions about whether they are prepared to love and care for a child brought into the world for this purpose just as they would love and care for any other son or daughter.

Infertility and assisted conception

The Bible presents human infertility as an unhappy and even traumatic state of affairs. If children signify hope, childlessness is a synonym for despair; the birth of a longed-for and prayed-for child is grounds for great joy (Genesis 15:2, 21:6–7, and 30:1; I Samuel 2; and elsewhere). The Biblical Hebrew word that denotes the infertile person (*akar/h*, 'the barren one') suggests that a life without children is a sad and empty existence. Thus, the prophet utilizes the language of infertility to depict the sacred history of Israel. Jerusalem, lifeless in exile, is portrayed as a childless woman, while God's redemption is heralded in the call: 'Rejoice, O barren one, who has not given birth…for the children of the desolate one will outnumber those of the one who is married' (Isaiah 54:1). Children, by contrast, are among the rewards promised to Israel for observing God's commandments (Exodus 23:26; Deuteronomy 7:14). Fertility therefore ensures the future of Israel as a people, as well as of individual progenitors. The best summary of this attitude might be the Talmud's blunt (if metaphorical) statement: 'One who is without children is considered as though dead.'[14]

These sentiments, along with the Jewish teaching that procreation is a *mitzvah*, a religious duty, support a strong presumption in favour of the use of 'artificial' methods as a remedy to infertility. Judaism, in other words, does not condemn, *a priori*, technological intervention into the sphere of human conception as a violation of the will of God or the law of nature. The history of the Jewish attitude toward the practice of medicine is a useful analogy here. In ancient times, the propriety of resorting to physicians in cases of illness was a matter of great contention. Did not the practice of natural healing signify a lack of faith in God as the source of all healing? Did not the proper response to illness consist of the classic steps of reconciliation with God, such as prayer, repentance, and the giving of alms (*tzedakah*)? Over the centuries, these questions were answered in the negative, and Judaism became comfortable with the notion that the physician, in fighting disease, is actually performing God's will and not subverting it. Indeed, the practice of medicine became identified as the primary means of fulfilling the *mitzvah*, a duty imposed by God, to save life. In the same way, some would define assisted conception as medicine, as a response to the 'disease' of infertility, even though that condition does not in any obvious way threaten the life of the infertile person. Even if not defined as 'medicine,' assisted conception has come to be viewed in Jewish circles as a thoroughly appropriate means of fulfilling the commandment to 'be fruitful and multiply' when persons or couples cannot conceive by natural means. Science therefore remains an accepted and welcome aid in fulfilling the Jewish religious duty – as well as the deep, powerful, and legitimate human desire – to bear children.

The above, it bears emphasis, is a general statement. As we shall see, some authorities raise objections to specific technologies from the standpoint of Jewish law and ethics. Moreover, one encounters viewpoints in the halachic literature that do express reservations toward the propriety of technological intervention into matters of human fertility. In the view of most authorities, however, the specific objections can be met, and the reservations appear to reflect a decidedly minority opinion. Reform Judaism, in particular, as a consciously modern religious movement, tends to see the advance of science as evidence of human progress and generally looks with favour upon technological breakthroughs that herald improvements in the human condition.

Yet 'modern' is not a synonym for 'naive.' Reform tempers its progressive attitude with the caveat that not every achievement of laboratory science constitutes an unmixed blessing. Like other religious traditions, Reform Judaism urges caution with respect to technology, especially given the concern that humanity's moral maturity might not be a match for its scientific accomplishments (Washofsky 2001, pp.232–233).

Given that Judaism views reproductive technologies either as medicine (that is, as therapeutic responses to a disease called infertility) or as appropriate means toward the fulfillment of a religious duty, it might follow that the infertile individual or couple bear a positive obligation to avail themselves of such technologies. This would subject them to considerable financial expense and (particularly in the case of IVF) physical discomfort, with no guarantee that the procedures would result in successful conception and childbirth. Reform Judaism rejects this conclusion. This position is based, in part, upon Reform's general tendency to uphold freedom of individual choice, but that rationale alone is insufficient. After all, Reform Judaism accepts the traditional Jewish teaching that one is morally obligated to seek out medical treatment for disease; why then should this obligation not apply to treatments for infertility? The difference, however, is that Jewish tradition considers 'obligatory' only those procedures regarded as 'proven' or 'tested therapies' (*refu'ah bedukah* or *refu'ah vada'it*). Therapies that do not rise to this threshold of certainty may be permissible, even though they offer but a slim chance of success and even if they pose a significant degree of risk to the patient, but they are not in any sense 'obligatory.' Weighing all the relevant factors – the (at best) uncertain prospects of successful conception, the medically acceptable yet not insignificant risk of complications from the procedure, the financial expense, and the prospect that repeated and unsuccessful efforts at fertilization would increase the emotional stress and anguish for the individual or the couple – Reform Judaism holds that infertile persons should not be counselled that, on religious grounds, they *must* undertake technologies of assisted conception (CCAR Responsum 1998b).

Artificial insemination

We can better understand how Jewish tradition approaches the issue of assisted conception, along with Reform Judaism's contributions to and modifications of traditional doctrine, by considering specific reproductive technologies in some detail (Abraham 2004, 3, pp.7*ff*; Dorff 1998, pp.47*ff*; Rosner, Bleich, and Brayer 1999; Washofsky 2001, pp.233–241 and pp.447–449).

The first of these is artificial insemination, a technology that has attracted rabbinical comment since its development in the mid-nineteenth century. Halachic authorities generally look with favour upon the version of this procedure known as AIH, that is, when the semen donor is the husband of the woman to be impregnated. In cases where the husband is impotent or where his sperm count is low, this might well be the only way in which he can fulfill the *mitzvah* of procreation.

As is frequently the case in *halachah*, dissenting views exist. Some rabbinical scholars hold that legal paternity is established only when a child is conceived in the 'natural' manner. Since the child conceived by AIH would not, therefore, be considered the offspring of the semen donor under Jewish law, the donor would not thereby fulfill the duty of procreation, and accordingly, in the view of these scholars, the procedure would not be permitted. Others forbid artificial insemination as a case of prohibited masturbation ('the improper emission of seed'). Most authorities, however, hold that the semen donor is in fact the legal father of a child conceived through artificial insemination. They, moreover, do not regard AIH as either unnatural or improper when, after all, its purpose is to conceive children. On the other hand, with one major exception (Feinstein 1961), Orthodox scholars overwhelmingly prohibit donor insemination (DI). They justify their opposition on various grounds. First, in this case the husband clearly does not fulfill his own duty to father children, so that, for Orthodox halakhists, the case for permitting the procedure is much less compelling. Second, if the donor is Jewish, there is a concern that the child might one day marry a forbidden biological relative.[15] Third, one can even argue that DI in the case of a married woman is an act of adultery (*cf.* Leviticus 18:20), though most authorities reject this suggestion. Finally, Orthodox opinion tends to condemn DI on frankly moral grounds, as a 'despicable' or 'disgusting' act that transgresses fundamental standards of sexual modesty and propriety.

Reform doctrine is much more accepting of both kinds of artificial insemination. Specifically, it rejects the reasons cited by Orthodox scholars for their opposition to DI. In the Reform Jewish view, there is simply no good, religiously based reason to forbid DI to those persons who are emotionally and psychologically ready for it. That the infertile husband does not fulfill his religious duty to procreate through this procedure is not a sufficient reason to prohibit it; Reform Judaism, as we have seen, holds that the female is also obligated to fulfill that *mitzvah*. More than that: the fundamental human desire of individuals and couples to bring children into their lives is in and of itself a positive good that cannot be reduced to the formal confines of a religious duty;[16] it ought rather to be welcomed and facilitated. The possibility that a child conceived through DI may unsuspectingly marry a biological relative is too unlikely to warrant the prohibition of the procedure. Orthodox discussions on this point assume that the child will never be informed of the identity of his/her biological father. This assumption is controversial at best, given the contemporary tendency, which

Reform Judaism supports, toward openness and full disclosure in such matters. And the determination by Orthodox authorities that DI is a 'despicable' or 'disgusting' practice is a value judgment that can be contrasted with opposing value judgments that can be and are argued just as forcefully. For their part, Reform scholars proceed from the assumption that the development of technologies like DI is a blessing, a gift of God through the medium of human intelligence, rather than an affront to decency and morality.

In vitro fertilization

This technique raises some of the same issues, from the Jewish legal standpoint, as does artificial insemination. One of these is the question of parentage. A leading Orthodox authority on medical issues (Waldenberg 1983) has ruled that a child conceived through IVF is the offspring of neither the semen donor nor the ovum donor. Given that the conception occurs outside its 'natural' place, the womb, the legal connection to both father and mother is irreparably severed. He also condemns IVF as morally repugnant, particularly for the frightening social consequences that, in his opinion, it portends: the consignment of human procreation to laboratory science, the production of 'humanoid' creatures that bear no relationship to families, to human mothers and fathers, and the like.

This negative opinion is not widely shared among Orthodox authorities, who generally permit IVF when there is no other option for a couple to conceive. In their view, the child is the legal offspring of its biological parents; the conception is 'natural' in that the semen still fertilizes the egg, regardless of the venue of the conception. As for the moral and social concerns, one can argue that rabbis have little or no influence over the development of technology and the policies adopted by the governmental and scientific establishments. What rabbis *can* influence is the happiness of the observant Jewish couples who come to them seeking relief from the tragedy of infertility. Should rabbis prohibit IVF, even on the basis of understandable social concerns, they will do nothing to halt the march of science, but they *will* condemn these couples to a life of sadness and lack of personal fulfillment.

Reform Judaism holds, once again, that this technology is a blessing. If we think of infertility as a disease, or at least as a biological condition that it is morally proper for human beings to regret and to seek to correct, then we must welcome IVF as we do the development of any other medical therapy. This should not be taken as a blanket statement of uncritical endorsement of the activities of scientists and technologists. Obviously, abuses can occur, and society is well advised to be on guard against them. The point is that Reform Judaism tends to classify such issues as practical matters, as problems to be solved in a positive way, rather than as formal religious arguments for prohibiting technologies that offer so much hope for human happiness.

With respect to lineage, Reform thought identifies the semen and ovum donor as the legal parents of the child. This holding is of particular importance with respect to the embryo implanted into the womb of a 'host mother,' a woman other than the ovum donor who carries the foetus to term. There is a debate within Orthodox halachic literature over the assignment of legal maternity in such a case (Bleich 1995, pp.237–272). A number of authorities hold that the child is the legal offspring of the birth ('host') mother rather than of the ovum donor. They base this decision upon a fascinating analogy to the pregnant woman who converts to Judaism.[17] In that instance, the fetus, though conceived as a non-Jew, becomes a Jew upon the woman's conversion. Since Talmudic tradition regards the proselyte as 'a newborn child'[18] whose legal and genealogical connections to his/her biological parents are thereby severed, the fetus at the moment of conversion ceases to be the legal offspring of its mother. Yet because, upon birth, the woman will be considered the mother of this child in all respects, it follows that maternity is established through birth and not through conception. Reform halachic thinking rejects this comparison as tortuous and out of place. Religious conversion is such a different case, characterized by such a unique set of circumstances, that it cannot serve as a precedential example for the status of a child born of a 'host mother.'

In the Reform view, questions such as this one reveal the outer limits of the method of analogical reasoning that is the essence of the traditional Jewish approach to law and ethics. Rabbinical scholars ought to acknowledge that, in matters relating to modern technologies of assisted conception, the drawing of dubious analogies to Talmudic 'precedents' strains the bonds of credulity (Ellenson 1995). It is more intellectually coherent to frame the determination of legal parenthood as a scientific question. Given that in all other cases Jewish law recognizes the biological parents as the legal parents of the child,[19] and given that here we know that the genetic material for this child was provided by two identifiable donors, Reform thought recognizes those donors as the parents of the child (CCAR Responsum 1997).

Surrogacy

In one sense, the genetic surrogacy arrangement is much simpler from the halachic standpoint than that of the gestational surrogacy arrangement. The genetic surrogate is without doubt the legal mother of the child, and the father's wife would have to adopt the child in order to be recognized as its legal mother. Yet there are serious ethical concerns attaching to this procedure. Rabbinical scholars, like all other moralists, will want to ask whether it is morally appropriate to bring in this manner a third party into the process of childbirth. The difficulty, from a Jewish perspective, is not that an 'outside' factor has intervened into the intimate sphere of marital relations. As we have seen, Judaism raises few principled objections to assisted conception, the involvement of technology in the process of human procreation. The problem, rather, is that the surrogate is *not* to be defined as a 'technology.' She is a human being, and it is arguably degrading for her to serve as a 'vessel for hire' by others who want children. True, she enters into this contractual relationship of her own free will, yet a poor person's free will is severely limited when it comes to gainful employment. We might rightfully be disturbed at the prospect of economically disadvantaged women being enticed to serve as childbearers for hire, enduring the physical demands of pregnancy and childbirth as well as the emotional trauma that may follow the birth of the child and its subsequent surrender. For that matter, the prospect may also be disturbing for the contracting couple or individual, since it can be argued that they have 'bought' this child on the open market. On the other hand, it can also be argued that they have fulfilled the *mitzvah* of childbearing in the only or best way open to them and that the surrogate has helped them to fulfill this worthy goal.

At first glance, the Biblical examples of Sarah (Genesis 16), Leah, and Rachel (Genesis 30) would seem to provide authoritative guidance. Each of these women permitted her husband to father a child through her maidservant. The maidservant acted as a surrogate, and the child was considered legally the offspring of the father's wife. The analogy is problematic, though, in that the maidservant was not *only* a surrogate. She also became the husband's concubine, a legal status similar though definitely not equal to that of his wife. The legal institution of concubinage no longer exists in Jewish practice, and we may not wish to invoke it even for purposes of analogy in our ethical reasoning. Moreover, those Biblical narratives also recount the domestic tensions that accompanied these relationships, which should make us think about the effects of such an arrangement upon the marriage of a couple that enters into it.

For these reasons, the existing Reform responsum on the subject (Jacob 1983, pp.505–507) views surrogacy as a medical procedure, akin to the technological methods of assisted conception, rather than as a direct descendant of a Biblical institution. This enables the responsum to grant its approval to the arrangement, in much the same way as Jewish thought generally accepts donor insemination and IVF as appropriate medical responses to infertility. The responsum, however, also expresses hesitancy about its decision, cautioning that it is necessary to 'await further clarification of medical and civil legal issues.' The medical issues should be understood to include the emotional and psychological effects of the arrangement upon the surrogate mother and those who contract for her services. Much careful thought and counselling must precede any decision to undertake such a relationship.

If surrogacy is permissible, albeit with certain provisos, that permit would apply *a forteriori* to the donation of eggs or embryos to prospective parents. Given the wide berth it grants to the exercise of an individual's 'informed choice' and personal religious autonomy, Reform Jewish thought would seem to raise no substantive objections to such donations. Still, the hesitancy that the movement's literature expresses with regard to surrogacy – that is, that the potential emotional and psychological effects upon the surrogate be carefully considered before a final decision is made – presumably adds a similar cautionary note to those contemplating the donation of eggs and embryos.

Gender selection

A similar tension pervades Reform's responses to the employment of technologies for gender selection. A responsum issued in 1941 (Jacob 1983, pp.508–509) offers tentative approval for 'the predetermination of sex in babies.' Although the question at the time was technologically 'premature,' the responsum noted that the rabbis had long ago prescribed various measures that couples might take to increase the chance that they would bear male children.[20] The responsum found nothing objectionable about this attitude: 'the desire of parents to predetermine, if possible, the sex of their progeny is not a reprehensible desire.' Thus, it endorsed the use of technological means 'yet to be discovered' that would enable the predetermination of gender. This support was conditioned, however, by the demand that these means would prove to be 'scientifically sound and morally unassailable.' Though it offered no criteria to determine the moral acceptability of such procedures, subsequent Reform thinkers have raised some substantive concerns. Some worry that the widespread use of efficient methods of gender predetermination might lead to gender imbalance within the society. Others ask whether, given Reform Judaism's overarching commitment to the principle of gender equality, it is morally appropriate to favour one gender over another in any significant way? One author (Schiff 1995) contends that gender predetermination is an example of a non-medical use of *in vitro* fertilization and is thereby unwarranted, since IVF is justified precisely because it is a remedy for infertility. Unanimity of views, therefore, does not exist. What we can say is that Reform thinkers would prefer gender preselection when it is carried out through pre-implantation genetic diagnosis, over the prenatal screening and abortion of fetuses of the unwanted gender. Abortion, as we have seen, requires a substantive medical warrant, and no matter how liberally we interpret that concept, it would not seem to extend to the selection of gender.

Conclusion

Reform's halachic literature has not spoken explicitly on every question of bioethics or, for that matter, on every subject that might be classified under the rubric 'fertility.' I hope, however, that the foregoing helps clarify the general lines of Reform Jewish discourse on our subject, that is, the manner in which the movement plants itself firmly within the parallel worlds of traditional Jewish thought (read: *halachah*) and of the ethical sensibilities of a consciously modern religious expression. The history of Reform Jewish moral thought is in large part the story of the effort to bring these two very different modes of thought into a common framework of argument. It is highly unlikely that such a combination will produce conclusions that enjoy the status of dogmatic certainty. The tension between these two worlds, along with the ambiguity that lies at the heart of the activity of textual interpretation, will guarantee a multiplicity of answers, a plural conception of moral truth. Reform Jewish thinkers tend to accept this reality as a positive good, as the destiny of Jews who intentionally – indeed, proudly – determine to live in both of those worlds at one and the same time.

Notes

1   The standard one-volume scholarly history is Meyer (1988). Plaut (1963 and 1965) has edited a two-volume documentary history covering the movement's formative period in Europe and America. Various monographs and studies cover the history of particular Reform or Liberal Jewish communities; see, for example, Kershen and Romain (1995).

2   Almost every statement of Reform Jewish doctrine stresses this point. A good example is the *Centenary Perspective*, a major declaration of Reform Jewish doctrine adopted in 1976 by the Central Conference of American Rabbis, the professional association of Reform rabbis in North America: 'Within each area of Jewish observance Reform Jews are called upon to confront the claims of Jewish tradition, however differently perceived, and to exercise their individual autonomy, choosing and creating on the basis of commitment and knowledge' (CCAR 1976).

3   For a comprehensive survey of the responsa literature, and for that matter of all forms of traditional halachic literature, see Elon (1994), p.1453–1528. The 'official' responsa of the North American Reform movement are those authored by the Responsa Committee of the Central Conference of American Rabbis. Many of those responsa are available at http://ccarnet.org/documentsandpositions/responsa.

4   See, for example, Knobel (1983); Maslin (1979); Polish and Plaut (1988); Washofsky (2001).

5   The *Sefer Hachinukh*, a thirteenth-century work that presents the *mitzvot* in the order that they appear in the Torah, begins its count with this one.

6   *M. Yevamot* 6:6; *BT Yevamot* 65b; *MT Ishut* 15:2. The Reform viewpoint concurs with that expressed in the Mishnah by R. Yochanan b. Beroka. Some traditional and Orthodox authorities hold that women, though not obligated to bear children under the rubric of Genesis 1:28, do observe a related requirement, to 'populate the world,' derived from Isaiah 45:18.

7   *M. Yevamot* 6:6; *BT Yevamot* 62b; *MT Ishut* 15:16.

8   See, in general, Feldman (1968).

9   This is true especially when the 'minimum requirement' for procreation – a son and a daughter – has been fulfilled. See, in general, *BT Yevamot* 12b and *Tosafot ad loc., s.v. veshalosh nashim*; Feinstein (1973).

10 See the classic text, *M. Ohalot* 7:6. Some versions of the text read 'its head' in place of 'the major part of it.'

11 R. Shmuel Halevy Wasner, *Resp. Shevet Halevy* 5:47 (1981, self-published): the *in vitro* embryo is not even a potential *nefesh*. Therefore, the prohibitions against

labour on the Sabbath, which are dispensed with when such action is necessary to save a human person (and even the potential person, the foetus), are not superseded in order to save the life of the *in vitro* embryo.

12   *Ibid.*

13   See *BT Sanhedrin* 74a: the saving of life supersedes all other obligations, but there are exceptions to this rule.

14   *BT Nedarim* 64b.

15   This assumes that the child will not be told the facts of his/her origin, an assumption that is fairly widespread among traditional authorities. Biological ties to non-Jews are irrelevant, from the standpoint of the *halachah*.

16   A similar point is made by Feinstein (1961), a leading Orthodox authority.

17   *BT Yevamot* 97b.

18   *BT Yevamot* 22a and elsewhere.

19   The topic of legal adoption is beyond the scope of this chapter. We might say, briefly, that classical Jewish law does not know of an institution called 'adoption,' in which individuals other than the biological progenitors become the legally recognized parents of a child (as opposed to its guardians). Nonetheless, over time Jewish law has found ways to make room for the institution. Reform thought is quite accepting of adoption, holding that one's adoptive parents are in all respects one's true parents. See CCAR Responsum (1993) (http://data.ccarnet.org/cgi-bin/respdisp.pl?file=12&year=5753).

20   See, among other passages, *BT Nidah* 31a–b and 70b–71a, *BT Berakhot* 5b, and *BT Shevu'ot* 18b.

References

Abraham, A.S. (2004) *Nishmat Avraham*. Brooklyn: Mesorah.

Bleich, J.D. (1995) *Contemporary Halakhic Problems*, 4. New York: Ktav.

Breitowitz, Y.A. (2003) 'What does halachah say about organ donation?' *Jewish Action 63*, 3, (Spring). Accessed 10/26/07 at www.ou.org/publications/ja/5764/5764fall/ORGANDON.PDF.

CCAR (1976) *Reform Judaism: A Centenary Perspective*. New York: Central Conference of American Rabbis. Accessed 06/06/07 at http://ccarnet.org/Articles/index.cfm?id=41&pge_prg_id=3032&pge_id=1656.

CCAR Report (1990) *Report of CCAR Ad Hoc Committee on 'Homosexuality and the Rabbinate.'* New York: Central Conference of American Rabbis. Accessed 06/06/07 at http://data.ccarnet.org/cgi-bin/resodisp.pl?file=hs&year=1990.

CCAR Resolution (2000) *Resolution on Same Gender Officiation*. New York: Central Conference of American Rabbis. Accessed 06/06/07 at http://data.ccarnet.org/cgi-bin/resodisp.pl?file=gender&year=2000.

CCAR Responsum (1993) *Kaddish for Adoptive and Biological Parents*. New York: Central Conference of American Rabbis. Accessed 06/06/07 at http://data.ccarnet.org/cgi-bin/respdisp.pl?file=12&year=5753.

CCAR Responsum (1996) *On Homosexual Marriage*. New York: Central Conference of American Rabbis. Accessed 06/06/07 at http://data.ccarnet.org/cgi-bin/respdisp.pl?file=8&year=5756.

CCAR Responsum (1997) *In Vitro Fertilization and the Status of the Embryo*. New York: Central Conference of American Rabbis. Accessed 06/06/07 at http://data.ccarnet.org/cgi-bin/respdisp.pl?file=2&year=5757.

CCAR Responsum (1998a) *Baby-naming for a Religiously-mixed Lesbian Couple.* New York: Central Conference of American Rabbis. Accessed 06/06/07 at http://data.ccarnet.org/cgi-bin/resp-disp.pl?file=2&year=5758.

CCAR Responsum (1998b) *In Vitro Fertilization and the Mitzvah of Childbearing.* New York: Central Conference of American Rabbis. Accessed 06/06/07 at http://data.ccarnet.org/cgi-bin/resp-disp.pl?file=3&year=5758.

CCAR Responsum (2001) *Human Stemcell Research.* New York: Central Conference of American Rabbis. Accessed 06/06/07 at http://data.ccarnet.org/cgi-bin/respdisp.pl?file=7&year=5761.

Dorff, E.N. (1998) *Matters of Life and Death.* Philadelphia, PA: Jewish Publication Society.

Ellenson, D. (1995) 'Artificial fertilization (*hafrayyah melakhotit*) and procreative autonomy.' In W. Jacob and M. Zemer (eds) *The Foetus and Fertility in Jewish Law.* Pittsburgh and Tel Aviv: Freehof Institute of Progressive Halakhah.

Elon, M. (1994) *Jewish Law: History, Sources, Principle.* Translated by Bernard Auerbach and Melvin J. Sykes. Philadelphia, PA: Jewish Publication Society of America.

Feldman, D. (1968) *Birth Control in Jewish Law.* New York: New York University Press.

Feinstein, M. (1961) *Resp. Igerot Moshe, Even Ha'ezer,* 1, nos. 10 and 71. New York: Balshon.

Feinstein, M. (1973) *Resp. Igerot Moshe, Even Ha'ezer,* 3, no. 24. New York: Balshon.

Jacob, W. (1983) *American Reform Responsa.* New York: Central Conference of American Rabbis.

Kershen, A.J. and Romain, J. (1995) *Tradition and Change: A History of Reform Judaism in Britain.* London: Valentine Mitchell.

Knobel, P.S. (1983) *Gates of the Seasons: A Guide to the Jewish Year.* New York: Central Conference of American Rabbis.

Maslin, S.J. (ed.) (1979) *Gates of Mitzvah: A Guide to the Jewish Life Cycle.* New York: Central Conference of American Rabbis.

Meyer, M.A. (1988) *Response to Modernity: A History of the Reform Movement in Judaism.* New York: Oxford University Press.

Plaut, W.G. (1963) *The Rise of Reform Judaism.* New York: World Union for Progressive Judaism.

Plaut, W.G. (1965) *The Growth of Reform Judaism.* New York: World Union for Progressive Judaism.

Polish, D. and Plaut, W.G. (eds) (1988) *Rabbi's Manual.* New York: Central Conference of American Rabbis.

Rosner, F., Bleich, J.D., and Brayer, M. (eds) (1999) *Jewish Bioethics.* New York: Ktav.

Schiff, D. (1995) 'Developing halakhic attitudes to sex preselection.' In W. Jacob and M. Zemer (eds) *The Foetus and Fertility in Jewish Law.* Pittsburgh and Tel Aviv: Freehof Institute of Progressive Halakhah.

Schiff, D. (2000) *Abortion in Judaism.* Cambridge: Cambridge University Press.

URJ (2007) *About the Union for Reform Judaism.* New York: Union for Reform Judaism. Accessed 06/06/07 at http://urj.org/about.

URJ Resolution (2003) *Stem Cell Research.* New York: Union for Reform Judaism. Accessed 06/06/07 at http://urj.org/Articles/index.cfm?id=7152&pge_prg_id=30698&pge_id=1625.

Waldenberg, E.Y. (1983) *Resp. Tzitz Eliezer* 15, no. 45. Jerusalem: Itah.

Washofsky, M. (2001) *Jewish Living: A Guide to Contemporary Reform Practice.* New York: URJ Press.

Abbreviations

BT – Babylonian Talmud

CCAR – Central Conference of American Rabbis

M – Mishnah

MT – *Mishneh Torah*, the Code of Maimonides (12th century)

Resp. – Responsa

URJ – Union of Reform Judaism

The Editors

Eric Blyth PhD is Professor of Social Work at the University of Huddersfield and Visiting Professor of Social Work at Hong Kong Polytechnic University. He studied Sociology at the University of York and obtained his professional social work qualification following postgraduate studies at Brunel University. He worked for 12 years in social work practice and management before taking up an academic post in the School of Human and Health Sciences at the University of Huddersfield in 1983. Since the mid-1980s he has pursued his research and scholarly activities in the field of infertility and assisted conception. He is the author of several dozen scholarly works, has presented papers on his research at conferences in Europe, North and South America, Australasia and Asia, and has acted as policy advisor to consumer groups, professional bodies and national governments and regulatory bodies.

Ruth Landau PhD is Associate Professor of Social Work at the Paul Baerwald School of Social Work and Social Welfare, the Hebrew University of Jerusalem, Israel. She obtained a BA in Sociology and Political Science at the Hebrew University and gained another BA in Social Work (*cum laude*) from Haifa University. She graduated from the Master's Program and wrote her dissertation for the PhD degree at Rutgers, the State University of New Jersey, USA. She has worked for over 20 years in social work practice, including eight years as the Executive Director of the Israeli Family Planning Association. She has published numerous articles on assisted conception and ethics in leading professional journals and addressed conferences in Israel, the UK, the Netherlands, and the USA. Presently she is the Chair of the Central Ethics Committee of the Hebrew University of Jerusalem.

Eric Blyth and Ruth Landau have previously co-edited *Third-Party Assisted Conception across Cultures: Social, Legal and Ethical Perspectives*, published by Jessica Kingsley Publishers in 2004.

The Contributors

Titilayo O. Aderibigbe has conducted multidisciplinary collaborative research and published several papers internationally in the area of reproductive health, law, gender, adolescent sexuality with the Social Sciences and Reproductive Health Research Network (SSRHN) and the Nigerian Institute of Social and Economic Research (NISER). Research funding was by the Federal Government of Nigeria, the Ford, MacArthur and Packard Foundations, and the Netherlands–Israeli Development Research Programme (NIRP). She is currently the director of the legal department in NISER.

Gautam N. Allahbadia is the Director of Rotunda – The Center for Human Reproduction, the world-renowned infertility clinic at Bandra, Mumbai, India. Throughout his career Gautam Allahbadia has been instrumental in developing new fertility-enhancing protocols and propagating the use of ultrasound in embryo transfer procedures. He was responsible for India's first trans-ethnic surrogate pregnancy involving a Chinese couple's baby delivered by an unrelated Indian surrogate. He also has to his credit India's first same-sex couple pregnancy and delivery of twins. He has organised seven International Congresses in the subject and was recently made a visiting lecturer to the University of Tel Aviv Sackler School of Medicine – the first Indian to be given such a position.

Swati Allahbadia currently works as a panel doctor with the Asian Heart Institute and is an Honorary at the Nowrosjee Wadia Maternity Hospital – a premier teaching institute in Mumbai, besides working out of the family-owned Rotunda Hospital. She has a general obstetrics and gynaecologic practice with focus on endoscopy. She has been Associate Professor of Gynaecology with Bombay University. She trained in endoscopy in Germany and the US and has been on the faculty of the Aesculap Academy, a gynaecological endoscopy institute within the Prince Aly Khan Hospital. Besides gynaecology and endoscopy she is interested in reading and travelling.

Sulbha Arora is the scientific director of the Deccan Fertility Clinic and Keyhole Surgery Center at Mumbai, India. She has authored 16 chapters in different medical text books. She has been the joint organising secretary for four international conferences on infertility and assisted reproduction. She has conducted a number of IUI training programmes and has also been the course coordinator for 12 workshops on gynaecologic endoscopy. She is currently the academic programme coordinator for the Rotunda-Deccan Fellowships.

Michael G. Barnhart is a full professor in the Department of History, Philosophy, and Political Science at Kingsborough Community College of the City University of New York. He teaches courses in all areas of philosophy, but his research centres on issues in comparative philosophy and ethics, about which he has written numerous articles and published a book, *Varieties of Ethical Reflection: New Directions for Ethics in a Global Context* (Lanham, MD: Lexington Books, 2002).

Cecilia Lai Wan Chan is Si Yuan Professor in Health and Social Work, Department of Social Work and Social Administration, and director of the Centre on Behavioral Health at the University of Hong Kong. She is renowned for her creative innovations in integrating Eastern concepts into her integrative therapy, and for her work on psychosocial oncology, end-of-life and bereavement care, as well as her Strength-focused and Meaning-oriented Approach for Resilience and Transformation (SMART) model of empowering clients in transforming loss and trauma.

Celia Hoi Yan Chan is the teaching consultant at the Centre on Behavioral Health, University of Hong Kong. She is one of the infertility counsellors in Hong Kong, establishing the psychosocial counselling service at the Assisted Reproduction Unit, Queen Mary Hospital, Hong Kong. She offers counselling for, and conducts psychosocial research on, people experiencing infertility and undergoing *in vitro* fertilisation.

Phyllis Creighton is a Research Associate in the Faculty of Divinity at Trinity College, University of Toronto. She has served on several task forces of the Anglican Church of Canada and has written extensively on abortion, donor insemination, sexuality, IVF, surrogacy, and the human embryo. A recipient of its Anglican Award of Merit, she is also a longtime elected lay member of the ACC General Synod. Author of conference papers and briefs to government bodies, she served on Health Canada's Advisory Committee on Reproductive and Genetic Technologies (1995–2004), which advised on legislation.

Elizabeth Wai-Hing Choi Hui is Teaching Consultant, Department of Nursing Studies at the University of Hong Kong. She was a midwife for some years before teaching midwifery courses in the department in the last ten years. Her research studies focus on psychosocial issues in childbearing.

Mohammad Iqbal began his career as an advocate and later on opted for industry as legal adviser/group company secretary. He was elected District Governor of Rotary International District 1120. He is currently engaged, at University College London, in researching human reproduction and the traditional cultural, ethical, moral, social and religious status of Muslim infertile couples when living in secular societies.

Geok Ling Lee worked as a part-time member of teaching staff at the National University of Singapore in the Department of Social Work. She is currently a PhD candidate with the University of Hong Kong in the Department of Social Work. Her current research includes examining the psychosocial aspects of couples living with infertility and a longitudinal study on the psychosocial well-being of orphaned children in rural China.

Ray Noble graduated with honours from the University of Manchester in 1976 and obtained his doctorate at the University of Edinburgh in 1981. In 1989 he was awarded a Rockefeller Senior Fellowship at University College London and is now director of the Centre for Reproductive Ethics and Rights at the UCL Institute for Women's Health. His work is focused on ethical issues acting as barriers to health care for women in the UK, India and Africa.

The Reverend Jim Richards has been CEO of the Catholic Children's Society in England for 18 years. After qualifying as a probation officer, he then had several management positions in local authority child care, followed by becoming Deputy Principal Advisor for the London Boroughs Children's Regional Planning Committee. During this period he obtained an MA and had a period of secondment with the Social Services Inspectorate. He has contributed a chapter on the ethical issues of the major faiths in *Assisted Human Reproduction* (D. Singer and M Hunter, eds. London: Whurr Publishers, 2003). He is a past trustee of the National Council of Voluntary Child Care Organisations (NCVCCO) (now Children England) and a trustee of the Cardinal Hume Centre and is a governor of a Catholic primary school. He was ordained deacon in the Catholic Church in 2006. Jim is married with children and grandchildren.

Mark Washofsky is the Solomon B. Freehof Professor of Jewish Law at Hebrew Union College–Jewish Institute of Religion in Cincinnati, Ohio. He specialises in the literature of Jewish law (*halachah*) and the application of legal theory to the understanding of the Jewish legal process. His publications deal with such subjects as the history of the *halachah*, the nature of rabbinical decision making, and issues of medical ethics in Jewish law. He serves as chair of the Responsa Committee of the Central Conference of American Rabbis, which issues advisory opinions on questions of Jewish practice. He is the author of *Jewish Living: A Guide to Contemporary Reform Practice* (New York: URJ Press, 2001) and, along with W. Gunther Plaut, of *Teshuvot for the Nineties* (New York: CCAR Press, 1997), the latest printed collection of Reform responsa.

Rabbi Gideon Weitzman is the Head of the English-speaking section of the Puah Institute and director of Puah USA, where he counsels thousands of couples worldwide in all areas of fertility and gynaecology as they relate to Jewish law. He has published numerous articles and several book chapters on the subject. In addition he is the Rabbi of the Merkaz Modiin Community in Israel and is a visiting associate professor in the Albert Einstein College of Medicine. He has written three books on the philosophy of Rabbi A.I. Kook and teaches in various educational institutions in Israel. He has lectured in a wide variety of forums and has addressed medical conferences and rabbinic groups, as well as many synagogues and communities. Rabbi Weitzman is married to Rivka and they have five children.

Subject Index

Author Index